Second Edition

The Hawker Typhoon
Including the Hawker Tornado

A Complete Guide To The RAF's Classic Ground-Attack Fighter

by Richard A. Franks

Airframe & Miniature No.2: Second Edition
The Hawker Typhoon (including the Hawker Tornado)
A Guide to the RAF's Ground-Attack Fighter
by Richard A. Franks

Second Edition published in 2015
First published in 2011 by Valiant Wings Publishing Ltd
8 West Grove, Bedford MK40 4BT
Tel: +44 (0)1234 273434
valiant-wings@btconnect.com
www.valiant-wings.co.uk

© Richard A. Franks 2011/2015
© Richard J. Caruana - Colour Profiles
© Jacek Jackiewicz - Isometric Lineart, Side Profiles & Scale Plans

© Crown Copyright used with the permission of Her Majesty's Stationary Office (HMSO)

The right of Richard A. Franks to be identified as the author of this work has been asserted in accordance with sections 77 and 78 of the Copyright Designs and Patents Act, 1988.

'Airframe & Miniature' and the 'AirMin' brands, along with the concept of the series, are the copyright of Richard A. Franks as defined by the Copyright Designs and Patents Act, 1988 and are used by Valiant Wings Publishing Ltd by agreement with the copyright holder.

All rights reserved. No part of this publication may be reproduced or transmitted in any form or by any means, electronic or mechanical, including photocopy, recording, or any other information storage and retrieval system, without permission in writing from the publishers.

ISBN 978-0-9930908-8-2

Acknowledgments

The author would like to thank the Department of Records and Information Services at the RAF Museum, Hendon, Bob Brown of Model Design Construction and Trevor Brockington of Napier for their assistance. A special word of thanks must go to Steve A. Evans, Libor Jekl and Daniel Zamarbide for their excellent builds and to Richard J, Caruana, Jacek Jackiewicz and Jerry Boucher for their superb artwork. We would also like to thank the following companies for their support of this title:

Aviaeology by Skygrid
123 Church Street, Kitchener, Ontario, Canada, N2G 2S3
Tel: +1 (519) 742 6965
www.aviaeology.com

CMK Kits s.r.o.
Mezilesi 718, 193 00 Praha 9, Czech Republic
Tel: +420 2 8192 3909
www.cmkkits.com

Hornby Hobbies Ltd
3rd Floor, The Gateway, Innovation Way, Discovery Park, Sandwich, Kent, CT13 9FF
Tel: +44 (0)1843 233525
www.hornby.com

Model Design Construction
Unit 3 Hillstown Small Business Centre, Mansfield Road, Hillstown, Bolsover, Chesterfield, Derbyshire, S44 6LE
Tel: +44 (0)1246 827755
www.modeldesignconstruction.co.uk

Special Thanks

I cannot complete this book without mention of Ian Mason. I had the pleasure of working with Ian at the RAF Museum Reserve Collection & Restoration Centre in the 1990s. He was a skilled ex-RAF engineer with many years of service and a dedicated aircraft restorer, having been a founder member of Russ Snadden's 'Black 6' Bf 109 restoration team. Sadly Ian is no longer with us, as he succumbed to cancer, but his skill, workmanship and attention to detail were an inspiration to me and I learnt a lot about the Typhoon and Tempest talking to him whilst he restored Tempest NV778. Certain people make an indelible mark on your life and for me Ian is one of them. So, the next time you are at Hendon and you look at Black 6 or Tempest TT.5 NV778, just spare a thought for Ian, for without men like him aircraft of the past would be nothing more than distant memories - Richard A. Franks

Note

There are many different ways of writing aircraft designation, however for consistency throughout this title we have stuck with one style (e.g. Mk Ia, Mk Ib etc.)

Cover

The cover artwork depicts JP925, ZH•J, flown by Flying Officer Norman Lucas of No.266 Squadron, when on the 9th February 1944 he and F/O Miller shot down a Do 24T-1 (W/Nr.0015, KK+T1 of Seenotstaffel 1) near Evreux. This artwork was specially commissioned for this title.
© J. Boucher 2015

Hawker Typhoon Mk Ib from No.56 Squadron does an engine run at its base at Matlask, Norfolk, before undertaking a 'Rhubarb' operation over Holland (©British Official)

Contents

Airframe Chapters

1	Evolution – Tornado	6
2	Evolution – Typhoon	12
3	Typhoon Production Variants	17
4	Drawing-Board Projects	26
5	Camouflage & Markings	31
6	Survivor	41
	Colour Profiles	44

Miniature Chapters

7	Hawker Typhoon Kits	52
8	Building a Selection	71
9	Building a Collection	110
10	In Detail: The Hawker Typhoon	120

Appendices

I	Tornado & Typhoon Kit List	160
II	Tornado & Typhoon Accessory List	162
III	Typhoon Decal List	168
IV	Tornado & Typhoon Production	173
V	Bibliography	175

Glossary

A&AEE .... Aeroplane & Armament Experimental Establishment
CO........ Commanding Officer
Flt .... Flight
ft .... Foot
GP .... General Purpose
HQ........ Headquarters
IFF........ Identification Friend or Foe
in .... Inch
lb .... Pound
Mk........ Mark
Mod....... Modification
mph....... Miles Per Hour
MU .... Maintenance Unit (RAF)
No........ Number
P/Off ..... Pilot Officer
RAE....... Royal Aircraft Establishment
RAF ...... Royal Air Force
RP .... Rocket Projectile
SOC....... Struck Off Charge
Sqn ...... Squadron
UK........ United Kingdom

Typhoon Mk Ib, R8762 with unfaired cannon recoil springs and fitted with 45Imp. Gal. drop tanks during performance trials at A&AEE in January 1943
(©A&AEE/Crown Copyright)

Dedication

This title is dedicated to the memory of Stephen Thompson. Stephen's design work was superb and he worked with me on five other titles prior to the Messerschmitt Me 262 for Valiant Wings in 2010. His style was one I very much liked, and the passion with which he pursued his work was an example to all. He had that rare combination in a designer of creating style with function that allowed his work to be effortlessly accessible, whilst retaining a great individual style that was truly beautiful to behold.

Stephen fought health issues for many years but his sudden death in his sleep in March 2011 was a great shock to us all. Our world is less without him and he will be sadly missed not just by all of us that had the joy of knowing him as a friend, but by many who never had the chance of actually meeting and getting to know him, but who nonetheless still loved his work.

Richard A. Franks
May 2011

Preface

Rapid development of fighters, escort fighters and ground-attack aircraft during the latter stages of the 1930s led to such aircraft as the Hurricane, Spitfire, Defiant and Whirlwind. The former were designed to deal with bombers and lightly-armoured, heavily-armed fighters, but once the Air Ministry learnt that the Luftwaffe had within its arsenal a heavy fighter in the shape of the Bf 110 it was obvious that something had to be done to create such a machine for the RAF.

Development of the Oerlikon and Hispano 20mm cannon for fitment in aircraft was well developed by this stage, but their use was limited by the lack of a suitable engine to power an aircraft at sufficient speed. Rolls-Royce were working on their twelve-cylinder Peregrine for the Whirlwind and from this they proposed a 24-cylinder version in an 'X' layout that basically saw one Peregrine mounted underneath the other. Napier on the other hand had great success with the 'H' layout in their Dagger, so from this they worked on a new 24-cylinder version that was almost an 'H' engine on its side. From these developments came the Vulture from Rolls-Royce and the Sabre from Napier, and with the promise of all this power the Air Staff issued Specification F.18/37 in 1937 for a new heavily-armed fighter powered by these new engines.

Around this time at Hawker, production of the first batch of Hurricanes was well under way and its designer, Sydney Camm, was already

looking towards the type's replacement. His design team therefore started work on new designs that would be tendered to meet F.18/37. In March 1938 the two designs, one using the Sabre and the other the Vulture, were accepted by the Air Ministry and contracts were issued for the production of two prototypes of each. At this stage flight clearance of the new 20mm cannon was not available, so with this in mind these first prototypes were envisaged armed with twelve 0.303in Browning machine-guns.

Hawker Typhoon Mk Ib, EK286, slips behind the photographers' photo plane during a photo-call in April 1943
(Hawker-Siddeley Ltd)

Two brand-new Typhoons (EK286 and EK288) at the Gloster factory at Hucclecote, Gloucestershire on the 16th April 1943, prior to delivery
(©Hawker-Siddeley Ltd)

Chapter 1: Evolution - Tornado

The Vulture installation in the prototype Tornado. The carburettor intake trunking can be seen at the top, above the upper engine mount bracket, while the central intake in the ventral radiator used in the Sabre version is blanked off
(©British Aerospace)

Tornado Prototype #1

Serial Number P5219

Camouflage & Markings

On the 24th and 29th April 1939, five months prior to the first flight of this machine, the Air Ministry issued new Orders with regard to the camouflage of military aircraft. These Orders were A.M.O. A.154/39 and Amendment A.298/39, both of which affected how P5219 was thus painted. The new Temperate Land Scheme was used so that the upper surfaces were in a disruptive pattern of Dark Earth and Dark Green, while the undersides should have been split 50/50 white (starboard) and black (port) with the division for these two colours extending along the centreline of the aircraft's belly. However P5219 did not have the demarcation in this way, instead the white/black stopped at the point where the forward section of the aft monocoque joins the centre section. It has been said by many authors that the area aft of this point was painted silver (aluminium) as were the undersides of the tailplanes, however a close study of the existing images of P5219 prior to its first flight do not show any contract under the aft fuselage, even when manipulated by photographic software, so it would appear that this area was painted in the same colours as the upper surfaces. You can just see a lighter shade at the leading edge of the tailplane, so it looks as if they were silver (aluminium) and the ventral radiator unit and forward nose section are definitely white in starboard side views, so we presume they were black on the port side with the demarcation split along the same centreline as the wings. A 35in diameter Type A roundel was applied either side of the fuselage, below the extreme end of the dorsal spine, while the aircraft serial number in 6in high black characters was applied on either side of the rear

The first Tornado prototype, P5219 in its original form with the radiator unit beneath the fuselage centre section
(©Hawker-Siddeley Ltd)

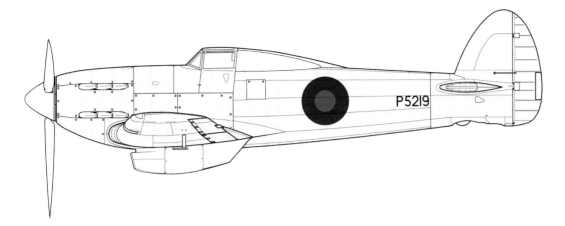

Tornado P5219

fuselage, forward and 4-6in below the tailplane centreline. No roundels were applied to the underside of the wings, nor was there a flash on either side of the vertical fin. It is probable that the upper wings had 50in diameter Type B roundels applied, with their centres 84 inches from the wingtips. Both propeller and spinner were painted black, with the 4in tips of the former in yellow. The walkways on the wing roots were painted with Cerrux Grey primer.

- The first flight was undertaken on the 6th October 1939
- This first prototype had no radio fitted, so there is no mast aft of the cockpit on the dorsal spine, nor any leads from the aft fuselage to the leading edges of the taiplanes
- The wheels featured five-spoke hubs and there were two small blisters aft of the upper set of exhaust stacks on either side of the nose
- The vertical fin and rudder were of the initial smaller shape and the latter featured a navigational light below the trim tab
- It was discovered that the ventral radiator unit created poor airflow, so the airframe was modified and the radiator unit repositioned under the nose
- In this revised form P5219 flew again on the 6th December 1939

- The aircraft was destroyed shortly afterwards in an accident,
- SOC finally 25/08/1943

Tornado Prototype #2

Serial Number P5224

Camouflage & Markings

This aircraft also featured the Temperate Land Scheme of Dark Earth and Dark Green, however for some strange reason the pattern used was a 'mirror image' of the official scheme, while the colours themselves were transposed with Dark Green in place of Dark Earth and Dark Earth in place of Dark Green? By the time of its first flight in December 1940 the new directive of 6th June 1940 was in force whereby "All new aircraft types not generally known will have yellow undersides". Initially the aircraft featured the revised Type A1 fuselage roundels, with their extra yellow outer ring, while the upper wing roundels remained Type B (50in). The serial number remained in black but was now in 8in high characters, albeit that its position remained unchanged. A flash was added to the vertical fin and although the width seems correct at 24in (equal stripes of red/white/blue) the height is certainly not 24in and seems to

The second Tornado prototype P5224 at Boscombe Down. The linkage for the rudder on the vertical fin is evident
(©Air Ministry)

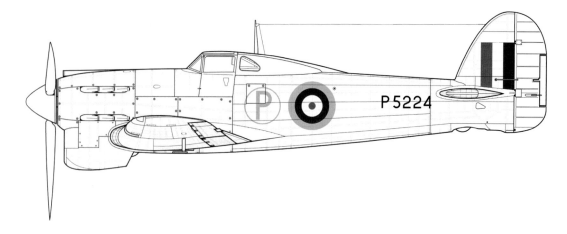

Tornado P5224

The second Tornado prototype P5224 photographed at A&AEE, of note is the intake on top of the cowling, what looks like a blanking plate in the centre of the radiator unit and the demarcation line of the upper and lower colours on the chin cowling
(©Air Ministry/Crown Copyright)

run from just above the fin fillet at the base to the top hinge point on the rudder. Type A roundels of 42in diameter were applied under each wingtip with their centres approximatelty 56in inboard. The spinner and propeller remained black, with the latter having 4in tips in yellow. Later the aircraft gained the new prototype 'P' marking in yellow within a 25in diameter yellow ring, as stipulated in the new regulations of 11th July 1941. This marking was applied forward of the roundel on either side of the fuselage and the 'P' was positioned to point forward on the starboard side and aft on the port side. The demarcation between the upper and lower fuselage colours was determined by a 60° angle from the centreline, so that when this struck the side of the fuselage that was the point of demarcation. With this machine that rule seems to have been applied to the aft fuselage, but the demarcation on the nose is a simple carry-forward from the centreline demarcation on the wing leading edges, it did not slope towards the front as seen on production Typhoons.

- Initially fitted with Vulture II engine, this was replaced in March 1941 with the Vulture V intended for the production Tornado
- The ventral radiator unit of the first prototype was under the chin, as seen on R5219 once modified
- The vertical fin was slightly enlarged and the rudder was also broader in chord and did not have a navigation light below the trim tab
- The aircraft was fitted with a TR.9 transmitter, so there is an aerial mast on the upper dorsal spine and a corresponding lead from the top of it to a point parallel on the leading edge of the verical fin
- The dorsal spine features small windows in either side, aft of the car door
- The wheels had four-spoke hubs
- The rudder had the balance linkage to the fin on the port side only
- The upper cowling featured an air intake at the top, aft of the spinner
- The wings had provision for the fitment of four 20mm cannon, although it probably only ever flew with ballast in lieu of the actual guns as no images have been found showing it with barrel fairings on the wing leading edges
- The aircraft was finally SOC 20/09/44

Production Tornado

Serial Number R7936

Camouflage & Markings

By the time of its first flight this machine was in the standard Temperate Land Scheme of Dark Earth and Dark Green in a disruptive camouflage pattern on the upper surfaces and Sky underneath. The demarcation was similar to that seen on P5224 although that on each side of the chin cowling dropped towards the intake leading edge in a straight line. The spinner and propeller were black, the latter having 4in yellow tips to each blade. Roundels comprised the enlarged 40in Type A1 on the fuselage, plus the standard Type B on the upper wings and Type A underneath. The fin flash was the 24in wide by 27in high version comprising equal (8in) stripes of red (forward), white and blue. The serial number was in 8in high black characters and was applied on either side of the aft fuselage, below and slightly ahead of the tailplane leading edge (forward of the transit join line). Later in its career whilst testing propellers at Rotol's Staverton airfield the markings changed and the underwing roundels were 25in Type C1 (still with their centres approx. 56in from the wing tip) while the fin flash changed to the 24in square version with the 2in white centre stripe separating the 11in wide red and blue sections. It is most likely the fuselage roundel also changed to a Type C1, but the upper wing ones probably remained Type B.

- First Flight 29th August 1941
- Delivered to Rotol at Staverton on the 31st August 1941
- The aircraft was used by both Rotol and de Havilland for various propeller tests including contra-rotating units for the next 18 months
- The aircraft was probably scrapped once all design work on such propellers ceased with the dawn of the jet age

Tornado P5224 in flight, viewed from this angle the underwing roundels are well illustrated and in the original print the blanking plates for the cannon are visible in the wing leading edge
(©Air Ministry/Crown Copyright)

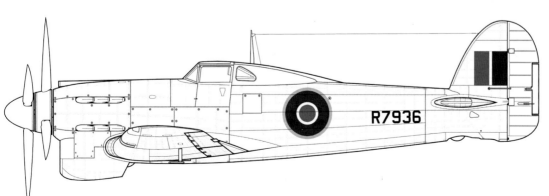

The only production Tornado R7936, seen here ar Rotol's Staverton airfield and fitted with a contra-rotating Rotol propeller unit
(©Rotol)

Tornado R7936

This is the only Centaurus-powered Tornado HG641, in this instance in its original form with the first cowling and the external exhaust stack
(©Hawker-Siddeley)

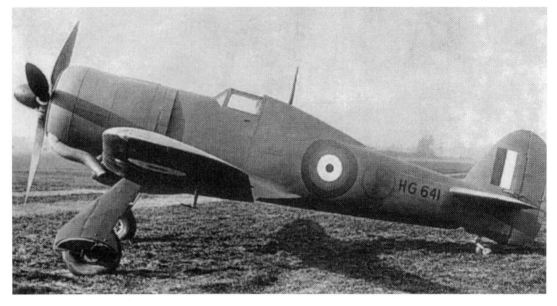

Tornado (Centaurus)

Serial Number HG641

Camouflage & Markings

Again this machine featured the Temperate Land Scheme of Dark Earth and Dark Green in a disruptive camouflage pattern on the upper surfaces, but as a prototype the undersides were probably yellow. The demarcation is standard, but the lower surface colour does not extend to the base of the rudder, which remains entirely in the upper camouflage colours. Initial photos show the 40in Type A1 roundel on the fuselage, plus the standard Type B on the upper wings and Type A underneath. The fin flash was the 24in x 27in version and the serial number was in 8in high black characters applied on either side of the aft fuselage, below and slightly ahead of the tailplane leading edge. Initially we thought that this serial was applied in an odd manner, as photos of the port side showed a distinct gap between the 'HG' and '641' elements, however a very close study of all such images shows that there is a distinct 'box' shape around the serial and it is our belief therefore that this serial was added via a photo-touch-up as the original either did not have it applied, or the prints were censored. Both the three- and four-blade propellers were black with 4in yellow tips to each blade, and when the spinner was fitted that too was black (and in this latter instance both propeller and spinner look very glossy). A prototype 'P' in yellow within a 25in yellow ring was applied aft of the fuselage roundel and forward of the serial number. The 'P' faced aft on the port side and forward on the starboard. By the time the aircraft was modified with the new cowling the fuselage marking was revised to the 35in Type C1 and the fin flash also changed to the 24in square version with a 2in stripe of white separating the 11in wide red and blue elements. At this time the machine seemed to have machine-guns fitted and the area around these shows signs of the red doped linen often applied to seal off the gun ports. At this stage there also seems to be a lighter coloured (or unpainted?) band around the aft fuselage, on the transit joint; the jacking stencil is clearly visible over the top of this band, so it is either a deliberately painted band or bare metal that the stencil was applied over? Study of existing photos shows

Centaurus Tornado HG641 in its revised form, with the new cowling, four-bladed propeller with spinner and exhausts behind the louvres on the fuselage side. The line on the aft fuselage is very prominent, as is the revised vertical fin and rudder
(Hawker-Siddeley)

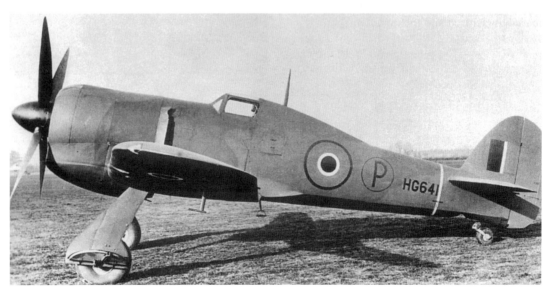

Evolution - Tornado

Tornado HG641 - 1st stage

Tornado HG641 - 2nd stage

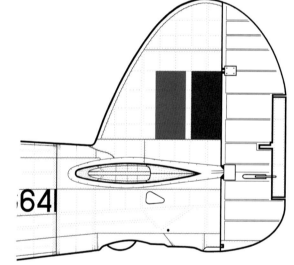

Tornado HG641 - Tempest tail

this to be clearly evident on both sides (see comments on the tail unit below).

- As far back as January 1940 Sydney Camm had considered a radial-powered Tornado and in April 1940 a prototype was ordered
- The first example was not a new build, it used wings from stock and the aft fuselage from the Langley production line, only the centre section was new
- First flown with Centaurus C.E.4S engine by P. Lucas on the 23rd October 1941
- Initially the aircraft featured a Rotol three-blade propeller without spinner
- Cooling problems led to a major redesign of the cowling, with the oil cooler intake moved from underneath the fuselage at the wing leading edge to the bottom lip of the cowling. The exhaust pipe seen on the first cowling was removed, with the new cowling featuring exhausts stacks that ported out of the rear louvres, like the Tempest and Sea Fury
- At the same time a four-blade Rotol propeller with spinner was installed
- Note that as the wings came from store, this machine featured the 'D' doors as part of the main undercarriage cover as per the first Typhoon prototype
- These wings were twelve-gun units and the weapons seemed to have been fitted, going by photos, as the ports are shown open and this is unlikely to have been done if no guns were installed
- Photos of the aircraft before and after modification seem to indicate that the tail unit was revised, initially the rounder, broader unit as seen on the later Tornado and Typhoon prototypes is fitted, but once modified the unit is taller with a pronouced point to the tip more akin to a Tempest? This may be an optical illusion, but it also may explain the light-coloured band visible at the transit joint in some photos - was a new tail unit fitted? - Please check photos to make your on decision on this
- Although the type offered great potential the Tornado design had been abandoned by this stage so the Centaurus engine was projected for use in the Typhoon as the Mk II, which eventually became the Tempest, but that is another story!

Chapter 2: Evolution - Typhoon

Typhoon Prototype #1

Serial Number P5212
Contract Number 815124/38

Colour & Markings

By the time this machine first flew it was painted in the Temperate Land Scheme of Dark Green and Dark Earth applied in a disruptive pattern on the upper surfaces. It should be noted that in the past various well known authors have quoted various other colours, Francis Mason stated that P5212 was for a time painted 'mid-blue/grey' on the upper surfaces (Arthur Bentley also listed this colour on his scale plans in 1974, as did Mike Bowyers in 'Fighting Colours', although in his article in Airfix Magazine in 1961 he stated the Dark Green/Dark Earth scheme was used?), while others have claimed the use of NIVO (a colour deleted in 1935) and a few have started to speculate on the use of a grey primer (often quoted as 'UP1' and 'UP2'). As we write this the bulk of people seem to come down on the side of the official scheme of the period, the problem is that all surviving images seem to indicate no colour demarcation, even from a high resolution image that is manipulated to give high contrast, so was the upper surface camouflaged or one colour - we will probably never know for sure.

The underside saw the port wing in black and the starboard one white. Period images seem to indicate that the underside of the fuselage was in the upper colours (see above), but the radiator cowling was certainly white/black so it is most likely that the demarcation followed the line of the wing fillets and ended at the front edge of the rear monocoque structure. It should be noted that the colour inside the nose intake was white, not black/white. With some confusion about the demarcation of the lower surface colours at this stage, it is no surprise to find that the undersides of the tailplanes were silver (aluminium). A 35in Type A roundel was applied to either side of the fuselage, directly below the end of the dorsal hump behind the canopy. The serial number was applied in black 8in high characters on either side of the aft fuselage, placed in front of and below (probably 6in) the centreline of the tailplane leading edge. No fin flash was applied, nor were there roundels under the wings. There are no published photos of the upper surfaces, so one can only assume that 50in Type B roundels were used as some sources state they have unpublished images confirming this even though regulations at the time specified Type A? Both the spinner and propeller blades were black.

Once modified after the structural failure and with the twelve machine-guns fitted the regulations had changed (as from 6th June 1940) so this meant that the undersides were now painted yellow. There is a well-known image that is often mis-identified as being the 2nd prototype, but in fact was of P5212 taken by the A&AEE during tests at Langley after modification and this shows that a fin flash was added, initially with the blue and white in 7in wide stripes and the remaining forward area of the fin in red. From the 1st August 1940 the regulations stipulated that the fin flash be 24in square with 11in bands of blue and red separated by a 2in white band in the middle. The new style fin flash was placed 1/2in forward of the rudder hinge line. 42in Type A roundels were placed under each outer wing panel, approximately 56in from the wingtip. There is a single image of P5212 showing it after modification and with a large number '6' on the forward port side of the nose, just below the front edge of the exhaust stacks. What is

The Napier Sabre I installation in the first Typhoon prototype. The engine bearing framework, ventral radiator and header tank around the front gearbox/propeller shaft are all noteworthy
(©British Aerospace)

The prototype Typhoon P5212 nearing completion at Langley in 1939. The three-stack exhausts and access panel and ports for the machine guns can be clearly seen
(©British Aerospace)

also strange is that by this stage it also seems to be sporting a revised location for the serial number, as it is a lot higher up the fuselage side than seen on previous images, almost in line with the centre of the tailplane, not below it? By July 1944 P5212 was still in the same overall scheme but had the prototype 'P' added in a yellow ring of 25in diameter aft of the fuselage roundel. It also had a Sky spinner and no armament was installed. The type had prominent strengthening plates on the rear fuselage and these were apparently painted black for some reason?

- Built at Hawker's Kingston plant
- First flight 24th February 1940
- Featured main wheels with five-spoke hubs
- The undercarriage only had main doors, attached to the oleo leg, there were no secondary doors so the tyres and parts of the bay were open once the undercarriage was retracted
- The engine had three-stack exhausts
- No radio was fitted, so no mast or lead was installed
- Exhibited directional instability so it was returned to Hawker for enlargement of the vertical fin and rudder
- During one test flight on the 9th May 1940 at 10,500ft and 270mph Lucas felt a severe lurch and heard a loud bang behind his seat. The vertical tube at the rear of the port longeron and the diagonal compression strut between the joint of the longeron and the top of the main fuselage had failed, resulting in severe buckling and tearing of the skinning as far as the wing trailing edge. Even though the main load-bearing elements of the monocoque were compromised Lucas was able to nurse the aircraft safely back (he had no radio on board so could not tell those at Langley what was going on) and was subsequently awarded the George Medal (gazetted in September 1940) for saving such an important prototype
- After modification the aircraft flew again on the 7th July, but suffered an engine failure resulting in a crash-landing

The first Typhoon prototype P5212 in its original colours and markings, include a lack of any fin flash or roundel under the wings
(©Air Ministry)

14   Evolution - Typhoon

This view of P5212 taken in March 1940 allows you to see the Type B roundels on the upper wings and the prominent wing root walkways
(© Air Ministry)

- Whilst it was being repaired a thicker and enlarged fin was installed, having been first tested on the Tornado
- This still did not give sufficient improvement in the stability of the type, so a larger rudder with a trim tab was installed
- By the time the fourth engine was installed the three-stack exhausts were deleted and six-stack units appeared in an attempt to reduce carbon monoxide ingression into the cockpit. This did not work, so the exhaust stacks were lengthened slightly but this also failed so the original style exhausts returned and louvres were installed
- It is probably at this point that the tailwheel gained doors and the main undercarriage doors were modified to have D-shaped doors added to the bottom section of each main door
- The type had 12 machine-guns fitted, as period images show the open ports in the leading edge as well as the spent cartridge case ejector ports below each wing

- The small windows in the decking behind the cockpit were installed, as was a TR.9D radio mast and aerial lead running from its top parallel to the leading edge of the vertical fin
- At this stage P5212 began a three week series of trials by the A&AEE, but carried out at Hawker's airfield at Langley from 25th September 1940. The pilot detached to complete this was Flt Lt Sammy Wroath and he was joined at Langley by Dr G. Hislop, the technical representative for the Typhoon project at the Air Ministry
- With only one complete Typhoon most of the testing fell to P5212 and in a six-month period before it was joined by P5216 in May 1941 it undertook various trials during 72 flight hours
- The aircraft later went to Northolt for further trials, returning to the A&AEE at their Boscombe Down base

Note: It is claimed that at some stage during testing this airframe received the revised upper engine cowl-

Typhoon P5212

Typhoon P5212 - with window

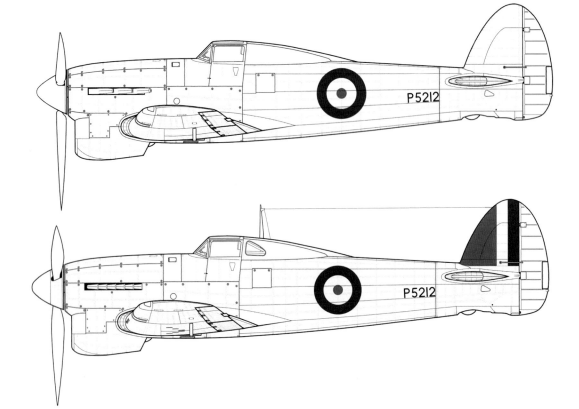

ing that became standard on the Tempest; this had a more rounded profile than the 'flatter' one seen on the early production (and prototype) machines.
- Damaged at A&AEE Boscombe Down on hitting the concrete compass base in July 1941. It is not known if it was repaired, or development work taken over by P5216
- SOC for static tests, date unknown

Typhoon Prototype #2

Serial Number P5216
Contract Number 815124/38

Colour & Markings

The second prototype was definitely finished in the Temperate Land Scheme of Dark Green and Dark Earth applied in a disruptive pattern on the upper surfaces. All of the undersurfaces including the tailplanes were yellow and this extended back to the bottom of the rudder, although the demarcation of this was not in line with that seen on the fuselage. The demarcation on the chin cowling was different from that seen on P5212 or later production machines in that it was low down on the unit, probably using the usual 60° method of working out the demarcation point on the aft fuselage? It should be noted that this method of setting the demarcation means that the line on the chin cowling is at an angle, being higher at the front edge than at the back. 35in Type A1 roundels were applied on both fuselage sides plus the 24x24in fin flash on both sides of the vertical fin. The serial number, in 8in black characters, was applied on both sides of the aft fuselage and again this was slightly below (approx. 6in) and in front of the leading edge of the tailplane. The underwing roundels were 42in diameter Type A with their centres positioned approx. 56in inboard of the wingtip, while those on the upper surfaces were Type B. The propeller and spinner were once again black.

- First flew on the 3rd May 1941
- Some sources have stated that it initially had the twelve-gun armament, but this is due to mis-identification of a photo of P5212
- The enlarged rudder had linkage with the vertical fin visible on the port side
- There were no windows in the decking behind the cockpit

In this front view of P5212 you can see the white/black undersides and the fact that the whole of the inside of the air intake is white

This photo is often quoted as being P5216, but this is P5212 at Langley after modification. Of note are the secondary doors added to the main undercarriage covers, the tailwheel doors, radio mast, twelve-gun wing and 6-stack exhausts
(©British Aerospace)

16 Evolution - Typhoon

This is the second Typhoon prototype P5216 and as you can see this was nearer to Mk Ib standard with the 20mm cannon with exposed recoil spring, the inner set of undercarriage doors and the lack of doors for the tailwheel. The vertical fin and rudder is the larger unit
(©British Aerospace)

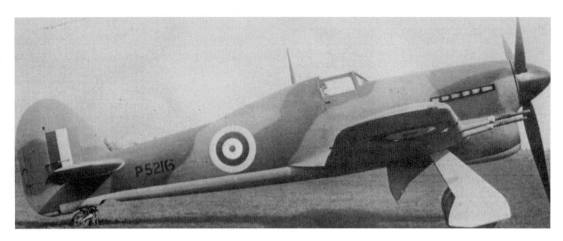

Typhoon P5216

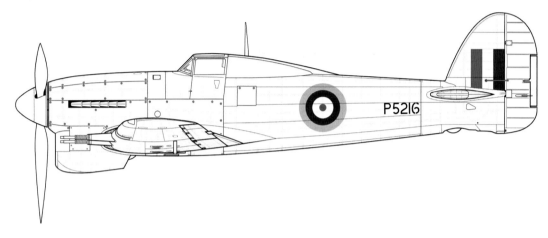

Typhoon P5216 seen here, probably at Langley, shows how similar to the production Mk Ib it was. The 20mm cannon, six-stack exhausts and inboard undercarriage doors are all visible (©BAE)

- A three-blade propeller was fitted
- Five-spoke main wheel hubs
- The secondary undercarriage doors were removed from the bottom of the main door and mounted separately outboard of the centreline on the inner edge of the wheel well. This type of undercarriage door arrangement remained for all future versions of the Typhoon
- The tailwheel doors seen on P5212 were deleted
- Although an aerial mast can be seen in photos, there is no pulley at the top, nor any sign of the coupling at the top edge of the fin, so we suspect no radio was installed

- Armed with four 20mm cannon, although these had the recoil springs visible at the front of each fairing in the wing leading edge, it also had many other modifications that made it more like the production Mk Ib
- Its testing life was limited as just twenty-four days after it flew for the first time the first production Mk Ia (R7576) took to the air
- P5216 spent the remainder of its career with Hawker or at the A&AEE along with periods testing propellers at Rotol
- Finally SOC on the 25th February 1945

Chapter 3: Typhoon Production

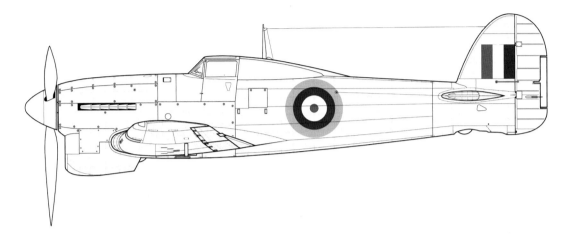

Typhoon Ia - First Production Batch

What follows is a listing of all the variations seen in the Mk Ia and Mk Ib production batches. For camouflage and marking data on these production machines see Chapter 5, while a full list of all the production batches can be found at Appendix IV.

Typhoon Ia - First Production Batch

The exact number of these early productions examples is, as yet, not confirmed, but is at least R7576 to R7635, although it is possibly that it affects airframes up to R7645

- The decking behind the cockpit did not feature the small windows
- TR1133 radio transmitter/receiver installed along with its associated mast The aerial lead ran from the top of the mast parallel to a point on the leading edge of the vertical fin
- IFF leads from the fuselage side to the tips of the tailplane leading edge

An unidentified early Typhoon Mk Ib with unfaired cannon recoil springs and 45Imp. Gal. drop tanks. The text in the bottom corner denotes this as an official 'identification' image, probably taken at A&AEE or RAE *(©Crown Copyright)*

- The rudder had the balance linkage visible on both sides of the vertical fin
- Three-bladed propeller fitted with a blunter shape to the spinner in comparison with previous machines
- Armed with twelve machine guns with their associated access panels in the upper surface plus the spent cartridge ejector ports in the lower surface

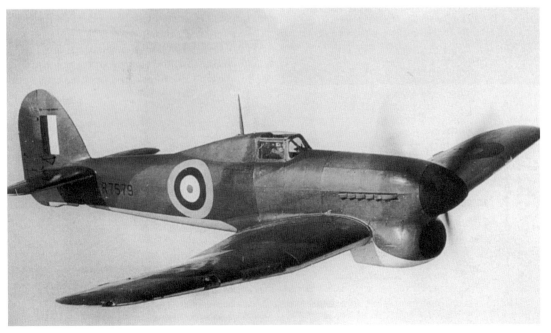

R7579 was one of the first Mk Ias and is seen here in flight devoid of unit markings but in the Dark Green/Dark Earth over Black/White scheme *(©British Aerospace)*

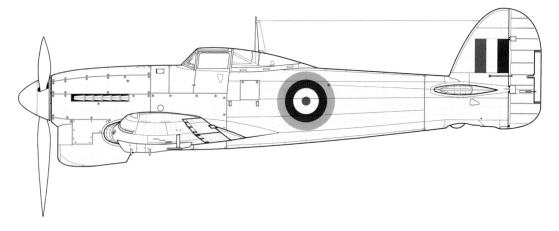

Typhoon Ia - 2nd Production Batch

Typhoon Mk Ib, EK286, 'Fiji V, Morris Hedstrom Ltd, Fiji' was a presentation aircraft and is seen here at Hucclecote on the 16th April 1943. This aircraft survived the war and was SOC in 1946 (©Hawker-Siddeley)

Typhoon Ia - 2nd Production Batch

As with the initial production batch the exact number of these later production examples is, as yet, not confirmed. Certainly R7681 and R7684 are late production machines

- The decking behind the cockpit was replaced with a clear section to improve rearward vision
- TR1133 radio transmitter/receiver installed along with its associated mast The aerial lead ran from the top of the mast parallel to a point on the leading edge of the vertical fin
- No IFF leads seen in photographs, but these may have been installed
- The rudder had the balance linkage visible on both sides of the vertical fin
- Three-bladed propeller fitted
- Armed with twelve machine guns and capacity to carry bombs via a rack under each wing

Typhoon Ib - 1st Production Batch

- The canopy had the solid aft decking
- The rudder had the external balance linkage
- Fitted with three-blade propeller that seems to have had a blunter spinner in comparison with those seen on the prototypes
- Six-stack exhausts
- Fitted with TR 9D radio with mast antenna on decking behind canopy and aerial lead running from top of mast to a point parallel with it on the leading edge of the vertical fin
- IFF aerials from the mid-fuselage to the outer tip of the leading edge of each tailplane
- Armed with four cannon, which did not have the covers for the exposed recoil springs

Typhoon Ib - Early Production Batch #1

- The solid aft canopy section was replaced with a clear plexiglass unit
- The rudder had the external balance linkage
- Fitted with three-blade propeller and the blunter style spinner
- Fitted with TR 9D radio with mast antenna on decking behind canopy and aerial lead running from top of mast to a point parallel with

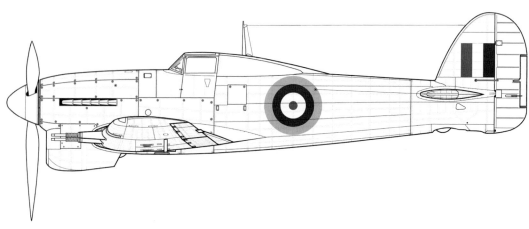

Typhoon Ib - 1st Production Batch

Typhoon Production   19

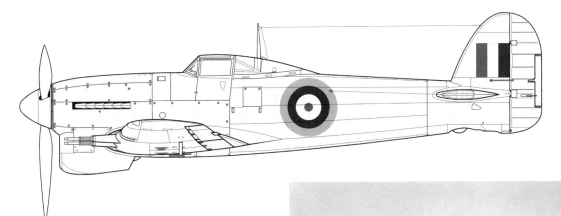

Typhoon Ib - Early Production Batch #1

- it on the leading edge of the vertical fin
- IFF aerials from the mid-fuselage to the outer tip of the leading edge of each tailplane
- Armed with four cannon, which did not have the covers for the exposed recoil springs

Typhoon Ib - Early Production Batch #2
- Car Door canopy, clear rear section
- The rudder did not have the external balance linkage
- Fitted with three-blade propeller and the blunter style spinner
- Fitted with TR 1133 radio with mast antenna on decking behind canopy but no aerial lead
- IFF aerials from the mid-fuselage to the outer tip of the leading edge of each tailplane

- Armed with four cannon with front fairings covering the recoil springs

Presentation aircraft 'Fiji V, Morris Hedstrom Ltd, Fiji', EK286 awaiting a test flight at Hucclecote on the 16th April 1943
(©Hawker-Siddeley Ltd)

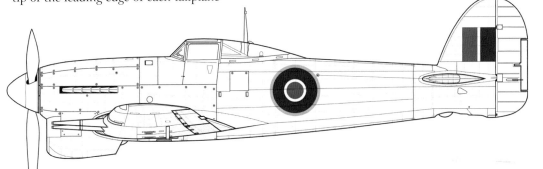

Typhoon Ib - Early Production Batch #2

Early production Mk Ib R7881 was used by the RAE and also saw service with No.3 Tactical Exercise Unit before being SOC in 1946
(©British Aerospace)

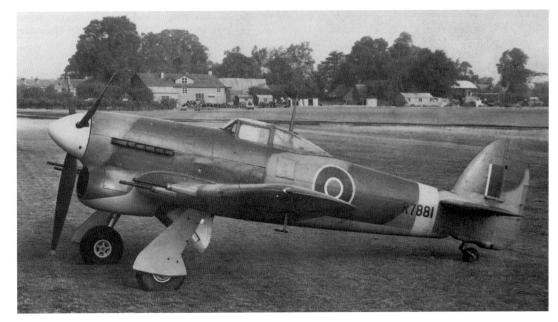

Typhoon Ib - Early-mid Production Batches [Spring 1943]

A formation of Typhoon Mk Ibs including DN317 (US•C), EK183 (US•A), R8825 (US•Y), R8721 (US•X), R8224 (US•H) and R8220 (US•D) all from No.56 Squadron based at Matlask in April 1943
(©Air Ministry/Crown Copyright)

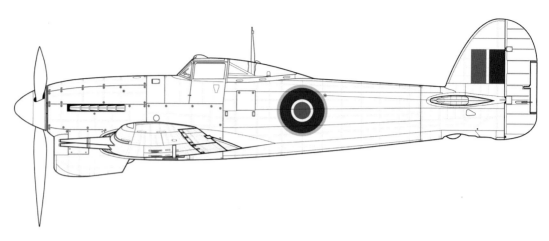

Typhoon Ib - Early-mid Production Batches [Spring 1943]
- Car Door canopy with mirror added to blister in the top section
- No external rudder balance linkage
- Fitted with three-blade propeller and the blunter style spinner
- Fitted with TR 1133 radio with mast antenna on decking behind canopy but no aerial lead
- IFF aerials from the mid-fuselage to the outer tip of the leading edge of each tailplane
- Armed with four cannon with front fairings covering the recoil springs

Typhoon Ib - Mid-production Batches
- Car Door canopy (no mirror)
- External reinforcing 'fish plates' rivetted over the rear transit joint
- No external rudder balance linkage
- Fitted with three-blade propeller and the blunter style spinner
- Fitted with TR 1133 radio with mast antenna on decking behind canopy but no aerial lead
- IFF aerials from the mid-fuselage to the outer tip of the leading edge of each tailplane
- Armed with four cannon with front fairings covering the recoil springs
- Note that some aircraft were later retrofitted with Tempest (enlarged) horizontal tailplanes

Groundcrew push out Typhoon Mk Ib, EK183, US•A, of No.56 Squadron at Matlask on the 21st April 1943. The groundcrews' nicknames, including 'Ozzy', 'Reg' & 'Dutch' are on the back of their overalls
(©Air Ministry/Crown Copyright)

Typhoon Ib - Mid-production Batches

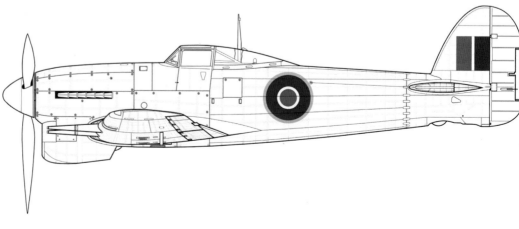

Typhoon Production   21

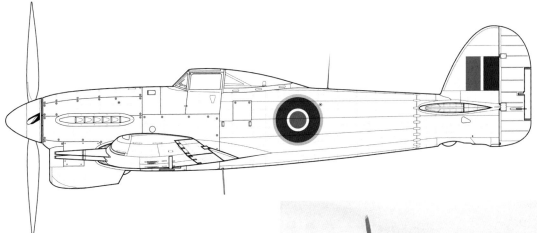

Typhoon Ib - Mid-production (last with 'car-door' canopy)

Typhoon Ib - Mid-production (last with 'car-door' canopy)

- Car Door canopy (no mirror)
- External reinforcing 'fish plates' rivetted over the rear transit joint
- No external rudder balance linkage
- Fitted with four-blade propeller (D.H. or Rotol)
- TR 1133 replaced with TR 1143 so mast antenna deleted and whip antenna added to dorsal spine
- No IFF aerials from the mid-fuselage to the tailplane, instead an IFF rod antenna was fitted under the fuselage, just aft of the wing root trailing edge, off-set to port
- Armed with four cannon with front fairings covering the recoil springs
- Sometimes fitted with Tempest (enlarged) horizontal tailplanes, plus many were retrofitted in service
- Exhausts stacks were usually fitted with a shroud in the factory, but this was normally removed in service as it reduced speed and complicated servicing

This shot of Mk Ib, EK183, US•A of No.56 Squadron was taken at Matlask on the 21st April 1943 for the officially revealing of the type to the press *(©Air Ministry/Crown Copyright)*

No 198 Squadron Typhoons on B.7 at Rucqueville-Martragny, France, in July 1944. Note that MN526, TP•V has the larger Tempest tailplane and a four-blade propeller

This shot shows JR333, a late-production Mk Ib with the Tempest taiplanes, four-blade propeller, whip antenna on the dorsal spine and IFF rod antenna underneath
(©Gloster Aircraft Ltd)

Typhoon Ib - Mid-production (first with 'bubble-top' canopy)

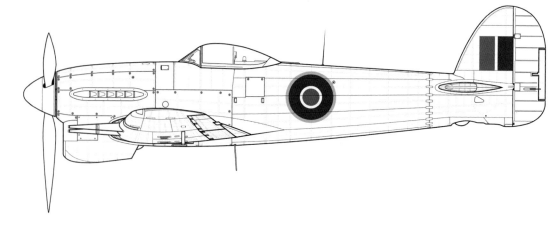

Typhoon Ib - Mid-production (first with 'bubble-top' canopy)

- New clear-view 'bubbletop' canopy replaces 'Car Door' version
- Car door removed on port side and area skinned over during manufacture
- The car door on the starboard side was modified and retained as a knock-out emergency exit
- External reinforcing 'fish plates' rivetted over the rear transit joint
- No external rudder balance linkage
- Fitted with three-blade propeller (D.H. or Rotol)
- TR 1143 radio with whip antenna added to dorsal spine
- IFF rod antenna under the fuselage, just aft of the wing root trailing edge, off-set to port
- Armed with four cannon with front fairings covering the recoil springs
- Exhausts stacks were usually fitted with a shroud in the factory, but this was normally removed in service as it reduced speed and complicated servicing

Typhoon FR Mk Ib - Conversions

- Bubbletop canopy, car door removed on port side and modified on starboard as an emergency exit
- External reinforcing 'fish plates' rivetted over the rear transit joint
- No external rudder balance linkage

This shot shows Typhoon Mk Ib MN180 at the Gloster factory at Hucclecote prior to a test flight on the 10th January 1944
(©Hawker-Siddeley Ltd)

Typhoon FR Mk Ib, EK427 of No.268 Sqn photographed in 1945. Note the truncated inboard cannon barrel fairing where the horizontal camera was installed
(©via R. Sturtivant)

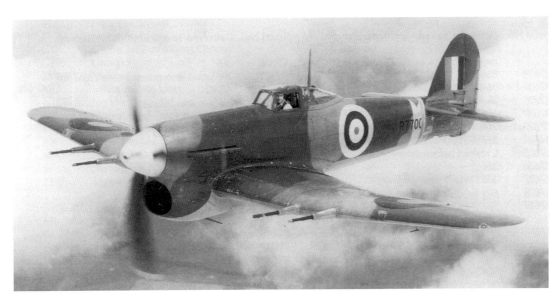

A lovely in-flight shot of R7700, an early Mk Ib probably on a flight for the A&AEE. The aircraft is devoid of squadron markings but does have a Sky fuselage band on the top of which can be seen a gas-detection diamond (this is a mustard-yellow colour)
(©British Official/Crown Copyright)

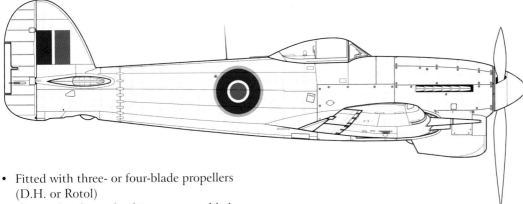

Typhoon FR Mk Ib - Conversions

- Fitted with three- or four-blade propellers (D.H. or Rotol)
- TR 1143 radio with whip antenna added to dorsal spine
- IFF rod antenna under the fuselage, just aft of the wing root trailing edge, off-set to port
- Armament reduced to two cannon (one per wing)
- Two or three cameras mounted vertically in the port wing cannon bay
- One camera mounted horizontally in the inner starboard cannon bay with the lens sighting out through the modified remains of the cannon fairing
- Unshrouded exhausts

I8•P of No.440 Squadron is probably seen here at Eindhoven in March 1945. It is configured as a fighter-bomber as you can see bomb racks under the wing

Another very well known machine, this is R7752, PR•G of No.609 Squadron, an early Mk Ib with unfaired cannon recoil springs, this scheme was used in the original Revell 1/32nd kit. Note that the fuselage Sky band is applied over the serial number
(©via R. Sturtivant)

Typhoon Ib - Late Production

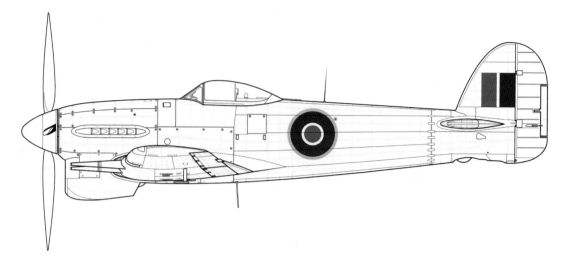

Typhoon Ib - Late Production
- Bubbletop canopy, car door removed on port side and modified on starboard as an emergency exit
- External reinforcing 'fish plates' rivetted over the rear transit joint
- No external rudder balance linkage
- Fitted with four-blade propeller (D.H. or Rotol)
- TR 1143 radio with whip antenna added to dorsal spine
- IFF rod antenna under the fuselage, just aft of the wing root trailing edge, off-set to port
- Armed with four cannon
- Shrouded exhausts (usually removed in service)
- Revised tailwheel unit with anti-shimmy tyre

Note: It is claimed that most of the late production Typhoons shared the revised upper engine cowling that became standard on the Tempest (this has a more rounded profile than the 'flatter' one seen on earlier machines [and tested at some stage on the 1st Typhoon prototype]). The exact point at which this took place in production (if at all) is, as yet, undetermined.

Typhoon Ib - Last Production Batches
- Bubbletop canopy, car door removed on port side and modified on starboard as an emergency exit
- External reinforcing 'fish plates' rivetted over the rear transit joint
- No external rudder balance linkage
- Fitted with four-blade propeller (D.H. or Rotol)
- TR 1143 radio with whip antenna added to dorsal spine
- IFF rod antenna under the fuselage, just aft of the wing root trailing edge, off-set to port
- Armed with four cannon
- Shrouded exhausts (usually removed in service)
- Tempest (enlarged) horizontal tailplanes as standard
- Revised tailwheel unit with anti-shimmy tyre

Note: It is claimed that most of the late production Typhoons shared the revised upper engine cowling that became standard on the Tempest (this has a more rounded profile than the 'flatter' one seen on

A good shot of a late production Mk Ib, of note are the 'anti-shimmy' tailwheel and the fact that this rocket-armed Tiffie has no landing light in the wing leading edge. This was often the case with RP Typhoons, as it was feared that the jet efflux would smash the glazing and the airflow would enter the wing interior

Typhoon Ib - Last Production Batches

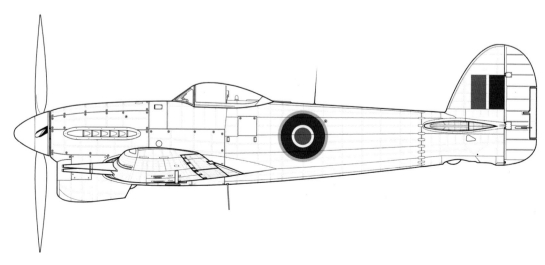

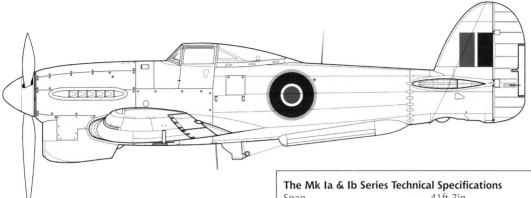

Typhoon TT - Converted Aircraft

earlier machines [and tested at some stage on the 1st Typhoon prototype]). The exact point at which this took place in production (if at all) is, as yet, undetermined.

Typhoon TT - Converted Aircraft

- Car Door canopy (no mirror)
- External reinforcing 'fish plates' rivetted over the rear transit joint
- No external rudder balance linkage
- Fitted with four-blade propeller (D.H. or Rotol)
- TR 1143 radio with whip antenna on dorsal spine
- No IFF aerials
- All armament removed, fairings removed and ports in wings faired over
- Shrouded exhausts
- Target-tug equipment (drogue container and wire guides) installed under rear fuselage - no winch used as target streamed and cable cutter used to release once back over the airfield - various types of such equipment are known via photos, so that shown is only one example
- Protection wires fitted around horizontal tailplanes and vertical fin and rudder, to reduce risk of target cable fouling

The Mk Ia & Ib Series Technical Specifications

Span	-	41ft 7in
Length	-	31ft 10in
Height	-	15ft 4in
Track	-	13ft 6 3/4in
Inner Wing Anhedral	-	1° 11'
Outer Wing Dihedral	-	5° 30'
Incidence	-	0°
Engine Early Machines	-	2,100hp Napier Sabre I 24-cylinder H-type sleeve-valve, liquid-cooled piston engine with D.H. 3-blade propeller
Engine Later Machines	-	Either 2,180hp Sabre IIA, 2,200hp Sabre IIB or 2,260hp Sabre IIC 24-cylinder H-type sleeve-valve liquid-cooled piston engines with D.H. or Rotol 3- or 4-blade propellers [Dia. 14ft 0in]
Performance		
Max. Speed	[Sabre IA @18,000ft]	- 405mph
	[Sabre IIB @19,000ft]	- 412mph
Climb to 15,000ft	[Sabre IIB]	- 5 min 50 seconds
Range with 2x500lb bombs	[Sabre IIB]	- 510 miles
Range with aux drop tanks	[Sabre IIB]	- 980 miles
Service Ceiling	[Sabre IIA]	- 34,000ft
	[Sabre IIB]	- 35,200ft
Weights		
Empty	-	8,840lb
Max Take-off	-	13.250lb [late aircraft with 2x 1,000lb bombs and D.H. 4-blade propeller]
Armament		
Mk Ia	-	Twelve Browing 0.303in machine guns with 500 rounds per gun
Mk Ib	-	Four Hispano 20mm cannon with 140 rounds per gun plus provision for up to eight 3in unguided rocket projectiles with 60lb heads or two 1,000lb bombs under the wings

As the Typhoon was a British aircraft it was built and all its performance was measured by Imperial standards so we have refrained from offering the above data in any other format

A very well known shot, but worth including nonetheless as it clearly shows a bubbletop Mk Ib (JR128, HF•L) of No.54 Squadron with Sky spinner and fuselage band plus yellow wing leading edges but devoid of any other 'recognition' markings (©via R. Sturtivant)

Chapter 4: Projects & Drawing-Board Projects

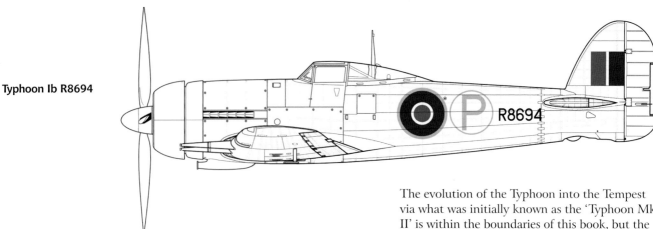

Typhoon Ib R8694

The evolution of the Typhoon into the Tempest via what was initially known as the 'Typhoon Mk II' is within the boundaries of this book, but the actual Tempest variants are not. What follows therefore is a list of all those Typhoons that were modified and became prototypes for Tempest variants, as well as the one-off annual cowl and night-fighter Typhoons and the projected naval version.

Typhoon Ib R8694
- Test-bed for annular radiator cowling
- Front cowling replaced with experimental annular radiator
- Carburettor air intake via scoop under the revised nose
- Car-door canopy with clear rear section
- The fuselage/tail joint featured the 'fish plate' reinforcement
- Rudder without the external balance linkage
- Four-blade propeller with very small spinner
- TR 1133 radio with mast, but no aerial lead
- No IFF leads or rod mast
- Retained the four-cannon armament
- Fitted with Tempest (enlarged) style horizontal tailplanes

Close-up of the annular radiator arrangement fitted to R8694 *(©Napier)*

Typhoon R8694 with the annual cowling installed, seen here at Napier's Luton airfield *(©Napier)*

Typhoon NF Mk I R7881 port side, note the shrouded exhausts and the fact that it looks as if just one blister remains on the upper wing surface (©British Aerospace)

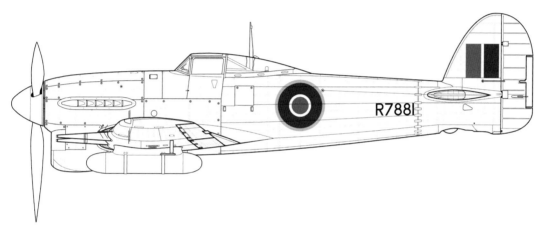

Typhoon NF Ib R7881

Typhoon NF Ib R7881
- Prototype Night Fighter, March 1943

- Car-door canopy with clear rear section
- The fuselage/tail joint featured the 'fish plate' reinforcement
- Rudder with external balance linkage
- Three-blade propeller
- TR 1133 radio with mast, but no aerial lead
- IFF leads from fuselage side to leading edge of each horizontal tailplane
- Four-cannon armament
- Outer port landing light removed and hole covered for fitment of AI Mk VI 'arrow' transmitter unit
- Corresponding transmitter antennae fitted above and below starboard wing, mid-chord, outboard of cannon bay
- AI Mk VI receiving rod antennae installed towards tip of both wings on upper and lower surfaces
- 44Imp. Gal. drop tank and associated pylon fitted below each wing
- Shrouded exhausts

The only Typhoon NF Mk I, R7881. The AI radar masts can be seen in the leading edge of the port wing as well as at each wingtip. The 44Imp. Gall. drop tanks we suspect were the same as used on the Hurricane night fighter
(©Hawker-Siddeley Ltd)

Sea Typhoon

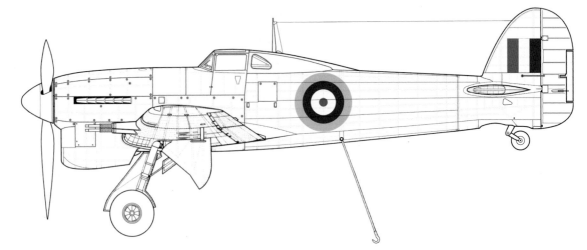

Sea Typhoon
- Project P.1009 for carrier-based fighter [never built]
- Car door canopy, solid aft fairing with small windows either side
- TR.9D radio with mast and lead at point parallel on the leading edge of the vertical fin
- Rudder with external balance linkage
- Three-blade propeller
- Unshrouded exhausts
- Fuselage lengthened forward of cockpit in fuel tank area and again in the aft monocoque
- Increased wing span with wing fold
- Undercarriage relocated and undercarriage legs set to retract outwards
- Arrestor hook and strengthening under rear fuselage
- Fitted with four cannon, recoil springs exposed

Typhoon II HM595
- Prototype for Tempest V in its initial form, September 1942 (1st stage)
- Car door canopy with clear aft section
- Rear fuselage/tail transit joint featured 'fish

Typhoon II HM595 - 1st stage

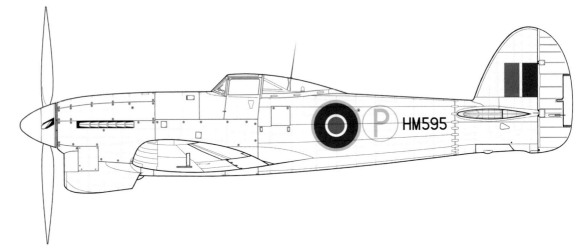

Typhoon HM595, the Tempest V prototype seen here in its initial form
(©Hawker-Siddeley Ltd)

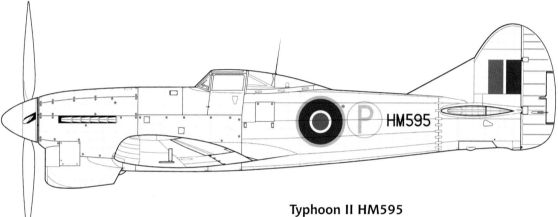

This shot of HM595 in flight shows it fitted with the interim fin fillet
(©British Aerospace)

**Typhoon II
HM595
- 2nd stage**

plate' reinforcement
- Fuselage lengthened forward of cockpit in fuel tank bay
- The vertical fin and rudder were enlarged
- Tempest style (enlarged) horizontal tailplanes
- New laminar flow wing
- Four-blade propeller
- TR 1143 radio with whip antenna on top of the aft clear section of the canopy
- The new wing did not feature armament, so there were no access panels or associated bulges or fairings

Typhoon II HM595
- Prototype for Tempest V in its later form, early 1943 (2nd stage)

Identical to it in its initial form except:
- Interim-style fin fillet fitted
- Armed with four cannon with revised (shorter) barrels that projected from wing leading edge (no fairings)

Typhoon II HM599
- Prototype for Tempest I in its initial form, February 1943 (1st stage)

- Car-door canopy with clear aft section
- Rear fuselage/tail transit joint featured 'fish plate' reinforcement

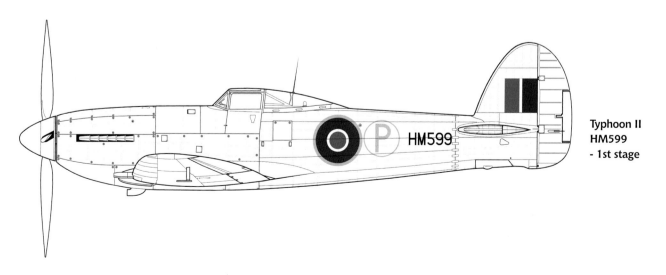

**Typhoon II
HM599
- 1st stage**

The Typhoon Mk II HM599 seen in its initial form with the car-door style canopy. Note the leading edge radiators and short cannon fairings
(©British Aerospace)

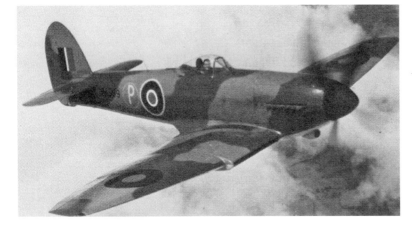

HM599 in flight in its revised form with the bubble canopy and the intake moved further forward under the nose
(©Hawker-Siddeley Ltd)

- Fuselage lengthened forward of cockpit in fuel tank bay
- The vertical fin and rudder were enlarged
- Tempest style (enlarged) horizontal tailplanes
- New laminar flow wing
- Combined oil/water radiator units in inboard wing leading edge of both wings
- Carburettor air intake via small scoop under chin
- Four-blade propeller

- TR 1143 radio with whip antenna on dorsal spine
- Armed with four cannon with revised (shorter) barrels and fairings

Typhoon II HM599
- Prototype for Tempest I in its initial form, February 1943 (2nd stage)

- Identical to it in its initial form except:
- Carburettor air intake moved forward under the chin
- Car-door canopy replaced by the newer 'bubbletop' version
- All armament removed and the ports in the wing leading edges faired over

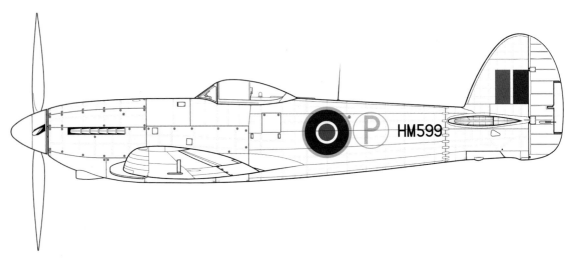

Typhoon II HM599 - 2nd stage

Chapter 5: Camouflage & Markings

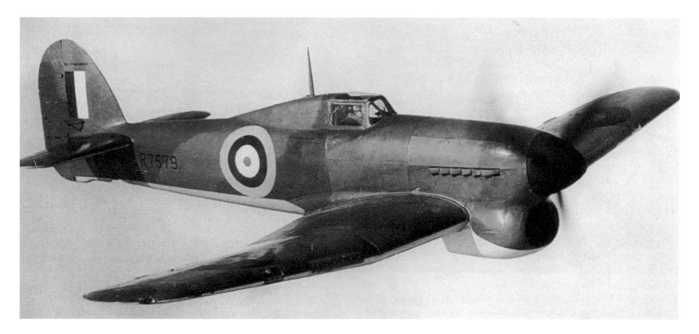

Here is R7579, one of the first Mk Ias, the overall scheme is the Dark Green/Dark Earth over Black/White scheme. The Type A fuselage and Type B wing roundels are visible as is the fin flash with equal bands of blue/white/red *(©British Aerospace)*

Let us first start by saying that nothing is certain when trying to deduce colours from old black and white photographs. The best you can make is an educated, and with luck intelligent, guess using both photographic and documentary evidence. The regulations with regard to the camouflage and markings of RAF aircraft during the war period are well known and all survive, the problem is that at the front line when the regulations changed it was highly unlikely that the ground crew rushed out to paint every aircraft in their charge, it was simply not practical. As a result you will find many anomalies in period images, such as the Type A roundel being seen under the wings of Typhoons as late as early 1945! So be warned, nothing is an absolute when it comes to camouflage and markings, and therefore what follows is what should have been according to the regulations.

For the schemes applied to the Tornado and Typhoon prototypes, please see Chapters 1 and 2 respectively.

Note – Do not get confused by the date when changes took place in the camouflage and markings of the Typhoon and those when the official orders were promulgated. The former usually happened well before the latter, as the pace of war often meant the paperwork was well behind the actual event!

The whole issue of camouflage on RAF aircraft can be traced back to the research undertaken by the RAE at Farnborough after the Expansion Scheme of 1937/38. The RAE undertook research into the most effective paint colours as well as devising specific disruptive schemes to render the best camouflage over specific terrain. In 1937 the RAE obtained general arrangement drawings from all the aircraft manufacturers of all types then in production (including prototypes), and from these devised a series of paint and camouflage patterns. These diagrams were sent to each manufacturer who was instructed to follow them with all current and future aircraft production. From the RAE drawings Hawker set about applying a specific camouflage pattern to all their designs, and this included both the Tornado and Typhoon. Even though it was not until July 1941 that the firm produced the official diagram in response to A.M.O A.513/41 (see later), all Tornado (bar P5224) and all Typhoons (bar P5216) built followed the initial patterns established by the RAE in 1937.

When the first production Typhoon R7576 flew on the 26th May 1941 it was painted in the standard Temperate Land Scheme that had come into force on the 12th December 1940 (A.M.O. A926/40). This comprised Dark Green and Dark Earth in the prescribed disruptive scheme on the upper surfaces, vertical fin/rudder and fuselage sides to a demarcation determined by the point at which a 60° angle from the centreline struck the fuselage side. With the Typhoon the demarcation line on the chin cowling arced down from a point at the wing root leading edge to the front of the cowling, probably at a point determined by the previously mentioned 60° method. The lower surfaces were Sky and the spinner and propeller were usually black, the latter having 4in of each tip in yellow. In accordance with (IAW), the Order dated 1st May 1940, the Type A fuselage roundels changed to the 42in Type A1 by the addition of a 12in yellow outer ring with this marking centred on the bottom edge of the radio

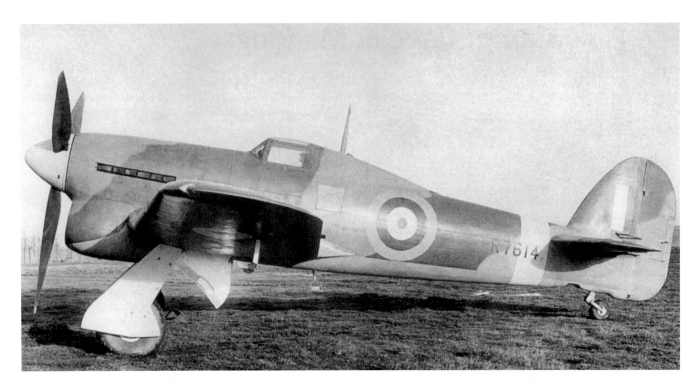

R7614 is a Mk Ia with Sky spinner and aft fuselage band, the contrast of which confirms the overall scheme as Dark Green/Ocean Grey over Medium Sea Grey. The fuselage Type A1 and underwing Type A roundels can be seen. You can also see how the fuselage roundel's centre is on the panel line that is at the bottom of the radio access hatch (© Hawker-Siddeley)

access door on the port side. The upper wing roundels were 50in blue and red Type B, while the underwing roundels remained 42in Type A with the centres of both these markings placed 1/6th of the span (84in) inboard of the wingtip; the regulations stated this latter marking was only to be applied on 'fighters', which at this stage the Typhoon was still considered to be. The serial number remained in 8in high black characters and these were applied mid-fuselage just forward of the transit joint for the tail; the regulations just stated that this marking had to be applied "at the rear end of the fuselage", so there is potential for variation. The fin flash was applied in accordance with the A.M.O dated 1st August 1940 that saw a 24x27in unit with equal (8in) bands of red/white/blue and with the red section facing forward on both sides;

Mk Ib EK183 seen here in service with No.609 Squadron, of note are the light coloured (sky?) tip to the black spinner and the black and white ID bands under the wings; the application of the white puts this photo as after 19th November 1943, but prior to February 1944. The underwing roundel is Type C1 (©Hawker-Siddeley)

Camouflage & Markings 33

This is a nice underside shot, showing the 12in/24in black/white ID stripes on the underside, the aft fuselage Sky band, Sky spinner, Type C roundel under the wing and Type C1 on the fuselage. Note that the rudder is in the upper surface colours even underneath. The small black item near the wing trailing edge on the port fuselage underside is a 'boat antenna' a Bakelite structure for a radio mast *(©Hawker-Siddeley)*

This view from the rear of the Typhoon clearly shows the single 12in wide yellow bands applied to the upper wings in line with the inner cannon barrel. The port wing root walkway looks to be grey? The wing roundels are Type B, while the fuselage roundel is Type C1 *(©Air Ministry/Crown Copyright)*

Recognise this? It's the photo of King George VI and his entourage of senior RAF officers walking over to Hawker Typhoon Mark IB, MN454, HF•S of No.183 Squadron, while inspecting aircraft and equipment at Northolt to be used in the invasion of Normandy, and it is what the box art for the Brengun kit is based upon! *(©Air Ministry/British Official)*

Under the supervision of their Flight Sergeant, armourers of No.609 Squadron RAF lift 3in. Rocket Projectiles fitted with 60lb warheads to load onto the Mk Ibs at Thorney Island, Hampshire. In the background can be seen JR379, PR•L, which has already received its rockets *(©Air Ministry/British Official)*

In this shot of MN658, I8•E of No.440 Sqn on the 22nd January 1945 you can clearly see that the upper wing roundels have been modified to Type C1 but that a yellow ring has been added, something that the official regulations did not allow *(©Public Archives of Canada)*

those on the Typhoon were usually done to 24x24in, though. The camouflage patterns used throughout the RAF were clarified in A.513/41 dated 10th July 1941 that stated "A series of five patterns has been prepared defining the various camouflage and colouring schemes, they are applicable to all aircraft irrespective of the peculiarities of each type". This resulted in all aircraft manufacturers preparing camouflage pattern diagrams using the Air Ministry pattern specified for that aircraft type (e.g. fighter etc), even though these disruptive patterns had been devised and stipulated by the RAE back in 1937. Those relating to the Typhoon were created by Hawker Aircraft and are Drawing No. D.114155.

All of the above is rather superfluous, though, as very few early Typhoon Mk Ia or Ib ever saw operation in the Dark Green/Dark Earth/Sky scheme, because by the time the type was taken on charge with the RAF (R7579 at the CFS on the 27th August 1941) Hawker were already using a new set of colours. They had already been working with new camouflage colours for the Hurricane and on the 24th July 1941 they produced drawings for the Hurricane that saw the Dark Earth replaced with a colour called 'Ocean Grey', while the underside Sky was replaced with Medium Sea Grey. This new scheme for the Hurricane was finalised on the 26th August 1941 and with Hawker already having deliveries of the new Ocean Grey it is not surprising that Typhoons coming off the Gloster production line at that time were painted with the new colours. There were no official regulations covering the use of the new colours at this stage, but all the machines issued to Nos.56, 266 and 609 Squadrons as they worked-up on the type at Duxford during

late 1941 and into May 1942 all had the Dark Green/Ocean Grey/Medium Sea Grey scheme. As early as September 1941 the Typhoons with the AFDU at Duxford had an 18in wide band of Sky applied around the aft fuselage, 6in forward of the tailplane leading edge, plus the spinner was also in this colour although the amendment to the regulations to make this latter item official did not happen until the 23rd January 1943. Squadron code letters applied to the Typhoon were in Sky and 24in high characters, with the squadron two-digit codes (US, UO & RP) applied forward of the roundel on the port side and aft on the starboard, and the individual aircraft code letter applied aft of the roundel on the port and forward on the starboard. As always there are exceptions, as photos of No.193 Typhoons show them with the squadron codes behind the roundel on the port side?

After the shooting down in error of two No.56 squadron Typhoons by Spitfires on the 1st June 1942 due to confusion with the Focke-Wulf Fw 190, it was felt necessary to add an additional identification marking to the Typhoon. This marking comprised a 12in wide yellow chordwise band running back in line from the

Mk Ib, EK183, US•A of No.56 Squadron at Matlask on the 21st April 1943. Of note are the application of the yellow bands on the upper wing and the fact that the individual aircraft letter ('A') seems to be in a different style and size to the squadron code ('US')? *(©Crown Copyright)*

The famous MP197 with its sharkmouth artwork, seen here from the rear to confirm the tail checkers and the odd patch below the windscreen *(©via Internet)*

MP197 in all its ferocious glory *(©via Internet)*

Another view of MP197, confirming the fitment of the Mk III rocket rails on this particular machine *(©via Internet)*

A No.175 Squadron Typhoon returns from a mission with its rocket rails empty and taxies between the trees at le Fresne-Camilly (B.5) airfield in the post D-Day period *(©British Official)*

Ground crew working on a Typhoon on the continent after D-Day as another one flies overhead returning from a mission *(©Air Ministry)*

Nice in-flight shot of JP853, SA•K of No.486 Squadron *(©Crown Copyright)*

This is an early-production Mk Ib without the forward cannon barrel fairings (R8224) in which you can clearly see that the spaces between the black stripes on the underside are still Medium Sea Grey, not white. The nose in a vertical line from the wing leading edge is white, in an attempt to stop confusion between the Typhoon and Fw 190. The film used has resulted in the yellow ring of the Type C1 fuselage roundel turning into a dark shade (©British Aerospace)

inboard cannon fairing; Michael J.F. Bowyer states in Fighting Colours that during a visit to Duxford in August 1942 he saw Typhoons with two of these bands on each wing, the second in line with the outer cannon fairing. No official order was ever released specifying the date by which these bands had to be removed, but by mid-1943 nearly all Typhoons no longer had the marking. The regulations officially changed, however, with the release on the 2nd July 1942 of A.M.O. A664/42, which specified the Dark Green and Ocean Grey over Medium Sea Grey scheme for all day fighters. These regulations also saw the replacement of the Type A and A1 roundels with the new Type C and C1, the former being the Type C with a yellow outer ring added, albeit that this marking was in common use from May 1942. These new roundels came in three sizes, the first being of just 18in diameter (16in Type C) and the second of 36in diameter (32in Type C) and the largest of 54in (48in Type C). The Type C was used under the wings, while the Type C1 became the standard fuselage roundel from this point. The fin flash also changed and although it remained 24x24in, the red and blue sections were expanded to 11in and the central white element reduced to 2in. Spinners were to be Sky and an 18in wide band of Sky was to be applied around the rear fuselage "immediately forward of the tail unit". A yellow stripe was added to the leading edge of each wing, running from the landing light and tapering to 3/4 the initial width by the tip light. The width of this band was again determined by an angle, this time 80° from the leading edge centreline, so that where it struck the wing was

Many Typhoons found themselves in second-line duties once they had been used at the front line. Here is a good example, JR193 ex-No.182 Squadron, and seen here in storage after the war still wearing its markings from No.3 Tactical Exercise Unit (©via R. Sturtivant)

This posed press image (hence Lt Erik Haabjoern's hand over the squadron number - it's No.56), does at least show up a few detail points such as the anti-creep marks on the tyres, the black/white stripes under the wings with these carefully painted around the cannon barrel fairing bases and the fact that the top part of the inboard cannon fairing is green as a carry-on from the camouflage pattern on the wing. The barrel ports are taped closed (©Public Archive of Canada)

This shot of MN180 at Hucclecote on the 10th January 1944 does highlight a few things, namely that the wings are built and painted with the ID bands on them at this stage, as the panels covering the wing leading edge tanks were added at the end of assembly and they are unpainted. Note also that the propeller and spinner are very matt indeed (©Gloster Aircraft Ltd/Hawker-Siddeley Ltd)

This is a nice underside shot of Typhoon Mk Ib, EK286, showing the 12in/24in black/white ID stripes on the underside, the aft fuselage Sky band, Sky spinner, Type C roundel under the wing and Type C1 on the fuselage (©Hawker-Siddeley)

the outer perimeter of the yellow marking. Code letters remained in Sky and the serial number in black (or Night).

Due to the confusion of the Typhoon with the Fw 190 an additional recognition marking was stipulated in November 1942. This resulted in the whole of the lower chin intake cowling plus 1/2 of the upper engine cowlings being painted white, along with the spinner; the exception here being No.181 Squadron who had the nose of their Typhoons in line with the centreline of the wing leading edge painted Sky. The white-painted nose was considered experimental and another measure tried at the time saw four black (Night) 12in bands applied below the wings 24in apart, positioned with the outboard band aligned against the inboard edge of the ailerons. As a result of this the 32in diameter Type C roundel was moved 6in away from the outer-most band (thus 78in from the wingtip). On the 19th November this order was amended and called for the areas between the black bands to be painted white. On the 5th December 1942 the white nose marking was deleted and the black/white stripes were officially introduced.

Plans for the Allied invasion of Europe had been considered from mid-1943 and a special section was set up to determine suitable recognition aids that could be applied quickly to Allied aircraft on the night before the invasion. As a result of this in an Order dated 3rd February 1944 it stated that "with effect from first light 7th February *[note that some sources state this was the 7th February 1945?]*, the Typhoon is to revert to Standard Day Fighter markings, the Black and White under wing bands to be painted out on aircraft in service and omitted from new production machines'. As a result all Typhoons reverted to the standard scheme of Dark Green/Ocean Grey over Medium Sea Grey, with Sky spinners and aft fuselage bands, yellow wing leading edges, 36in Type C1 fuselage, 32in Type C underwing and 50in Type B upper wing roundels and 24x24in Type C fin flash. The first Tempests came into RAF service not long after this change in the regulations, but they somehow retained the black/white identification markings under the wings until replaced by the D-Day markings on the night of the 5th/6th June 1944.

The A.A.E.F Invasion Stripes (D-Day) markings for the Typhoon consisted of 18in wide stripes (three white and two black) applied around the wings, starting at a point 6in inboard of the upper wing roundel. Three white and two black 18in bands were also applied to the rear fuselage, with the first band applied 18in forward of the leading edge of the tailplane. This latter marking caused confusion and there are many instances where the first band forward of the tailplane obscured the Sky fuselage band, or was not applied as a result of the existence of the Sky band in that location. The bands remained until the regulations stipulated

Camouflage & Markings 39

ABCD P HM 1234567890
P HM 1234567890

24" high
Sky fuselage codes
(Standard style)

8" high
Night fuselage serials
(Standard styles)

National Markings
1/48 scale
©Richard J. Caruana 2011

National Markings Up To May 1942

50" diameter
Blue/Red roundel
above wings

42" diameter
Blue/White/Red roundel
below wings

35" diameter
Yellow/Blue/White/Red
fuselage roundel

24" X 27"
Blue/White/Red
fin flash

National Markings Post May 1942

50" diameter
Blue/Red roundel
above wings

32" diameter
Blue/White/Red roundel
below wings

36" diameter
Yellow/Blue/White/Red
fuselage roundel

24" X 24"
Blue/White/Red
fin flash

National Markings Post January 1945

50" diameter Blue/White/Red
roundel above wings
(Modified from Blue/Red)

32" diameter
Blue/White/Red roundel
below wings

36" diameter
Yellow/Blue/White/Red
fuselage roundel

24" X 24"
Blue/White/Red
fin flash

that they were to be removed from the upper wing and fuselage surfaces in the period of the 2nd August to 10th October 1944. The underwing and lower fuselage stripes remained in place until early 1945, by which time most had been removed without any official order to that effect. On the 3rd January 1945 the 2nd TAF issued orders that all aircraft attached to the Command were to have their spinners painted black or camouflaged instead of Sky or the individual Squadron or Flight colours, and the Sky rear fuselage band was also to be deleted.

At the same time an order was issued to modify the upper wing 50in Type B roundel to Type C standard by adding a white band 1/2 the diameter of the blue with a red circle 3/8 the total diameter inside that.

There are instances at this time of Typhoons with a white or yellow outer ring to the upper wing roundel, but this was never official and in the orders released on the 7th January 1945 any such band had to be removed. As the Typhoon squadrons moved through Europe in late 1944/early 1945 the problems with dust

40 Camouflage & Markings

Typhoon RB389 of No.440 Sqn clearly shows the changes in 2nd TAF marking regulations in early 1945, as the spinner has been painted black and the aft fuselage Sky band has been overpainted in green *(©Public Archives of Canada)*

A very informative photo of a Mk Ib from No.56 Squadron at Matlask on the 21st April 1943. Note the ID stripes carefully painted around the cannon fairing bases, to the extent that the outer one is still Medium Sea Grey on the lower half. The propeller tips are clearly marked in yellow (4in) and the spinner seems to be 50/50 Sky and black. The hooks under the wings are bomb shackle pick-ups *(©Gloster Aircraft Ltd/Crown Copyright)*

resulted in Napier staff coming up with a dome filter for the air intake; in service this unit was usually painted Medium Sea Grey and often carried the individual code letter of the aircraft on it in black.

Operational Markings

See the colour profiles on pages 42–49 for a selection of unit markings and insignia applied to the Typhoon. We would also recommend the following titles for those wishing to read more on this complex subject

- **British Aviation Colours of World War Two: The Official Camouflage, Colours and Markings of RAF Aircraft 1939-1945**, RAF Museum Series Vol.3 (Arms & Armour Press 1976 ISBN: 0-85368-271-2
- **Camouflage & Markings: RAF Fighter Command Northern Europe 1936-1945** by James Goulding and Robert Jones (Ducimus Books Ltd 1970-71)
- **Fighting Colours: RAF Fighter Camouflage and Markings 1937-1969** by Michael J.F. Bowyer (Patrick Stephens Ltd 1969 SBN: 85059-041-8)

Bubbletop MN180 at Hucclecote, 10th January 1944. Of note are the unpainted inboard wing leading edges, which cover the tanks and we presume were thus only fitted once the wings were on the aircraft, and the wings themselves were probably pre-painted prior to assembly to the current regs. (hence the ID stripes and roundel). The doped patch on the side of the cowling is the camera-gun port as the camera would not be added until the aircraft was in service *(©Gloster Aircraft Ltd/Crown Copyright)*

Chapter 6: Survivor

Today, of the 3,317 Typhoons built, just one complete example survives, so we thought it fitting to offer a concise history of this unique example.

- Ordered from Hawker Aircraft Ltd by the Air Ministry against contact No.943/SAS/C.23(A)

- Work sub-contracted by Hawker to Gloster Aeroplane Company Ltd under sub-contract No.B.12148/39

- Built during 1944 at Gloster's Hucclecote factory in Gloucestershire. Given airframe number 153219 it was fitted with a Napier Sabre IIA engine and formed part of the 5th production batch (MN229 to MN269), which were delivered between December 1943 and June 1944

- First flight took place at Hucclecote on the 8th February 1944 with Sqn Ldr Allan H. Smith DFC at the controls. So good was the aircraft that he signed it 'off test' with no rectification work required before the aircraft was taken on charge by the RAF

- The aircraft was released by Gloster on the 16th February 1944 and allocated to No.51 Maintenance Unit (MU) Lichfield for storage

- During March 1944 the airframe was allocated for flight evaluation in the USA. The evaluation was in response to the USAAF's interest in the type as a fighter-bomber and for trials relating to increased fuel capacity

- On the 12th March 1944 the aircraft was sent to No.47 MU at RAF Sealand, Cheshire, for packing prior to shipment by sea

- Loaded aboard the SS American Manufacturer on the 24th March 1944 for shipment to the USA

- The SS American Manufacturer arrived at New York on the 16th April 1944, where the aircraft was unloaded and shipped by road to Wright Field at Dayton, Ohio.

- Arrived at Wright Field on the 6th May 1944

- At some stage (exact date unknown) the aircraft was allocated the serial number FE491, later changed to T2-491. The 'FE' denoted Foreign Experimental and was applied to both Allied and Axis types tested in the USA.

- On the 6th June 1944 MN235 was photographed at Freeman Field (Photo Ref #NA164)

- Due to changing requirements MN235 did not undertake the test programme originally envisaged and following a minor accident it was placed into storage

- On the 24th July 1944 at Freeman Field the engine was crated for storage, at which time it had only nine hours flying time on it.

- By the 3rd January 1949 the crated airframe and engine were in store at the ex-Douglas Aircraft facility at Orchard Field Airport, Park Ridge, Illinois and ownership was passed from the USAAF to the new 'National

Air Museum', which had been created by an act of Congress on the 12th August 1946 and later went on to be known as the National Air & Space Museum.

- The site at Orchard Field was renamed O'Hare International Airport in 1949 but the ex-Douglas Aircraft site was re-activated by the USAAF in 1950 with the commencement of the Korean War and many of the aircraft stored there were moved outside.

- In a letter in UK magazine Air Pictorial in August 1953 the aircraft was spotted at Orchard Field Airport (actually already renamed O'Hare International Airport by this time) by Keith Boyer.

- By 1955 commercial flights started at O'Hare International Airport which meant that the aircraft stored there could no longer remain on site, so all (including MN235) were

Photographed on the 6th June 1944 at Freeman Field, of note are the lack of landing lights in the wing leading edge, the shrouded exhausts and the basic markings *(©USAF)*

Photographed in 1994 after inclusion in the D-Day exhibition at Hendon when the black/white Invasion Stripes had been applied
(©RAF Museum, Hendon)

moved to the newly acquired storage site at Silver Hill, Suitland, Maryland. This site was named the 'Paul E. Garber Preservation, Restoration and Storage Facility' not long after opening and MN235 remained in storage there until 1967

- By the late 1960s the idea of a dedicated aircraft museum in the UK was being headed by Dr John Tanner and in April 1967 a request was made by the MOD via the British Government to the American Government for the return of MN235

- In July 1967 MN235 was officially presented to the proposed Royal Air Force Museum by the Smithsonian Institute (of whom the National Air & Space Museum is a part)

- The aircraft was shipped back to the UK from Baltimore on the SS Samaria, arriving at Liverpool Docks in late 1967

- By the 4th January 1968 the airframe was taken by road to No.71 MU, RAF Bicester for survey work to establish the amount of work needed to restore the airframe for museum display

- On the 9th April 1968 the airframe was transported by road by No.71 MU to No.27 MU, RAF Shawbury for restoration to display standard by a mainly civilian team.

- When the aircraft arrived back from the USA it was found to be missing one 20mm cannon, most of the engine cowlings, the spinner, starboard aileron, various undercarriage parts, the radiator/oil cooler unit, side panels below the cockpit and various inspection panels. The cannon was found in RAFM stock, while the spinner was adapted from a Handley-Page Hastings unit, and all other missing parts were made by the team at Shawbury. The other major deficiencey was the radiator unit and a visual dummy was made by cutting down a truck radiator. Recent excavations at the old Freeman Field site in the USA have unearthed what is misidentified as a German aero-engine component, but is in fact the missing Typhoon unit. If it can be preserved and if it will ever be reunited with MN235 is something we will just will have to wait and see?

- It had been intended to complete MN235 in time for display at the Royal Review at RAF Abingdon in June 1968 and on Horse Guards Parade in September 1968 but delays caused by the above mentioned missing parts meant it did not appear at either event.

- The aircraft was completed and formally handed over to Dr. Tanner by Wg Cdr D.A. Grifkins, the CO of No.27 MU, on the 19th November 1968. The aircraft remained in store at Shawbury awaiting the creation of the new RAF Museum.

- In February 1972 the airframe was repainted at Shawbury

- By November 1972 the aircraft had moved to the new RAF Museum, Hendon site and was placed in the Sydney Camm Hall (this area later became known as the Fighter Hall)

- In 1994 the aircraft was made the centrepiece of a new display called 'D-Day' and invasion stripes were applied. The aircraft was moved slightly from its original location and the tail was lifted up and placed on a support to put the airframe in an 'in flight' position.

- In 2011 with the arrival of a Tornado F Mk 3, MN235 was moved once again to a position directly behind the Tornado.

- 4th November 2013 dismantling underway for move to MBCC RAFM Cosford for attention. Removal of the cannon fairings revealed traces of the original wartime paint scheme on the wing leading edge – yellow leading edge band, upper surface grey and even clearly delineated black underside stripes.

- 7th November 2013, by road to MBCC at RAFM Cosford.

- November 2013, excavations by the volunteer Freeman Field Recovery team found the complete missing Typhoon radiator core and at least one engine cowling amongst other buried aircraft parts at this American test site.

- 8th May 2014, despatched by road to RAF Brize Norton en route to Canada for loan to the Canada Aviation and Space Museum, Rockliffe, Ottawa.

- 17th May 2014, flown out to Canada by RCAF in an C-17.

- 4th June 2014, following assembly at Rockliffe, towed from the conservation hangar to the main display hall. Formally unveiling on the 6th June 2014 to mark the 70th anniversary of D-Day.

This side view taken on the 6th June confirms that MN235 was supplied with the TR1143 whip aerial and IFF rod antenna installed (©USAF)

Other Typhoon Sections & Replicas

- There is a complete Typhoon cockpit section on display at the IWM, Duxford

- There are cockpit sections from Mk IA, R7708 and Mk IB, EJ922 at the BofB Museum, Hawkinge [Note - no photography is allowed within this museum]

- Mk IB, JR505 cockpit section is now owned by Mr Brian Barnes in Coventry, where it had previously been seen on display in the Midland Air Museum

- Unidentified Mk IB cockpit section at the D-Day Aviation Museum, Shoreham Airport (complete with engine)

- A cockpit/fuselage section using parts from JP843 is currently being constructed by Roger Marley at Sleap with the Wartime Aircraft Recovery Group Aviation Museum

- An unidentified Mk Ib forward fuselage found in a scrapyard is now with the Gloucesterhire Aviation Collection

- An unidentified cockpit section is part of the Air Defence Collection at A&AEE Boscombe Down

- Mk Ib, RB396 rear fuselage section is part of the Luchtvaarmuseum at at Fort Veldhuis in Holland

- A Mk Ib replica marked as JP656, BR•S can been seen suspended from the roof at Memorial de la Poix, Caen

44 Colour Profiles

Hawker Typhoon Mk Ib, R7752, PR•G, flown by Squadron Leader R.P. Beamont, No.609 Squadron, Manson, February 1943. Ocean Grey and Dark Green. Nose art consists of five German crosses, 19 locomotives and a naval vessel in white, outlined in black (except for smoke of locomotives); 'Tally-Ho' in white over a Dark Green base and the unit badge above it. Rank pennant below windscreen

Hawker Typhoon Mk Ia, R7684, JG•, flown by Wing Commander John Grandy, OC Duxford Wing, June 1942. Ocean Grey and Dark Green upper surfaces with Medium Sea Grey undersides. Sky spinner, rear fuselage band and pilot's initials 'JG' on fuselage sides. Rank pennant on cockpit door. Standard early style markings in all positions

Hawker Typhoon Mk Ib, R8893, XM•M, No.182 Squadron, late 1942. Ocean Grey and Dark Green upper surfaces with Medium Sea Grey undersides. Codes and fuselage band in Sky. Night (30cm/12") and white (46cm/18") ident bands below wings. White nose used temporarily as high visibility marking. Note unfaired front section of cannon

Hawker Typhoon Mk Ia, R7681, OV•Z, No.197 Squadron, March 1943. Ocean Grey and Dark Green upper surfaces with Medium Sea Grey undersides; Sky spinner, codes and rear fuselage band. Night/white bands below wings; previous white nose area covered in Dark Green. Standard national markings of the period

©Richard J. Caruana 2011/2015

Hawker Typhoon Mk Ia (converted to Mk Ib standard), R7855, PR•D, flown by Fg Off Lallemant, No.609 Squadron, Manston, April 1944. Ocean Grey and Dark Green upper surfaces with Medium Sea Grey undersides. Sky codes, front of spinner, and rear fuselage band; rear of spinner red. Standard period markings except for retention of early-style underwing roundels. Night (30cm/12") and White (46cm/18") ident bands under wings. Note unshrouded front section of cannon. Personal emblem on starboard only; codes other side read PR•D

©Richard J. Caruana 2011/2015

Hawker Typhoon Mk. Ib, EK183, US•A, No.56 Squadron, March 1943. Ocean Grey and Dark Green upper surfaces with Medium Sea Grey undersides. Codes, front of spinner and rear fuselage band in Sky; rear of spinner black. Standard period markings; Night (30cm/12") and White (47cm/18") ident bands below wings, and yellow 30cm (12") chordwise bands above wings

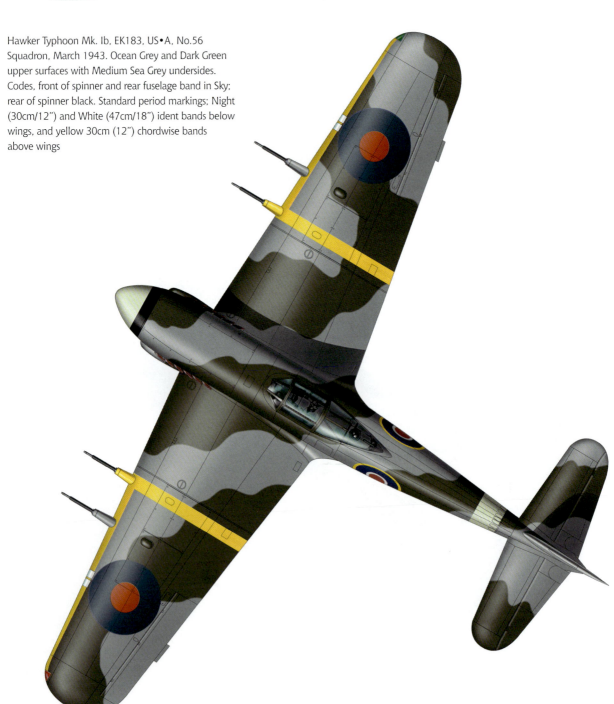

©Richard J. Caruana 2011/2015

Hawker Typhoon Mk Ib, R8742, EL•A, No.181 Squadron, March 1943. Ocean Grey and Dark Green upper surfaces, Medium Sea Grey undersides. Codes, spinner and fuselage band in Sky. Night (30cm/12") and White (46cm/18") ident bands under starboard wing only, port undersides Night. White 'Exercise Spartan' identification markings on fuselage sides

Hawker Typhoon Mk Ib, R7715, PR•Z, No.609 Squadron. Ocean Grey and Dark Green upper surfaces with Medium Sea Grey undersides; Sky codes and rear fuselage band. Red/white spinner; Night/white bands below wings (the Night area extended underneath cannon fairings) and Yellow wing leading edges. Blue/Red roundels above wings; non-standard large early-style roundels under wings. Squadron crest on cowling

Hawker Typhoon Mk Ib, EK176, JX•K, No.1 Squadron, Lympne, July 1943. Ocean Grey and Dark Green upper surfaces with Medium Sea Grey undersides; Sky spinner, rear fuselage band and codes. Night/white bands below wings and Yellow wing leading edges. Blue/Red roundels above wings; three-blade propeller

Hawker Typhoon Mk Ib, MN293, TP•D, No.198 Squadron, Thorney Island, June 1944. Ocean Grey and Dark Green upper surfaces with Medium Sea Grey undersides; Sky codes and rear fuselage band, red spinner with white backplate. Night/White bands below wings and around fuselage; serial partially overpainted. Note 'D' of code repositioned on engine cowling

©Richard J. Caruana 2011/2015

48 Colour Profiles

Hawker Typhoon Mk Ib, MN363, ZY•Y, No.247 Squadron, France, June 1944. Ocean Grey and Dark Green upper surfaces with Medium Sea Grey undersides wearing full D-Day stripes, 46cm (18") in Night and White around fuselage and wings. Sky spinner, codes and part of rear fuselage band

Hawker Typhoon Mk Ib, MN623, BR•W, No.184 Squadron, August 1944. Ocean Grey and Dark Green upper surfaces with Medium Sea Grey undersides; Sky spinner and rear fuselage band. Night/White bands below wings and around fuselage. Medium Sea Grey codes

Hawker Typhoon Mk Ib, MN526, TP•V, No.198 Squadron, Plumetot (France), July 1944. Ocean Grey and Dark Green upper surfaces with Medium Sea Grey undersides; Red spinner and 'TP' of code, Sky rear band and 'V' of code, 'V' repeated on fin in White. 46cm (18") Black and White bands under fuselage and wings. 'B' roundels above wings

Hawker Typhoon Mk Ib, MN582, HH•A, No.175 Squadron, B.5 airfield, August 1944. Ocean Grey and Dark Green upper surfaces with Medium Sea Grey underside; Sky codes and rear fuselage band. Night spinner and serials, Night/White bands around wings and below fuselage; Blue/Red roundels above wings. Enlarged (Tempest) tailplanes fitted

©Richard J. Caruana 2011/2015

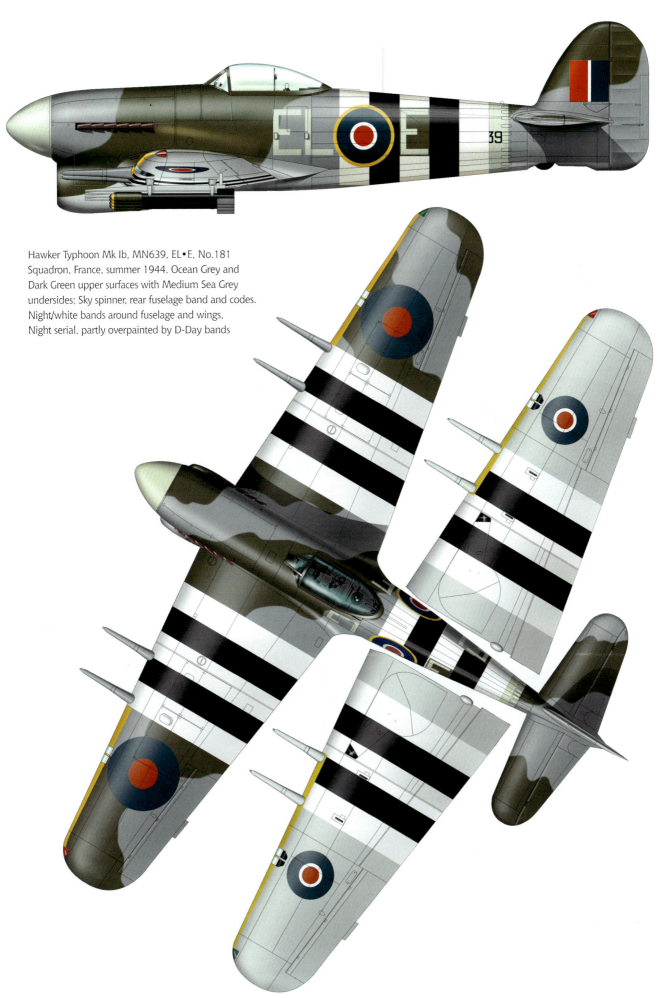

Hawker Typhoon Mk Ib, MN639, EL•E, No.181 Squadron, France, summer 1944. Ocean Grey and Dark Green upper surfaces with Medium Sea Grey undersides; Sky spinner, rear fuselage band and codes. Night/white bands around fuselage and wings, Night serial, partly overpainted by D-Day bands

Hawker Typhoon Mk Ib, MM955, FM•N, No.257 Squadron, Tangmere, March 1943. Ocean Grey and Dark Green upper surfaces with Medium Sea Grey undersides; Sky rear fuselage band, spinner and codes. Night serial; Blue/Red roundels above wings

Hawker Typhoon Mk Ib, R8925, •B, during tropical trials, Ismalia, early 1943. Dark Earth and Mid-Stone upper surfaces with Azure Blue undersides. Standard markings in all positions, except for yellow wing leading edge; red spinner

Hawker Typhoon Mk Ib, MN639, QC•S, No.168 Squadron, Eindhover, late 1944. Ocean Grey and Dark Green upper surfaces with Medium Sea Grey undersides; Sky rear fuselage band and codes. Night serials, Night/White stripes below rear fuselage only; yellow spinner and wing leading edges. Red/Blue roundels above wings

Hawker Typhoon Mk Ib, RB485, I8•E, No.440 Squadron, Flensburg, 1945. Ocean Grey and Dark Green upper surfaces with Medium Sea Grey undersides; Sky codes and Night serials. Red/white spinner (white rear plate). Yellow wing leading edges; enlarged (Tempest) tailplanes

©Richard J. Caruana 2011/2015

Colour Profiles 51

Hawker Typhoon Mk Ib, SW417, MR•X, No.245 Squadron, Germany, summer 1945. Ocean Grey and Dark Green upper surfaces with Medium Sea Grey undersides; Sky codes and white serials. Blue/white spinner and checks on rear fuselage. Blue/White/Red roundels above and below wings

Hawker Typhoon Mk Ib, SW433, DP•S, No.193 Squadron, Germany, August 1945. Ocean Grey and Dark Green upper surfaces with Medium Sea Grey undersides; Sky codes and Night serials. Red/white spinner, Yellow/Blue/White/Red roundels in six positions; yellow wing leading edges. Unit badge on fin within a white rectangle

Hawker Typhoon Mk Ib, SW411, PR•J, flown by flown by Sqn Ldr 'Pinkie' Stark of No.609 Squadron, Germany, summer 1945. Ocean Grey and Dark Green upper surfaces with Medium Sea Grey undersides; Sky codes and Night serials, Night spinner with yellow backplate. Yellow/Blue/White/Red roundels in six positions; yellow wing leading edges. Unit badge on front fuselage with Squadron Leader's pennant aft

Hawker Typhoon Mk Ib, T9+GK (probably ex-JP548 of No.174 Squadron), captured in France and repainted in Luftwaffe markings. Ocean Grey and Dark Green on upper surfaces with RLM 04 Gelb (yellow) undersides, extended to the whole rear fuselage; black spinner. Codes in white and black

©Richard J. Caruana 2011/2015

Chapter 7: Hawker Typhoon Kits

The Typhoon has been a popular subject with kit manufacturers over the years, so we thought we would have a look through the kits that we could find of the type and give you our assessment of them. We have not included the Tornado in this list, as the kits available for it are limited to low-volume resin and vacform kits or limited-run injection moulded plastic conversions.

1/72nd

Academy

This injection moulded kit of the Typhoon Mk Ib (#1664) was released by Academy in 1999. The neat box contains one clear and three grey-coloured plastic sprues, all of which have nicely recessed panel lines, but strangely no rivet detail. The aircraft components are nearly identical to the well known scale plans by Arthur Bentley, the only area where they deviate

Academy

is the profile of the leading edge of the rudder, which is a bit under size, but we are talking a tiny amount (1mm max.). The reinforcing plates on the rear fuselage are quiet prominent and there are too many, while the exhaust stacks are moulded in situ and are inaccurate as they don't look like the exposed versions or those with the shroud. The upper profile of the cowling looks wrong, mainly due to the fact that the nose overall is too short, which leads to the whole thing having rather odd proportions. A three-blade Rotol or a four-blade propeller are supplied and although they are close to the Bentley plans, they are not 100%; the spinner is definitely too short. The kit only offers the anti-shimmy tailwheel tyre, which is suitable for late production machines. The air intake/radiator unit is nicely detailed with an insert, but there is no filter fitted in the orifice, which was very likely considering the two decal options offered.

The cockpit interior is quite nice, with moulded sidewalls in the fuselage halves and a separate floor, control column, rudder pedals, seat, instrument panel and rear bulkhead. The Bentley plans do not clearly show the pilot's seat in detail, so the one in this kit is basic and thus not very accurate, while the head armour also suffers from being the wrong shape. The canopy however is too low in overall profile. The inner undercarriage doors (#A16 & A17) are correct in shape but the L-shape moulded into the inside is incorrect, as this is a wooden flat panel riveted to the area to act as a brake on the spinning wheels as the undercarriage retracts – fill the hole and paint the detail. The main problem is that the main undercarriage legs and doors are too long, by about 3mm, resulting in the completed model looking as if it is standing on tip-toes. The main undercarriage doors also have an odd shape to them, so will need to be reprofiled. The 3in rocket projectiles are moulded with the Mk I rails and both are well detailed, but the distance between the rocket and the rail is too great and the electrical connects ('pig tails') at the back are missing.

Things that need to be added are the whip antenna on the dorsal spine, IFF rod on the underside, 'boat antenna' housing on the underside, some detail in the back of the air intake/radiator plus linkage for the flap in this area, and there are also two pipes just visible in the top of the starboard upper cowling and one on the port. Truthfully you also have to replace the canopy, as the front windshield section is too steep and there is no way of correcting it save for replacement with the vacformed example in the Falcon set.

The kit offers markings for:
- MH582, HH•A of No.175 Squadron, August 1944
- SW493, DP•S of No.193 Squadron, August 1945

Both are in the standard Dark Green/Ocean Grey over Medium Sea Grey scheme and because both are post mid-1944 they have the Sky rear fuselage band but not the spinner. The first option has Invasion Stripes and these along with the fuselage band are supplied as decals but are best replaced with painted-on examples.

Verdict

The best injected kit in 1/72 at present, it needs a few corrections and a little extra work adding details such as an aftermarket cockpit interior to get the best from it, but even from the box it makes into a very nice Typhoon.

Airfix

This kit is the oldest Typhoon about, having first been released back in 1959. Its age shows, as it is a very basic kit and we have seen it in silver, light and dark grey-coloured plastic. The age of the kit is well illustrated by the fact it is made up of just one clear and twenty-seven coloured plastic parts. Surface detail is all raised for both rivets and panel lines. Compared with the Bentley plans there are a lot of anomalies, not a surprise as the plans were produced 15 years after this kit! The span is accurate, but the ailerons (separate) are short inboard while the blisters over the cannon bays are over-size and the wrong shape; the cannon barrels are separate and although long enough are a bit too

Airfix

thin. The panel lines of the wings are, on the whole, nothing like the real thing. The fuselage is very close on overall length (about 1mm out) but the underside of the chin intake is too flat and is moulded solid at the back with a solid 'wedge' to represent the flap in this area. There is no detail inside the intake, just a moulded bulkhead. The exhausts stacks seem to be an odd mix of shrouded and unshrouded with the flange of the former but the separate stacks of the latter? The tailplanes are the right span, but the panel and rivet detail is wrong, while the propeller and spinner is moulded as one part and although the latter is accurate in shape the propeller blades are short and not wide enough. The canopy is one-piece and is poorly moulded, being very thick and without any discernible framework, the top of the bubble section is also too high making it look wrong once in place. There is no interior detail save for a basic seat on pegs and a generic pilot figure. The wheel wells are just holes in the lower wing half opening into the interior of the upper section, the undercarriage legs are moulded with the thick doors, while the inner doors are similarly thick with simple tabs to mount them with. The mainwheels are just simple 'buttons' of plastic with a hole in the centre and the tailwheel and yoke are moulded in one piece but lack any accurate detail or shape. Bombs are included, but the racks are simple blisters moulded to the lower wing and the bombs themselves are generic lumps which bear little resemblance to the real items. It should be noted that the wings do not feature any tip or landing lights.

Throughout its life the kit seems to have only ever carried one decal option, that being JR128, HF•L of No.183 Squadron in 1943. This is a well known machine, as it was photographed numerous times during the war. The decals are simple but the white stripe in the fin flash looks too wide.

This kit has also been released by Airfix Corporation of America and Heller.

Verdict
A very basic kit that is really only of any interest to the collector depending on the packaging, or those getting all dewy-eyed about their youth. Be warned though, it will build and look as bad as it did when you made it all those years ago!

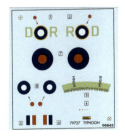

Heller

Airfix (new tool)

Airfix released their newly tooled Typhoon Mk Ib (#A02041) in April 2013 and it depicts a late series version with a four-blade propeller and 'Tempest' tailplanes. The kit comprises a single clear sprue and four moulded in a light grey-coloured plastic, offering a total of 74 parts. The panel lines are all engraved and quite subtle in places when compared with previous new toolings from Airfix (Hornby), however those on the fuselage mid/rear

Airfix (new tool)

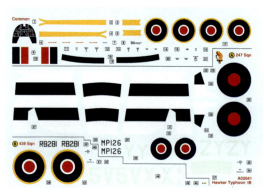

section are too deep, being more like those used to define the hinge lines of the control surfaces. There are numerous raised caps and covers as required, plus the 'fish plates' on the rear fuselage are correctly depicted, albeit a little too pronounced for this scale (sand them down slightly). The surface lacks any rivet detail, apart from the fixings for the cowls, which are all shown as engraved dimples, when these are raised rings for the Dzus fasteners.

The interior is well detailed, but the control column and rudder pedals are all simplified and the instrument panel is flat with a few dials on the edges and just a decal to reproduce the remainder, but these are all in the form of white outlines on a black background, so it is not 100% accurate. There is a separate gunsight moulded with the compass under the instrument panel, but it lacks the supporting framework that went from one side of the cockpit to the other. It is depicted without a clear lens unit, now this is the same as the altered Mk II unit in the cockpit section at Duxford, from which much of the Airfix research was taken, but that is not what the type necessarily carried, as most Typhoons initially used the Mk II* and that had a typical lens. Some ground-attack machines used a modified Mk II* with the screen removed and the graticule modified to a plain 100mph ring and dot. This became the Type I Mk III Projector Sight and was cleared for the Tempest in February 1944, subsequently being used on night-fighter and Typhoon squadrons, and once the Grade A armoured windscreens became available the sight was much improved due to the optically correct nature of the glass (previously the glass caused distortions). Definitely Hugh Fraser's RB281 had this type of sight fitted, but I can't find a confirming image for the other option in the kit. The seat features the standard quilted back panel, but there are no belts, not even as decals.

The quoted colour of Interior Grey/Green overall seems to be at odds because Gloster made most Typhoons and they had the upper section (above waist height) in grey/green, but the remainder below it was aluminium; the area for the battery below the seat was actually painted with an anti-acid glossy black paint and the instrument panel sections were anodised black, which has a distinct deep purple tint to it. The fuselage is 1.5-2mm short in comparison with the scale plans drawn by Arthur Bentley, but these were 1974 vintage and with such a minute 'error' (6 scale inches), it won't be of consequence to the majority. The handhold on the starboard upper edge below the cockpit is moulded as a raised oblong, when it should be an engraved outline, and the vent just ahead of the lower handhold is shown projecting slightly below it, when it should be slightly higher. The cine camera hole in the front, starboard side of the nose, is depicted as an outline with an ovoid dimple in the middle; this would be taped over if the camera was not installed, or the opening would be just that, so either drill or fill the oval dimple in the middle. The vertical fin has a pronounced bulge to the top leading edge, meaning that it slopes too far forward and it is also about 2mm higher than the aforementioned scale plans. Although not really an issue in this scale, the formation lights in the aft section of the root fairing for each tailplane should be clear.

The rear fuselage also looks to be about 1mm narrower than all commercial scale plans. The upper cowl profile is good, something that Academy got wrong, but the exhaust stacks are far too skinny and that is probably down to the world's only example at Hendon having the shrouds fitted, so the stacks were probably a bit of a 'guesstimation'. Many say that the main canopy looks too flat in profile, but I think the real problem is that the bubble canopy had pronounced bulges at the side and these are not in the kit part, probably down to the complex moulds needed to do this, and that results in the whole unit looking 'flat'. The radiator unit is depicted with the extended section around the oil cooler element in the middle, and truthfully in this scale, this is over-thick. You could leave it off, as many flew without it, but the recess in the radiator as depicted is too deep for this scale. The kit does not offer the Napier 'mushroom' style filter, nor the mesh screens used in the early D-Day period, nor the final 'cuckoo doors'. The wing span matches scale plans, as does the profile, and the kit features the cannon bays so that the access panels can be posed open. The oblong bulges outboard on the upper surface of each wing are present and correct, but the inboard teardrop-shaped ones are, as most kit manufacturers have done, too pronounced, as it is only the slightest bulge. I am not 100% convinced with the oval inspection panels inboard of the aileron hinge line, as these are raised and in 1/72nd that is probably too much? The footstep built into the trailing edge of the starboard wing root is shown in partial relief but this should just be an engraved outline, as the unit is spring-loaded and only 'open' when the pilot's foot is in it.

On the underside the cartridge ejector ports for the cannon are there, but the smaller ones inboard of them for the links are missing. The wings lack any landing lights, which are fine for most of the later series machines when carrying rockets, but not all. In early 1944 the starboard landing light was deleted from all in-service Typhoons, and at the time of D-Day many rocket-carrying ones had the port one plated over as well, but not all machines had this, so the option for the lights would have been better. The tip lights are moulded with each wing half and are thus solid. The centre-section of the underside of the fuselage is part of the lower wing half, and the oblong panel there is raised, when in this scale it is better engraved, plus the 'boat' antenna is oval with a flat top to it, when it should be oval in plan view and domed in profile. The downward ident lamps inboard of the undercarriage bay leading edges are just engraved rings, there are no clear covers, nor detail; this only applies to late production machines, but it's applicable to one decal option, so these should be clear parts. The undercarriage bays are well moulded with good depth, the retraction jacks are also moulded with the inner doors, but these seem to be just long tubes, when they should be a 'stepped' hydraulic ram; they also look too short. The 'scuff plate' inside the inner door is present on each, but really in this scale an engraved outline or decal would have been better, as it is just too pronounced/thick.

The undercarriage legs are nice, but they lack the towing bridle 'D' rings at the top/front and there are no brake lines, plus the main wheels are 'weighted', but actually look far too flat The tailwheel is a single-piece moulding and it is too big, has a poorly defined yoke and lacks the anti-shimmy style of wheel usually seen on the mid- and late-series machines. The kit features Mk Ib rocket rails and 3in rockets with 60lb HE heads and although the fins of the rockets are too thick, this is pretty standard with any injection moulded kits, however the rails themselves lack the distinctive guide tubes that run on each side down the entire length and these will need to be added from suitable diameter plastic rod; in the kit these 'rods' can be seen from the side of each rail, but from the front and viewed up underneath, the space in-between, that should be two separate 'rods', is solid. All the rocket/rails lack the connecting 'pigtail' cables.

The kit offers two decal options:
- MP126, ZY•Y, flown by Sqn Ldr B.G. Stapleton DFC, No.247 Sqn, No.124 Wing, 2nd TAF, Eindhoven, The Netherlands, December 1944
- RB281, 5V•X, flown by Fg Off A.H. Fraser, No.439 Sqn, No.143 Wing, 2nd TAF, Eindhoven, The Netherlands, February 1945

The decals include airframe stencils, yellow wing leading edges and D-Day stripes, as well as all the unique markings. The decal sheet has perfect colour and register, but the images are matt with opaque areas between the characters of the serial number and unit code letters.

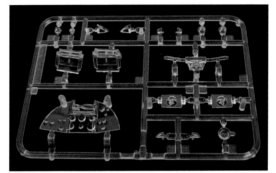

Clear parts

This kit has subsequently been released as a Starter Set (#A55208) with paints and glue, as a 'Dogfight Double' (#A50136) with the new-tooled Focke-Wulf Fw 190A-8 and with vehicles and figures in the 'D-Day Air Assault' gift set (#A50157). Both of the latter two, which we have, share a common single decal option, which comes from #A02041 anyway and that is MP126, ZY•Y, flown by Sqn Ldr B.G. Stapleton DFC of No.247 Sqn, No.124 Wing, 2nd TAF, Eindhoven, The Netherlands, December 1944.

Verdict

Nowadays this is 'the' choice for the type in this scale, albeit that the Brengun kits are better as far as overall accuracy and detail goes (plus thus far Brengun are the only ones to offer the earlier three-blade versions or the early A-series), they just lose out due to their limited production nature.

Aviation Usk

This limited-run injection moulded kit was first released in 1989, then reissued in 1997. It was also announced for reissue under the Xotic-72 label (the new owners of Aviation Usk) in 2004 but this never happened. When this kit was first released it must be understood that limited-run injection moulding technology was in its infancy, as a result this kit comes on one sprue of brown-coloured plastic that is very rough to the touch. There is a bit of flash and close examination of the components will show that they are covered in tiny scratches. The wing is correct in span and the engraved ailerons are accurate, although the panel

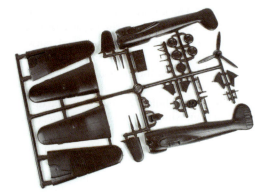

Aviation Usk

lines on both are a bit hit and miss – there is no engraved rivet detail. The smaller oval panel for the inboard cannon bay is depicted as an engraved outline, but there is conflict as to whether this is a bulge of just a panel anyway? The wheel wells are boxed in but feature no detail and the wing does not have the tip or landing lights. The fuselage is slightly short, almost the same as the Airfix kit, so we suspect this is what this kit was based on: the back of the chin intake is solid like Airfix as well. There are no reinforcing plates on the rear fuselage and the door is scribed at a slant. The tailplanes are moulded with the fillet, which is unique, but although the main panel lines are correct other details are missing. The cockpit has some basic detail moulded into the fuselage halves, a floor, control column, instrument panel and rudder pedals plus the seat with the head armour. None of this is very accurate and the latter item is extremely dubious with odd struts included to brace it? The propeller and spinner unit is moulded as one piece and although the blade length is accurate the lack of any definition between spinner and blade makes for a very basic-looking 'blob'. The gun barrel fairings are about 2mm too long, but they are at least thicker than the skinny ones from Airfix. The instructions show the exhaust stacks as separate parts, but they are moulded with the fuselage halves probably due to the limitations of the moulding method. The undercarriage doors are thick and without detail, while the oleo legs are basic tube struts and although the wheels have hub detail it is not that accurate. The canopy is vacformed clear plastic and although not bad it is not that clear and as it depicts a car-door example it does not have well defined framework for these elements.

The kit comes with a sheet of decals from the Usk range (#7104) that may have been sold separately. It offers markings for:
- DN406, PR•F, 'Mavis', No.609 Squadron, Manston, March 1943
- EK176, JK•X of No.1 Squadron in July 1943.

Both are Dark Green/Ocean Grey/Medium Sea Grey with Sky fuselage band and spinner (just the tip in the former option). Each has the ID white/black stripes on the undersides, but the instructions state that the white is 18in wide, not 24in as they should be.

Verdict

Another one really only for the collector as the detail and quality of the parts is so basic that it will take a great deal of effort to make anything worthwhile from it.

Brengun BRP72003

Brengun

Czech manufacturer Hauler produce a series of kits under their Brengun brand and these include kits of the Typhoon. The first two were released in late 2012 and offered the Hawker Typhoon Mk Ib 'mid-production with three-blade propeller' (#BRP72003) or the Hawker Typhoon Mk Ib 'late-production with four-blade propeller' #BRP72004. These were followed in 2014 by the Hawker Typhoon Mk Ib Car Doors 'Early Production' (#BRP72006), Hawker Typhoon Mk Ib Car Door 'Early/Mid and Mid Production' (#BRP72007) and the Hawker Typhoon Mk Ia 'Early & Late Production' (#BRP72012). We only have the first two here, so will confine our comments to them.

The first thing to remember is that these are limited-run, low-volume injection moulded kits, so you have none of the niceties of a mainstream kit such as locating tabs. Each kit is made up of a generic set of parts, the main sprue being common to all with, we suspect, revised fuselage and wing components being offered in the Early/Mid versions.

In these two you also have to cut off the entire tail section, so that the later 'Tempest' tailplanes can be installed (these are on the sprue containing the wing parts), but the instructions don't even mention this? The generic nature of the instructions mean that you have to take care in ensuring you use the right bits for the version you are building.

Surface detail is via fine engraved detail, but in places (e.g. the dorsal spine) these are only partial or damaged and you will thus have to rescribe them. No reinforcing 'fish plates' are included on the kit parts, nor on the small photo-etched fret in the kit. They are however on a separate etched set from Brengun, which is a bit much as they should have been on the kit fret from day 1.

The decals, although excellent, have some problems, those in #BRP72004 have a number of errors, namely only one of the four options is a rocket-equipped Typhoon, two of the others are bomb carriers and the last version (Wg Cdr J.C. Button) carried neither. The serial numbers on option A (JR149) and C (SW433) are wrong and the 'Pulverizer II' (Option A) scoreboard markings are completely fictitious! With #BRP72003, option A should have the 'S' on the top of the vertical tail in white, not Sky, plus period images of this machine at the date/location stated in the kit show it still fitted with the shrouds around the exhausts and the kit does not depict this. Option B (JR379) is shown in a well-known posed wartime image and it is rocket-armed, with no D-Day stripes but the size, style and location of the squadron codes are at odds with the decals (the kit ones are too small and set too far down the fuselage sides), plus the serial number location is wrong, Brengun depict it below the centreline, whilst the period photos shows it is on the centreline with only the smallest rear section of the '3' on the Sky band on the port side, not all of it. I also suspect that the spinner is neither Sky nor Medium Sea Grey, it may well be Dark Earth going by its tonal value? Oh yes, this machine too still retains the exhaust shrouds. The third option, MN454 is that which the cover art depicts, with the inspection of this airframe by King George VI, it is a late production machine with the Tempest tailplanes, it is rocket-armed and has no D-Day stripes. The spinner and tail band are Sky and it looks to have yellow wing leading edges, which are not shown in the kit. This machine did not have the exhaust shrouds fitted.

Overall dimensions are good, with the correct length and span, and the correct profile to the vertical fin, unlike the Airfix example. The detail in the cockpit is superior to the Airfix kit, with the tubular structure of the real thing well depicted and the seats having etched belts. The instrument panel lacks detail, though, plus it only has the mounting frame for the gunsight, the sight itself is missing. The wheel wells are well detailed and multi-part, but there are ejector towers projecting from the inner (wing) face that will have to be removed to get them inside each wing half (you will probably have to thin the whole roof area as well). The rocket rails are well moulded, with the guide rods on each side correctly depicted. The

rockets themselves are not bad, but the fins are thick and you have to get the separate etched fret from Brengun if you want to correct that. The cannon ejector ports under the wings are only semi-relief and the tip lights are moulded with the main wing, so these need to be removed and replaced with clear plastic. The canopy is two-part and well moulded, plus the sprue also contains the Car Door version that was used in subsequent releases. The formation light (#51) is not used on all machines, so check your references. The small etched fret also includes the foot step on the port side and the tailwheel unit is a lot better than the one in the Airfix kit, being the correct size, but it still lacks the anti-shimmy style of tyre.

Brengun BRP72004

Each kit offers the following decal options:
#BRP72003
- MN134, SF•S, No.137 Squadron, RAF Manston, June 1944
- JR379, No.609 Sqn, 2nd TAF, Summer 1944
- MN454, HF•S, No.183 Squadron, May 1944

#BRP72004
- JP149, I8•P, 'Pulverizer II', No.440 Squadron, Summer 1944
- SW564, HH•T, No.175 Squadron, Celle, April 1945
- SW433, DP•S, No.193 Sqn, August 1945
- RB431, •JCB, personal aircraft of Wg Cdr J.C. Button, No.123 Wing, April 1945

The decal sheet is beautifully printed, but there are various errors in the options as mentioned earlier.

Verdict

In respect of detail, this kit has the edge on even the new Airfix example, certainly the interior and things like the tailwheel are much better, as are the overall dimensions and shapes in comparison with commercial scale plans. The nature of the kit and the high asking price make the whole thing less appealing though, which is a shame. The lack of etched parts for the missing 'fishplates' and all the mix-ups with the decal options, are inexcusable.

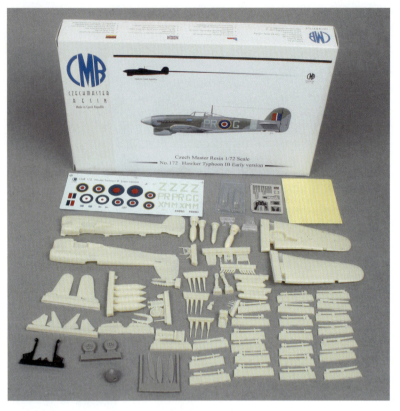

CzechMaster Resin 172

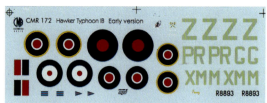

CzechMaster Resin

The CzechMaster Resin (CMR) range can trace its origins back to the generic Czechmaster range produced in Czechoslokavia before the fall of the Iron Curtain. Today CMR offer three Typhoon kits, the first being #159 that depicts the Typhoon Prototype and Mk Ia, the second is #172 depicting the Mk Ib Early Version and the third and final one (#181) is the NF Mk Ib. All kits use the same basic moulds, which are new ones created once the original Czechmaster versions were outdated. The kits have also been updated recently with the addition of pre-painted, photo-etched brass that is produced for CMR by Eduard M.A. As all three utilise the same basic parts they can be considered as one. The fuselage halves compared with the Bentley plans are spot-on, with all surface detail finely and accurately engraved. There are no fish plates on the aft fuselage/tail joint, while the exhaust stacks are separate and depict the correct style. The prototype kit comes with the three-stack exhausts as well as the usual six-stack and it also has the smaller chord rudder and the external balance linkage.

The wings are different in the Mk Ia and Mk Ib kits, which is correct, and the former have the machine-gun and ejector ports moulded into them, while the latter have the ports for the cannon bays and the cannon barrel fairings as separate parts. The only odd thing is that the panel lines etc. match the Bentley plans, but the landing light is too far outboard, thus moving all panels around it also outboard? The landing lights are separate clear resin parts. In the latest editions the propeller and spinner are made in a different manner from that shown on the instructions, the spinner shape and blade profiles are bang on, though. The main wheels are also newer parts moulded in grey resin and they are highly detailed representations of the five-spoke version, however the prototype/Mk Ia versions need four-spoke hubs. The prototype/Mk Ia kit comes with three different styles of canopy in vacformed clear plastic, so you get the solid aft fairing, the clear fairing or the clear version with the blister for the rearview mirror in the upper section.

CzechMaster Resin 181

The Mk Ib and NF versions just have two canopies and all kits have the car-door element as clear resin. You do get a wealth of ordnance, including 90 and 44Imp. Gal. drop tanks, 1,000lb, 500lb and 250lb bombs and racks, plus in the Mk Ib a set of 3in rocket projectiles and rails, the former offered with either 25lb or

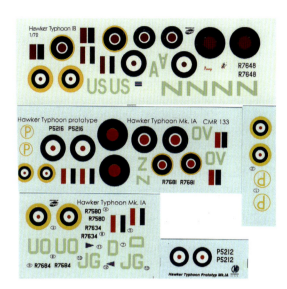

CzechMaster Resin 159

60lb heads. The cockpit interior for all kits is superb, with the combination of highly detailed resin parts and those pre-painted, photo-etched. The night fighter version has extended exhaust stacks as well as the six-stack and shrouded six-stack units, cannon barrel fairings with and without the end covers and you even get one set with the springs in an alternative position. The NF also only has the 44Imp. Gal. drop tanks but it does have the three- and four-blade propeller units.

The kits offer the following colour options:
- #159 – R7648, US•A, No.56 Squadron, Duxford, June 1942; prototype P5216, A&AEE, early 1942; Mk Ia, R7580, No.56 Squadron, Duxford, September 1941; Mk Ia, R7634, UO•D, No.26 Squadron, February-March 1942; Mk Ia, R7681, OV•Z, No.197 Squadron, March 1943; Mk Ia, R7684, •JG, OC Duxford Wing, June 1942; prototype P5212 in the much debated overall grey scheme
- #172 – Mk Ib, R8893, XM•M, No.182 Squadron, late 1942; Mk Ib, R7752, PR•G, No.609 Squadron, November 1942; Mk Ib, R7698, Z•Z, Duxford Wing, September 1942
- #181 – NF Mk Ib prototype, R7881, Langley, February 1943; NF Mk Ib, R7881, RAE Farnborough, April-September 1943; NF Mk Ib (w/o radar) R8697, SA•Z, No.486 Sqn, 1942.

Verdict

All three of these kits are superb, not cheap, but superb nonetheless. The quality of the moulding combined with the level of detail and accuracy make these the best Typhoons currently in 1/72nd.

Frog

These kits have been released many times, those we know of are AER, Air Lines, Alanger, Ark Models, Bienengraber, Chematic, DFI, Eastern Express, Hema, Herna, Maquette, Minicraft, Minix, Novo, NovoExport, Roly Toys, RPM and Tashigrushka. The two separate kits produced by Frog were the Typhoon Mk Ib 'Bubbletop' (#389P) from 1959 to 1964 and the Typhoon Mk Ib 'car door' (#F.231) from 1975 to 1977. We will look at both in turn.

#389P

Considering the age of this kit it is not far out in length and span, from there on though it's as you would expect. The panel lines are quite deep and do not accurately reflect those of the real aircraft. In this first version the national insignia and squadron codes are also engraved into the model surface, but that was very much a 'style' in the 1950s. The fish-plates on the rear fuselage/tail joint are not depicted. The wing does not feature the blister for the outer cannon bay, nor does it have the landing light either as an engraved line or separate clear part. The wingtip light is defined as an engraved line, but it's far too big, the ailerons are in the wrong place and slightly too short, also without a trim tab. The tailplane is a single piece, passing through the fuselage, but it is under scale in both span and overall shape.

The propeller is the three-blade Rotol unit and the blade length and profile is very accurate, the spinner however is too domed. There are not even undercarriage bays in the lower wing halves,

Novo

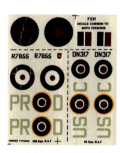

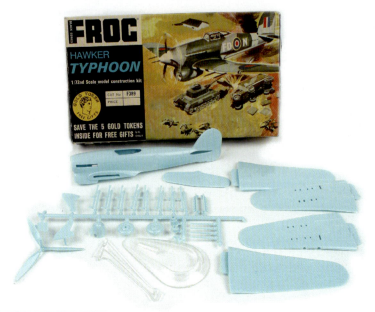

Frog 389P

just engraved lines. The undercarriage doors are thick and without detail, the main one has a basic strut for the oleo moulded to it. The main wheels are just basic 'buttons' with a hole in the middle and no hub detail. The cannon fairings are too long and a little skinny, while the rockets and rails are basic in detail and the 60lb heads

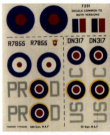

are decidedly skinny. The canopy is one-piece and although quite well moulded the mid-upper profile is too flat.

The single option in the kit is:
- NN454, FD•N, No.114 Squadron, this is of course a totally spurious scheme as NN454 was not a Typhoon serial and No.114 Squadron did not operate the type.

Frog F231

Verdict
One for the collectors only. Strangely the tooling reissued by Ark Models in early 2011 was this tooling, not the later #F231? The tooling had been modified to remove all the engraved markings, whilst the detail on the forward fuselage (the aft is smooth) and wings is now raised?

#F231

This kit was the new tooling produced by Frog to replace #389P and the one we had was moulded in a very dark blue plastic, although there are other examples in other colours. The surface detail is all raised lines, there are no rivets and the fuselage is spot on for length, and the surface detail matches the Bentley plans (which were produced the year before this kit was made). The rear fuselage has the fish-plates as raised detail and the exhaust stacks are moulded as part of the fuselage. There is no interior detail save for a basic seat and pilot figure, the radiator front is a separate insert that has basic detail and the rear of the unit is open but this just opens up inside the empty fuselage. The wings also have raised detail and match the Bentley plans except in one important point, the cannon fairings are in the wrong place, they are 4mm too far inboard? The ailerons are the correct shape and location and are supplied separately.

The wheel well is boxed in but has heavy basic and inaccurate detail on the roof, the bay is also very shallow. The landing light is engraved on the wings, as are the tip lights, the latter once again seeming over-size. The tailplanes are the right span and width but they feature only the basics of panel lines, while quite a few are missing. The canopy is one-piece and well moulded with clear canopy framework, but the aft section is too long, however this is because the side and top profiles for this in the Bentley plans are different and Frog seem to have followed the top view, which is longer. The kit comes with 3in rockets and rails but the latter are too long with the supports in the wrong places, while the rockets have too skinny 60lb heads. Only one propeller is included, the three-blade Rotol unit, but the blades are moulded with the spinner so lack detail at the roots. The undercarriage is basic, the doors are thick and without interior or exterior detail and the separate oleo legs are just featureless tubes. The wheels do feature five-spoke hubs but the detail is shallow and the big hole in the centre and plug in the oleo will look pretty inaccurate.

The kit offers two decal options:
- R7855, PR•D of No.609 Squadron, Manston, 1943
- DN317, US•C, No.56 Squadron, Matlaske, 1943

Both options are dark Green/Ocean Grey/Medium Sea Grey, while option 1 has the black/white ID bands under the wings and option 2 also has the yellow band on the upper wings.

Verdict
This is not actually that bad a kit and with a lot of work you could make a passable model from it, but Frog is more collectable than buildable nowadays and this one deserves to be kept unbuilt.

HobbyBoss

This kit was released by this Chinese manufacturer in their 'Easy Assembly' range in 2007. This range sees the production of a snap-together kit with solid wings and a partially solid fuselage, plus detail parts like a normal construction kit. The parts are beautifully moulded in a grey-coloured plastic and the panel lines are all engraved although there is no rivet detail. The kit is identical to the Bentley plans in fuselage length and profile, the panel lines are a bit at odds, though, as HobbyBoss have ignored the door on the starboard side, assuming this related only to the car-door version. The kit is basically identical in overall shape to the Academy example and thus replicates many of the errors in that kit, plus adding a few more. The rudder also has three hinges, when it should be just two. The wing is accurate in span and the wheel wells are boxed in and detailed. The panel lines on the wings are a little at odds with plans, the wingtip and landing lights are just engraved lines, but both are way too big. The cannon ejector ports are solid and the barrels are the right length but the panel lines at the base are at odds with plans (the outer ones are far too large circles).

Strangely the fishplates on the top and bottom of the fuselage are missing, even though the rest are there? The cockpit interior is basic with floor/seat/control column moulded as one piece and not accurately at that. The tailplanes are correct in span and all panel lines match the Bentley plans. The main wheels feature five-spoke hubs, but the diameter of these is too small, the inner doors also have the L-shaped recess instead of the flat scuff plate. The tailwheel and yoke is moulded as part of the fuselage, the tyre is anti-shimmy but is too narrow. The rockets and rails are nicely moulded but they are identical to the Academy ones, so the former is too far away from the latter. Both three- and four-blade propellers and spinners are included; the profile of the blades is a little blunt at the tips and both spinners are short. The kit only offers the early style tailplanes, so decal option MR•Z at least can't be built from the kit. The only real disappointment is the canopy, which is thick and one-piece and the top is flat and too low in overall profile, making the whole unit inaccurate.

The kit offers markings for the following options:
- MP195, DP•Z, 'Zipp X', No.193 Squadron, August 1944
- MR•Z of No.245 Squadron, April 1945.

Verdict
This is actually a neat kit, which offers a lot of detail parts that could be adapted to older examples. The overall package is designed for the more junior market, but it is not one to be ignored, as it would build up into a good rendition. Just remember to add some detail to the cockpit and get a replacement canopy, plus add some Tempest tailplanes if you intend to make MR•Z.

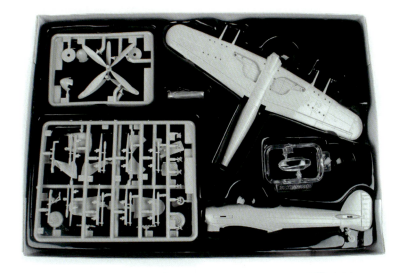

HobbyBoss

Pavla Models

This limited-run injection moulded kit was produced by this Czech firm in 2003. It is typical of the style of limited-run kit produced at this time so it combines resin detail parts and a vacformed canopy. Depicting a car-door Mk Ib the single sprue of grey-coloured plastic is well moulded with fine recessed panel lines but no rivet detail. The fuselage is bang on with the Bentley plans, as are all panel lines. The interior is a combination of plastic and resin parts and nicely detailed albeit difficult to get inside the fuselage due to the nature (thickness) of limited-run kits. The tailwheel unit is nicely defined but suffers a bit from flash; it fits into the rear fuselage before the fuselage halves are joined. The intake/radiator unit is resin and

62 Hawker Typhoon Kits

Pavla

Monogram

nicely formed and two styles of exhaust are included, shrouded or unshrouded, the former are poorly defined, though.

The wings match the Bentley plans nicely with the small teardrop-shaped covers for the inner cannon on the upper wing depicted as bulges, but again this area is open to dispute. The wheel wells are resin inserts and the landing lights are supplied as clear parts. You get the cannon barrel fairings with or without the recoil spring covers, the latter being resin parts. The propeller is made of separate blades mounted onto the hub/spinner and each is a little too broad. The canopy is supplied with or without the upper blister for the rearview mirror while the car door for the starboard side is supplied as a separate grey plastic part, although you will have to cut out the window section and glaze it somehow. The undercarriage doors are very nice, with accurate shape and interior detail (yes they have the L-shaped scuff panel) and to be truthful these are ideal to replace the ones in the Academy kit. The oleo legs are basic while the wheels are nicely detailed units depicting the five-spoke hubs. The kit does not offer any bombs, tanks or rockets. The neat thing is that Pavla supply the fish-plates for the rear fuselage as decals, which work really well in this smaller scale.

The kit offers the following colour options:
- R7752, PR•G, No.609 Squadron, Manston, March 1943
- EK273, JE•DT, No.195 Squadron, Ludham, July 1943
- R7698, Z•Z, Duxford Wing, Autumn 1942

Verdict

Although probably not worth the time and effort to build, as there are better options, this could add a lot of detail to the Academy kit and, with work, could allow you to convert the Academy kit to a car-door version?

1/48th

Monogram

This injection moulded kit from Monogram in the USA was first released in 1969 and has been reissued many times since, the most recent being in the 'Monogram Classics' range in 1999. This is also the tooling that was reissued by Hasegawa before they made their own new tooling.

The example we had was the 1999 reissue and it was moulded in an olive green-coloured plastic. All the parts feature fine raised panel lines and a limited number of fasteners. The fuselage length is good, the only item that looks odd is the profile of the vertical fin leading edge and top, which seems too pointed; a quick check

on enlarged plans proved this to be the case as the whole vertical fin is about 2mm too high and 1mm too narrow. The exhaust stacks are moulded with the fuselage halves and they depict the shrouded version, probably as the world's only example was fitted with them and was stored in the USA until 1967, but this type of cover was usually removed in service. The cockpit interior has detail moulded to the fuselage half interior combined with an instrument panel and a grossly inaccurate seat/bulkhead unit. The separate floor that is put in from underneath has a basic control column but no rudder pedals.

The wings are about 4 scale inches short in span and the panel lines are limited and do not correspond to the Bentley plans. The smaller set of cartridge ports (for the links) in the wing undersides are too far aft and the flaps lack visible hinge cut-outs. The wheel wells are boxed in and are nice and deep but the detail is very basic and comprises heavy ribs on the roof. The landing lights and wingtip lights are separate clear components and both are in the correct location on the wing leading edge, although the latter are once again too big. The tailplanes are the correct span but the panel lines are limited with a number missing and no rivet detail; the sloped cover over the trim tab gearbox inboard is missing.

The kit only offers the four-blade D.H. propeller and this is the correct diameter but is moulded with the spinner so it lacks definition at the blade roots (no spinner cut-outs etc.). The undercarriage is nicely detailed, with wheels that have five-spoke hubs and oleo legs that have detail and retraction linkage. The undercarriage doors have rivet detail on the outside (at odds with the wing surface) while the insides of the inner doors do include the scuff pads. The clear parts are well moulded, however the shape and profile of the sliding canopy section looks a bit flat on top even though the overall shape is sound.

The kit comes with two decal options in this 1999 edition:
- RB222, TP•F, No.198 Squadron, Battle of the Falaise Gap, August 1944
- JP149, I8•P, No.440 squadron, October 1945

The Sky for the codes and fuselage band is too grey, while the No.440 option should have Type C (or C1, which was unofficial) roundels on the upper wing surfaces instead of the supplied Type B and by October 1944 the aft Sky band was over-painted.

Verdict

For years this was the only game in town and it was a good one. It could be made into a car-door version thanks to the KMC conversion and even today the quality of the moulding and sound basic detail is still impressive. Out-shone by the Hasegawa kit today this one is still worth investing time and effort in if it can be found cheap secondhand.

Hasegawa JT59

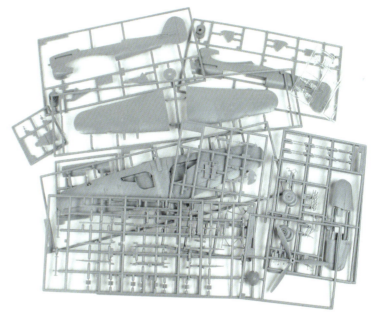

Hasegawa

Hasegawa initially reissued the Monogram kit in Japan, but in 1998 they produced an all-new tooling of the car-door Typhoon and followed this in 1999 with the bubbletop. As the main parts are common to all kits we will just look at the package as a whole, pointing out the differences between the car-door and bubbletop.

The Hasegawa kits are typical of their work in the late 1990s in that there are numerous small sprues with all the various parts to make the car-door or bubbletop versions from a common set of main parts. This did result in fuselage halves that have an insert for the upper cockpit/fuselage area, which means the insert has to fit well to work, although sadly sometimes it does not. All panel lines are engraved and there is rivet detail where necessary. The fish-plates on the aft fuselage are strangely oblong, when they should be a

Hasegawa clear parts common to all

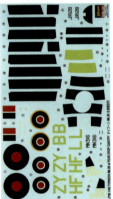

Hasegawa JT60

square-tipped diamond shape.

The cockpit interior is built up a bit like the real thing, with a framework that supports the floor plates, rudder pedals, control column, instrument panel, rear bulkhead and seat. The bulkhead shows the correct triangular shape on the car-door version, but there is no armoured glass in the gaps either side between it and the canopy – much debate rages about this, but some wartime photos clearly show thick glass in these areas. The upper decking under the lower canopy has some detail, but should have such things as the light and wiring. With the bubbletop a different rear bulkhead is used to correctly reflect this area, the upper fuselage decking inserts are also different. The radiator unit has detail back and front, but the former does not have the radiating support arms within the inner ring (there should be four).

The fuselage is about 3mm short and all of this deficiency is in vertical tail, mainly aft of the rudder post. Much debate lingers about the profile of the upper engine cowling, as it is claimed that the Typhoon late series machines had the upper cowl seen on all Tempests, which was more rounded than the 'flat' version seen on the initial and mid-production series. You have a look at the kit parts and decide, as most seem to feel that this area of the kit is too flat. The wing detail is correct, however Hasegawa have also opted to show the teardrop shaped cover as a bulge, something which is still open to debate. The cannon barrel fairings have the lower section moulded with the wings, while the outer sections are separate to allow the covered and uncovered recoil springs to

Hasegawa JT183

be offered (the early version only comes with the exposed spring units, although the others are still on the sprues). The landing and wingtip lights are all separate clear components and both are located correctly and of the right size. With the rocket-armed bubbletop it is best to check references as a lot of these machines had the landing lights plated over. Overall the span is 1–2mm short, with nearly all of this shortfall being at the wingtip. Underneath the IFF mast (#N10) is too long and thick, while the 'boat antenna' (#N9) was not carried by all machines, so check your refs. The tailwheel and yoke is a single assembly and the wheel is the original plain version, not the grooved anti-shimmy one seen on most machines from 1944. Bomb racks are included in the car-door kit, along with what are probably supposed to be 250lb bombs; these need replacing as they lack detail or profile. In the bubbletop version 3in rocket projectiles and rails are included with each rail made of two parts and the rockets are separate with individual tails. All of these look very accurate and are far superior to anyone else's attempts at these weapons.

The three-blade propeller in two versions has separate blades but the spinner cut-outs look a bit suspect; the kit was also released as a limited edition with the four-blade propeller. Two styles of exhaust are included in the car-door machine, shrouded or exposed, the latter being far too skinny and thus needs replacing. In the bubbletop version only the shrouded exhausts are included, which is a shame as most were removed in service. The undercarriage bays are boxed in and nicely detailed with far more subtle ribbing in the top. The undercarriage doors are nicely detailed inside, with the scuff plates on the inner set, while the main doors include the oval access panel only seen on mid- and late-production Typhoons. The limited edition 'Shark Teeth' kit included resin 'Tempest' tailplanes, with diagrams in the instructions of how to remove the existing style tailplane root fairings and fit these new parts. The kit also had a new radiator insert, which featured the 'cuckoo doors', but none of the struts supporting this unit are included (the box art shows them nicely, though). The upper nose profile of this machine should probably be the later (Tempest) style unit, but this area of the kit remains unchanged from the 'flat' style of the early and mid-production airframes.

We have four of the releases, so here are the decal options in each:
#JT59 Mk Ib Car Door
• EK139, HH•N, No.175 Squadron
• JR371, TP•R, No.198 Squadron

Both options are Dark Green/Ocean Grey/Medium Sea Grey, both have the lower wing ID stripes and Sky spinner and fuselage band plus yellow wing leading edges

#JT60 Mk Ib with Tear Drop Canopy
• MN316, ZY•B, No.247 Squadron
• JR128, HF•L, No.183 Squadron

Both are Dark Green/Ocean Grey/Medium Sea Grey, option one has Invasion Stripes around wings and fuselage and both have Sky spinner and fuselage band plus yellow wing leading edges

#JT183 Mk Ib Early Version
- R7752, PR•G, No.609 Squadron
- R7695, ZH•Z, No.266 Squadron

Both are Dark Green/Ocean Grey/Medium Sea Grey with Sky spinner and fuselage band plus yellow wing leading edges. Option 2 has Type C upper wing roundels with a yellow outline, something that was officially frowned upon at the time, but common on some units' machines.

#09978 Mk Ib 'Shark Teeth'
- MP197, MR•U, No.245 Squadron, June 1945
- RB326, 5V•V, No.439 Sqn, April 1945
- MN925, OV•Z, No.197 Sqn, September 1944

All these options are Dark Green and Ocean Grey over Medium Sea Grey, option 1 has the 'sharkmouth' and blue spinner, whilst option 3 has partial invasion stripes still. Option 1 should, apparently, have the inside of the undercarriage doors in the same blue/white checks as applied to the rear fuselage?

Verdict

This is an excellent kit, even with the complexity of the inserts to get both car-door and bubbletop out of a basic set of moulds. The detail and quality of parts make this the choice for the Typhoon in 1/48.

Italeri

This (#2734) is just a reissue of the Hasegawa Mk Ib 'bubbletop' kit (#JT60), with new decals, so all the comments in relationship to the Hasegawa original apply here also, as no changes were made to the tooling. The box top lists this as a 'Mk Ib Late', whilst the instructions are just 'Mk Ib', the upshot is that this is a mid-production Mk Ib with the three-blade propeller and early tailplanes, so it is not accurate as a 'Late' nor for some of the decal options.

The kit offers the following decal options:
- JP*16 ,PR•J, No.609 Sqn, RAF Thorney Island, 6th June 1944 - As a JP-series machine this has the early tailplane and three-blade propeller. Confirmation of the serial has currently not been possible, as the only likely option is JP916, which was EL•C with No.181 Squadron on D-Day?
- MN130, •PR, 'M', No.609 Sqn, RAF Thorney Island, 6th June 1944 - The serial number is wrong for this option, it was MN131; it does have the early tailplanes and three-blade propeller, so with modification to the serial number can be made from this kit
- MN570, •B, No.198 Sqn, No.123 Wing, RAF Thorney Island, 6th June 1944 - This was a late series airframe with a four-blade propeller and Tempest tailplanes, so can't be built from the kit
- MN363, ZY•Y, No.247 Sqn, France, June 1944 - This was also a late series airframe with a four-blade propeller and Tempest tailplanes, so can't be built from the kit

The decals are perfectly printed with excellent register and colour and they are glossy with lim-

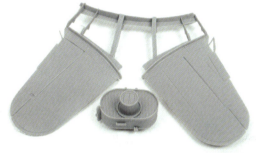

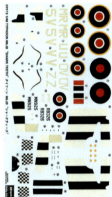

ited excess carrier film. They are thick, though, and require a bit of decal softener to settle down into the recessed panel lines etc.

Verdict

The high asking price of this kit here in the UK (£24.99) made many ignore this one we are sure, but with the reissued original now over £30 in the UK, it is well worth considering, especially with that superb decal sheet. Just be aware you cannot make a late-series example with the Tempest tailplanes and four-blade propeller needed for the last two decal options. Only Hasegawa in their 'Shark Teeth' kit (#09978) had the Tempest tailplanes and later carburettor intake with 'Cuckoo doors' as additional resin parts.

Hasegawa 09978

Italeri

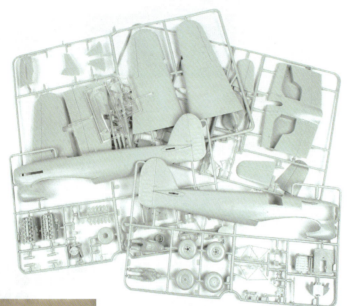

Revell (original)

1/32nd

Revell

Revell released their injection moulded Typhoon in this scale in 1973 and it has been reissued a couple of times since, the last being in 1996. We have an original version along with the one released in 1996, so we will note where they differ.

The first release was in a light grey-coloured plastic and all the detail was raised including lots of rivets. Even in this first edition there was a lot of flash evident. Detail in this larger scale is good, the fuselage is slightly short, but only by about 1mm. The linkage on the rudder

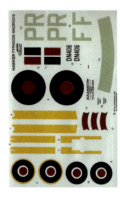

Revell (reissue)

is incorrect and that on the trim tab is over-simplified and needs replacing. The kit features a complete Sabre engine and radiator unit, but this is undersized to fit within the fuselage cowls. The cockpit interior is built up as a framework, but the shape of the head armour and seat is all wrong.

The wings are about 1.9cm short in span and again feature the teardrop-shaped panel as a bulge for the inboard cannon, while the outboard ones are elongated ovals when they should be oblong with rounded ends. The prominent foot step in the trailing edge of the starboard wing is omitted from the surface detail, so needs to be added. Underneath the smaller link ejector ports are too far aft and the two oval access panels under the wings tips are missing. The hinge cut-outs for the flap sections are missing and there is an odd oval-shaped bulge near the mid-section of the ailerons. The barrel fairings are a little long and they lack the detail (panel line and fixings) of the join for the forward section.

The inner undercarriage doors feature the scuff plates as recessed areas, so these need to be filled, while the oval access panel on the outside of the main door is missing if you are making a late-production machine. The wheel bays are boxed in and nice and deep but they are devoid of any accurate detail. The oleo legs are quite well detailed and include retraction linkage, while the wheels feature five-spoke hubs. The tailwheel is made up of separate yoke and wheel, each being two-part, but the latter is the grooved anti-shimmy version that is not applicable to the early Mk Ib. The bomb racks are moulded integrally with the bombs, so these are best replaced. No rockets or rails are included. The canopy comes with the car-door area separate, but the upper canopy section that is always open when the car door is, is moulded with the main canopy. The detail and armoured glass below the rear section of the canopy are not included in the kit.

The original kit came with one decal option: R7752, PR•G, No.609 Squadron. Study of period photos shows that when this machine was flown by Sqn Ldr Beamont it had covers over the cannon recoil springs but these were modified Spitfire units, not Typhoon ones. When reissued in 1996 the decal option was as follows: DN406, PR•F, flown by Fg Off L.W.F. 'Pinky' Stark, No.609 Squadron, Manston, early 1943. Period photos of this machine show that it did not carry the yellow bands on the upper wings and the kill markings were smaller and lower down the fuselage side than depicted in the decals.

Verdict
Although old now, this is still a good basis for a Typhoon if you do not like working with resin. One can only hope the aftermarket take pity on us and offer a series of update sets and detail parts.

Model Design Construction (MDC)

Released in 2006, this resin kit features metal, photo-etched brass and vacformed plastic components. Unlike the Revell kit this one depicts the bubbletop Mk Ib and the options of three- or four-blade propellers are included, but you only get the standard tailplanes so you can't make a late-series machine. The hollow-cast fuselage halves contrast with the solid wings, so the kit at times feels like a mainstream injection-moulded product.

Now five years old some of the panel lines on the fuselage halves are starting to fade, with those on the mid-starboard side being the worst affected. These almost fade to nothing, but a strong light will show where they should be so you can rescribe them. Mould separation marks are also present along the entire fuselage underside and, oddly, only at the top of the chin intake on the starboard side? These look like ragged, uneven ridges in the resin and will need filling, sanding and, where necessary, rescribing. You will also need to sand down the lump visible on the starboard cockpit side, where the door handle was on the car-door version, and rescribe the aft vertical panel line, as that has faded a bit.

The vertical fin area also needs some rescribing due to faded panel lines and again the starboard side is the worst affected. There are no foot or hand-holds engraved onto the starboard fuselage side, nor has either side got the vents below the cockpit area (two on the port side and one on the starboard). The wings are solid cast items with highly detailed undercarriage bays. The surface detail is fairly close to that on the Bentley plans, but there are areas that can be enhanced if you so choose and a few access panels that need to be redefined due to fading of the engraved detail. The foot step in the trailing edge of the starboard wing root is completely omitted, so this needs to be scribed on. The wheel wells are lovely, being highly detailed and nice and deep, the only omission is the compressed air bottle in each. These 750 litre bottles are very prominent, so they need to be added from scratch in a model this size. All the retraction jacks are separately moulded and the undercarriage oleos are white-metal, while the main wheels have the five-spoke hubs and are cast 'weighted'. Because the wheel wells have to be moulded 'open' initially the edges that overhang front inboard and rear outboard are separate, with the former having the downward ident lights moulded into them, but these only apply to the late production machines.

The cockpit interior is superb, being built-up as a tubular framework just like the real thing. Some of the complex shapes cause the parts to twist during curing, so in our sample the framework was thus effected; a quick dip in hot water and then taping them to a board to cool should return them to the correct shape, though. On top of the resin parts MDC include decals for the instrument panel and etched Sutton harness, either using etched belts of etched buckles with foil belts (you supply suitable foil).

Model Design Construction

No armament is included in the kit, the rockets being available separately, and this is simply because MDC offer various versions of the rails from the initial Mk 1 (CV32022 for HE and CV32023 for HE/SAP) through to the lightweight Mk 3 (CV32035 for AP and CV32036 for HE/AP) used from December 1944, so they thought it best to allow the modeller to pick which type he needs for the aircraft he is building. MDC also advise us that bomb racks will be produced as well shortly, so check their website for price and availability. They already offer the bombs for these racks, with the 500lb versions available as CV32050 or CV32052 and the 1,000lb version as CV32053.

The final medium in the kit is vacformed clear plastic for the canopy and a spare is included should you get things wrong. Also on the sheet are the wing leading-edge light covers, but MDC include an etched brass template to cut these from clear stock as an alternative. The carburettor intake features a superb separate filter unit, the front of which features the 'cuckoo doors', although that does means modellers will have to modify this to depict the initial domed unit designed by Napiers in haste in 1944. The modeller will also have to make from scratch the stone screens often fitted in the intake during operations from rough strips in Euope during the hectic days after the D-Day landings.

The decal sheet offers five options, none of them identified in any way but they are:
1. MR*?, No.245 Squadron, 2nd TAF, flown by Sqn Ldr J. Collins from B6 Coulombs airfield, Normandy in June 1944 – this is probably MN819; MN130, PR•M, No.609 Sqn, 2nd TAF. RAF Thorney Island, 6th June 1944; RB485, I8•E, No.440 Sqn, 2nd TAF. Flensburg, Germany, April 1945; SW593, 7L•C, No.59 Operational Training Unit, May 1945; RB382, BR•M

of No.184 Sqn, 2nd TAF, July 1945, flown by Fg Off A.E. Pavitt {note this should have a red 'M' on the intake filter doors}. The aforementioned instructions show each option only in port side profile, plus a generic camouflage pattern showing starboard side and top views, there are no other details about colours or markings, either general or specific. The instructions are the one thing that could do with improvement, as they are a little dis-jointed, the photographic style used does not duplicate well and they are, at times, confusing; especially when they refer to individual sets (CV32038 – wings, CV32030 – cockpit and CV32018 – undercarriage legs). The decal options also really need more data even for the average builder, and as the specific use of each option determines if the subject has rockets, bombs or neither, this is even more important.

Verdict

Currently the best option in 1/32, but it still needs careful assembly and skill to deal with some of the problems to get the very best from it.

1/24th

Airfix

Announced in late 2012 this new tooling did not become a reality until June 2014. Looking at this one in detail is difficult, as no commercial 1/24th scale plans exist and just doubling a set of 1/48th scale ones can cause all sorts of problems, especially with complex curves etc. We will therefore restrict our comments to the overall dimensions, the look of the airframe and the details.

Inside the huge box you will find fourteen grey-coloured and two clear sprues. The instructions come in the form of a 48-page, A4-size booklet and the 229-assembly stages give you an idea of how detailed the kit is. From this kit you can make a Tempest-tailed, mid- to late-production series machine with a three- or four-blade propeller, plus you have the options of bombs, rockets or drop tanks. The interior is an impressive little model in its own right, but the plastic seat belts, although a good attempt at this detail in plastic, are just too thick to be convincing and are best replaced with the modern paper or etched examples. The engine is another little marvel, and you can add an electric motor inside it to spin the propeller if you so wish. There are quite a few injector pin marks to deal with and alignment of the components is not without its problems. The issue of ejector pin marks is one that applied to many of the components in this kit, with these often being in very visible locations, plus you will have to spend quite a bit of time cleaning up the mould separation lines on things like the cockpit tubular framework. The radiator intake centre is quite nice, but it's a bit thick even in 1/24th scale, the 'cuckoo doors' are supplied as just the front section, there is no filter element in between, which means you are just left with a gaping hole at this point. There are also two versions of the simple mesh screen fitted into the chin intake, one with and one without the 'cuckoo doors'.

The exhausts stacks are separate and nicely detailed with the centre seams, but you do not have any of the shroud options in the kit, even though it is true that most were removed in service. The wing is a complex series of sections built up around the spars and you have the complete cannon bays with ammunition boxes and feed units, plus the fuel tanks, all of which will be lost forever if you close up the wing halves and cannon bays of course. The landing lights are included (#R13 and R09), but these parts are not used because all the decal options have these apparently blanked off, so you use 'solid' part #132 instead. The upper section of the aft fuselage and vertical fin are separate from the upper/rear sections of the fuselage, this is to allow the bigger 'Tempest' tailplanes to be used, as Airfix obviously had the Car Door version on the cards (now confirmed from them for 2016), which will need the earlier narrower tailplanes. The complex 'skin' approach to the fuselage and wings would seem potentially difficult, but all builds thus far seem to have coped with it well.

The starboard mid-upper cowling (#N03) does not have the two pipe stubs that project out of it about mid-way along, instead both port and starboard panels have a hole with a raised lip in this region. The elusive desert filter (#L14) is included for the last decal option, the operation of which has never been fully explained in my mind, but there must have been a modification to the existing air intake system to allow this to be 'closed' so that the engine could breath through this filter? The kit parts make no attempt at depicting what this might be, so I must assume Airfix could not find out either (there

Airfix

was probably an additional control added in the cockpit for this filter as well, but it's not there either). High marks to Airfix for including two styles of light cover for the formation light built into the rear of the tailplane fairings, one convex the other concave in outline. Wheel well detail is excellent, with all the pipework and the compressed air cylinder separate, plus the canvas bag for the wheel locks is nicely moulded on the rear bulkhead (spar). The wheels feature five-spoke hubs and the tyres are weighted, not too heavily, but some may prefer aftermarket alternatives. The oleo legs are well detailed, but lack any brake lines other than those bits that are moulded onto the undercarriage doors(!), nor the prominent towing 'D' eyelets on the front/upper edge. The tailwheel has the anti-shimmy type tyre and the yoke is separate from the wheel. The flaps can be depicted up or down and all the control surfaces can be positioned. The separate insert for the cockpit area is another giveaway to the future release of the Car Door version, as this is just how Hasegawa approached the situation with their 1/48th kit. The crash-bars and gunsight correctly depict the modified Mk II* unit used on many of the rocket-equipped squadrons, or its production version (Type 1 Mk III Projector), however some of the options may have retained the standard Mk II* sight, so it would have been nice to have it in the kit and Airfix will certainly need it for their Car Door version.

Both Mk Ib and Mk IIIb rails are included, the detail on these is not bad, but they lack certain aspects and we suspect most, having invested this much in the kit, will see the benefit of replacing the kit rockets with the superb Master Models examples. The 44 Imp. Gal. drop tanks are also well done, but they lack the filler caps on the top. Both 1,000lb and 500lb GP bombs are included, they lack the tail fuze-arming vanes, though, plus you will need to add the arming lanyard wires to them as well. The bomb racks are good and include separate sway braces. Both three- and four-blade propellers are included and it is interesting to note the two styles of spinner for the three-blade option, does this hint at the so-called 'Tempest' upper engine cowls revised profile? The final details include the IFF rod antenna, the crew access step and the pitot head. The 'boat antenna' is moulded with the ventral section of the mid/aft fuselage, but it has the rod part of it moulded in situ resulting it is being attached to the underside of the fuselage and in this scale it should really be separate; just chop it off, then drill and replace with a suitable length of rod or wire.

The kit offers four decal options:
- MN666, C•G, No.121 Wing, flown by Wg Cdr Charles Green, RAF Holmsley South and B.5 le Fresne-Camilly, France, June 1944
- DN252, ZY•N, No.247 Sqn, 2nd TAF, France and Belgium, June-September 1944. You will note from the image in the instructions of a built example that this machine has 'cuckoo

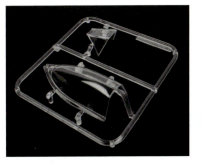
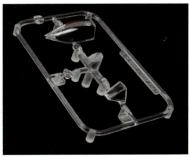

Clear parts

doors' on the intake, but the part included in the kit is just the front, the filter element in between is missing (there is just a gap!)
- MP197, MR•U, No.245 Sqn, 2nd TAF, Germany and RAF Warmwell, June-August 1945.
- JB389, I8•P, 'Pulverizer IV', No.440 Sqn, 2nd TAF, The Netherlands & Germany, February-May 1945. Oddly, this machine had 'SCO' hand-painted in white on the outer face of the outer cannon barrels, just forward of the half-way mark and this is not on the decals. The bombs should also have tail fuze arming vanes, which are not included, plus you need to add the arming wires. The type is also seen in many period images with anti-personnel bomb canisters, but these are not in the kit. I have to say that I feel that the width of the characters used for the 'Pulverizer IV' name are too thin in comparison with period images of this machine. Period images also show a kill marking, badge or stripped area of paint (?) on the starboard fuselage, just below the canopy sill, and the rear fuselage looks to have a painted-out Sky band, as the green paint in this area is much darker.

The decal sheet is well printed, with perfect register and colours, but as usual with Airfix the carrier film is opaque and quite obtrusive in certain areas (around the codes etc.) A full set of airframe and ordnance stencils is included, plus the dials for the instrument panel are also supplied as decals. The instructions include the 'scale' dimensions for the invasion stripes, which is always useful.

Verdict

As the only option in the scale, and likely to remain so, this is of course the choice if you want a 1/24th Tiffie in your collection. It is a superb piece of model engineering and should, therefore, be in most modellers' 'to do' list. With the announcement of the Car Door version as we close this updated edition, you will soon have to make space for another one, which is no bad thing!

Airfix A19002 alongside 72nd version!

Airfix

1/24th Typhoon Mk Ib 'Car Door'
(Planned for 2016)

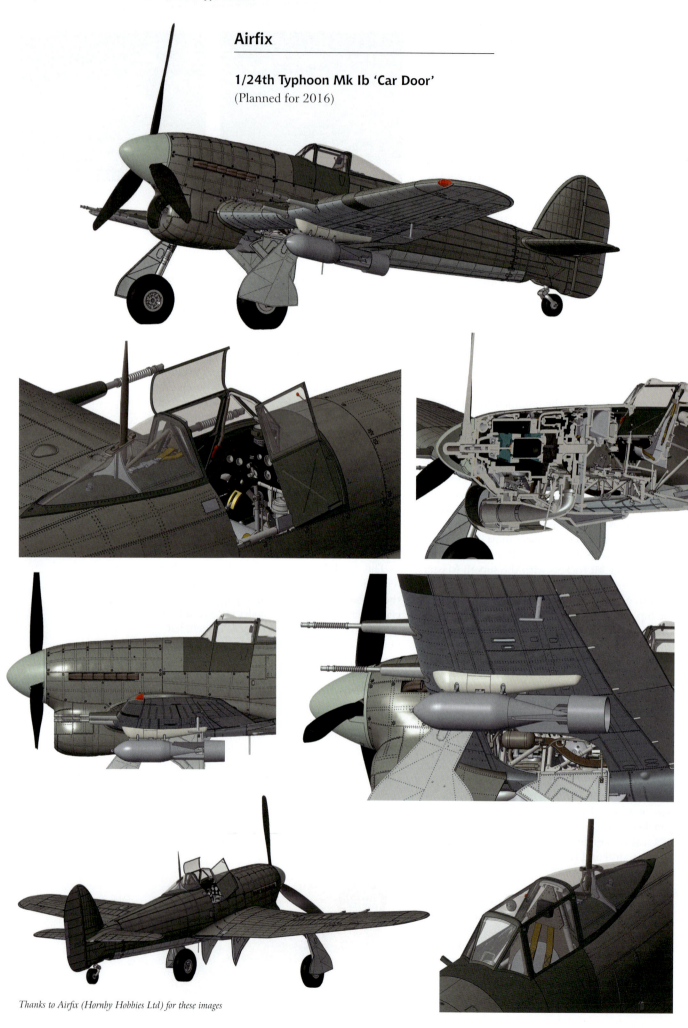

Thanks to Airfix (Hornby Hobbies Ltd) for these images

Chapter 8: Building a Selection

Having looked at what kits are and have been available of the Typhoon in the three major scales, we thought it would be a good idea to build those that we felt were the best in 1/72nd, 1/48th, 1/32nd and 1/24th.

Academy 1/72nd Typhoon Mk Ib

by Libor Jekl

In this kit Academy offers the late production Typhoon with the tear drop canopy and with so few competitive kits of this version (with the exception of the HobbyBoss kit in their 'Easy Assembly' range) this is the only reasonable choice in 1/72nd scale. The kit also offers excellent value when you consider the price versus the quality, as even though it has been on the market for quite some time it features high level of detail and easy assembly. The kit should satisfy both the less experienced or occasional modellers as well as experienced builders that can utilize a wide range of available aftermarket products.

The etched, resin or vacformed extras may also help to solve the most visible kit's inaccuracies such as the simplified main wheels, oversized exhausts, oddly shaped propeller and canopy.

For my kit I chose the famous 'sharkmouth' example from No.245 Squadron and after careful study I went for the following aftermarket products that substantially improved the look of the finished model and also helped to convert the kit to the late standard with larger (Tempest) tailplanes:
- CMK resin interior set
- Resin Art wheel and radiator set
- Resin Art 4-blade propeller

All photos © the authors 2011/2015

The completed and painted replacement cockpit set from CMK

Building a Selection

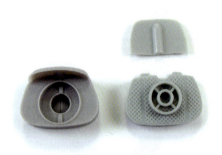
The kit radiator unit on the left with the excellent Resin Art replacement on the right

A specially-made photo-etched screen from Hauler

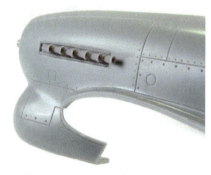
The Quickboost exhausts are a lot better than the kit detail

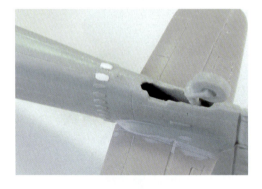
The reinforcing plates on the extreme underside and top need to be created from plasticard

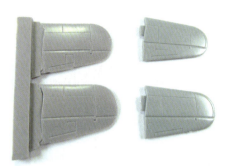
The replacement Tempest tailplanes from Quickboost (left) with the standard kit examples on the right

The kit wheels are OK (top), but the Resin Art ones are a lot better (bottom)

- Quickboost exhausts
- Quickboost Tempest tailplanes
- Falcon canopy
- Anti-dust screen (custom made at Hauler)
- Aviaeology decals

I commenced the build with the replacement exhausts as the kit exhausts look crude and do not correspond to any known Typhoon exhaust style. They were cut off using a fine razor saw and the fuselage was sanded smooth and polished. The Quickboost resin exhausts need openings in the fuselage so the required rectangular apertures were first pre-drilled and then opened with a scalpel blade. I recommend you insert the new exhausts at the end of the build otherwise the delicately cast items may be easily broken off. The interior of the kit looks basic, but it is quite adequate for a kit with a closed canopy. Since I had already decided to replace the canopy anyway, I needed to add more details and went for the CMK cockpit set that includes, besides the cast items, a small etched fret with instrument panel and other small details and a vacformed canopy. Unfortunately, the latter item

Building a Selection 73

was formed from oddly coloured and cloudy material and in addition it featured the same shape inaccuracy as the kit's item, having too sharp a slope of the windshield front that makes the whole canopy look too tall. Therefore, the canopy was sourced from the Falcon RAF set. The resin parts nicely matched the fuselage sides so they could be primed and sprayed black. Subsequently the Interior Green colour was applied in several thinned layers giving contrast around raised details; this 'patchy' look served as a base for further weathering techniques. The small cockpit opening does not allow enough light to come through and therefore adequate contrasts have to be created. Next I applied a black wash to all parts and all visible edges were accentuated with a light grey colour drybrushed on. The individual details were picked out in corresponding colours using acrylic paints and the complete lot could be inserted into the fuselage.

Now I moved on to the installation of the replacement radiator in the nose, which features the correctly shaped air intake and finer louvres. The part is designed as direct replacement so no other adjustments are necessary. 2nd TAF machines operating from field aerodromes had several types of anti-dust filters and screens fitted and the subject of this build was no exception. Unfortunately, there was no aftermarket item available, so it was custom made for me by a local etched part manufacturer. The fuselage and wing assembly was thankfully a perfect fit and quite straightforward. The wing openings for the spent cartridges are provided as raised lines only and these definitely benefit from being opened, so I drilled them out. The late-production Typhoons were equipped with larger tailplanes taken from Tempest production and these can be sourced either from a Tempest kit or Quickboost. I chose the latter as the tailplanes are cast pre-adjusted to fit the Academy kit and again they do not need any extra work except cleaning up prior to fitment. The Falcon canopy was cut into sections and the windshield was, after some

The 3mm taken out of the oleo leg can be seen in this shot with the original unit on the right and the modified one on the left

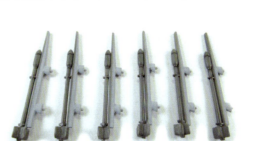

The modified and painted undercariage components

The rockets were separated from the rails then reattached closer - here you can see the modified units painted and weathered

trimming, glued to the fuselage.

Now the kit was ready for priming, which was done with Mr Surfacer 1000 and using my Rosie the Riveter tool the kit received a full riveting job. Then the kit's surface was sanded smooth with extra fine wet and dry and polished to a high gloss with polishing sticks. The camouflage was sprayed on using Gunze-Sangyo acrylics, the individual base shades were gently lightened and then post-shaded with darkened hues before being fixed with gloss varnish. The paint chipping was reproduced with a silver Prismacolor pencil on the upper surfaces and Vallejo dark acrylics underneath. The panel lines received MIG Production washes, the Dark Wash on the upper surfaces and the Neutral Wash underneath.

The Aviaeology decals are printed to the highest quality, having perfect register and good looking colours, and also included is a set of stencils. These decals reacted well to both Microscale and Gunze-Sangyo decal solutions and perfectly conformed to the kit's surface. The other plus point is that the instructions include a photographic supplement and very comprehen-

Building a Selection 75

sive narrative regarding the sharkmouth motive and its colouring. I went for the more moderate option without the red in the mouth section as to my eyes the red seems less probable.

Now I turned my attention to remaining bits. One of the most noticeable kit's inaccuracies is the high 'sit' of the finished model that is caused by overlong main undercarriage legs. The best point for cutting and shortening these is about in the middle so I cut off the centre portion and replaced it with brass tubing about 3mm shorter that was secured in the pre-drilled ends of both strut halves. The same odd look also applies to the undercarriage doors, especially along their bottom edge, which is at the wrong angle. This can be partially solved with a plasticard to extend the covers' overall length so they can then be cut to the proper shape. The rocket projectiles' attachment to the rails does not look the part either, because they are moulded on long pins; in reality they were very close to the rails. The chosen subject of this build is shown in period photographs with the later 'lightweight' style of rails, but these are not provided in the kit, however I believe the original variant may have been used too. The rockets were therefore cut off the rails and the pins were removed; at the same time I also thinned the fins that are moulded as separate components. From thin plastic wire I added the 'pig tails' wiring with a drop of paint at the end reproducing the plug. Photographs often show a combination of external fuel tanks and rockets, unfortunately the kit does not provide any other stores so the fuel tank was borrowed from a CMR kit and a few external details like the reinforcing strips and fuel cap were added using thin plastic sheet. After a final coat of matt varnish the antennae made of black fishing line was attached as well as the propeller unit. The exhaust stains were sprayed on with a mix of black and grey paint and the wheels were dusted with MIG Productions Light Dust pigment. Fresh fuel stains on the external fuel tank and around the filler caps were brushed on using AK Interactive Fuel Stains enamel mixture.

Verdict

Although the basic Academy kit has a few faults, these can all be overcome and with a little time and effort a superb little Typhoon can join your collection. Investing in the aftermarket items I used are well worth it if you want to add that little extra to your example.

After priming and painting of the wing leading edges the camouflage was masked with Blu-Tack and masking tape

The model once all the painting and decalling had been completed

Building a Selection

Airfix 1/72nd
Typhoon Mk Ib

(#A50136, Dogfight Double with Fw 190A-8)
by Steve A. Evans

Lovely box top art by Adam Tooby sets the scene for some neat looking plastic inside

Airfix has had something of a chequered history. Many years ago, deep in the mists of my childhood, they really were world leaders in plastic model aircraft kits. Then the doldrums took over and the once mighty name, products and reputation, went right down the tube. In the last couple of years, however, they have really made the effort to get back into the market and reclaim some of that lost glory. This small scale Typhoon is a perfect example of that recovery of their fortunes. It comes in a neat package, whether it's as the individual kit or, as here, the 'Dogfight Double' release, twined with their Fw 190A-8. The plastic is very well moulded in pale blue colour, with fine detail and neat panel lines. The interior detail is not bad, with the tubular construction of the real thing represented as moulded detail on the sidewalls, a padded seat and proper 'see-through' floor. There is some flash and mould lines to deal with but it's not overly intrusive and easy to remove with a sharp knife. The plastic itself is a little on the soft side but it's all perfectly formed with no sink holes or other blemishes. The only negative is a few warped parts, mainly the upper section of the right wing and the rocket rails. I have a feeling this is actually bad packaging where the two kits are both jammed into quite a small box. The rest of the Typhoon contents are the instructions, which are well drawn, with a full-colour, 4-view camouflage and painting guide and well drawn assembly stages. There is only one choice in this box but it's a superb one, with invasion stripes, red spinner and art on

the nose. The decals come on a single sheet and although well printed they look a little thick and very matt.

It starts just as you would expect with the interior. The fit of the parts is really good, not quite up to Tamiya standard but it's not far short of it, to be honest. Trial fits and trims are recommended but not actually necessary most of the time. The only bit to look out for is the slightly over-complicated way the undercarriage bays and the integral front radiator unit fit into the fuselage. It pays dividends to tidy up the mating surfaces here to get everything aligned properly. The fit of the other major parts is very good, with only a tiny mismatch at the wing roots to take care of, possibly as much to do with my haste to get it done than anything, I suspect. Detail-wise, you get the choice of the gun bays open on the wings. They are reasonably well detailed with gun breeches and ammunition runs but even in this scale are a little simplified, so are just a good starting point for

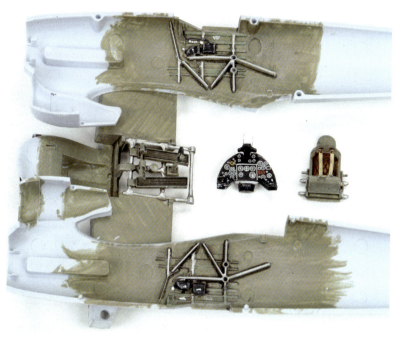

adding more detail. You also get the choice of bombs or rockets in the kit but be warned, you have to match the armament with the aircraft markings, there were bomb carriers and rocket carriers but they never swapped between the two because the fittings in the wing were entirely different.

As mentioned, in this box you only get the one colour scheme and I decided, right from the start, that I would only spray the main colours and use the Airfix decals for all the stripes and markings. This was pretty brave of me because in the past the decals found lurking in the bottom of Airfix boxes were loathsome things, in league with the devil and sent to us to destroy our faith in everything good and righteous.

The interior is reasonably well detailed, not that much of it will be seen on the finished model. The seat belts are Eduard's new 'Super Fabric' belts and they work beautifully.

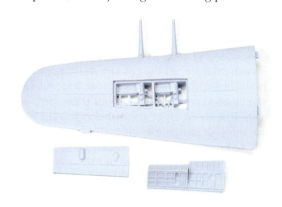

The wings come complete with gun bays, if you want to cut open the skin. They actually look half decent in this scale, so not a bad effort from Airfix here

78 Building a Selection

This bit is a little complicated, getting the wheel bays into place, so the time getting it right, is time well spent

Major construction is fast and easy, with only a bit of gapping around the wing-to-fuselage joint but this is probably as much my rushing things a bit, as much as it is the kit going wrong

Anyway, less of that, more of the painting. As you can imagine, all the colour codes are in Humbrol enamels but being classic RAF colours, there is no shortage of choice out there for them. Just about every paint maker has their own range of 'authentic' colours to choose from. I elected to use the colours called for on the sheets so the only real decision for me was on the demarcation lines. On the little Brengun Typhoon I did I opted for the soft look, so this time I went for the hard-edged pattern to see the difference. This made it a quick and easy process of masking and spraying, with the Humbrol enamels thinned with Baufix universal thinners which dry really quickly (almost acrylic quick!) and very matt.

Weathering followed of course and this was picking out a few small panels in lighter shades of the main colours, pastel dust for general scruffiness (especially on the underside behind that mucky engine) and some Tamiya X-19 Smoke along the panel lines, and sealing it all in.

Two coats of Johnson's Klear had it glossy enough for the decals and with not a little trepidation I set about putting the markings into place. The decals are neatly printed in perfect register and good colour density, with a heavy looking matt finish. The sheet includes all the national markings, the stencils and the identification bands: Sky, Black and White and Yellow. I used warm water to get them off the backing, which was rapid, they moved about on the kit reasonably well and they even fitted where they were supposed to, so the sizes are just about right. I then slathered them in Microscale softening solution and sat back to watch the horror show commence. To my surprise they acted just like old fashioned decals used to by wrinkling up and becoming horrid messes but remembering the lessons of the past,

Building a Selection 79

Halfords Plastic Primer is good for finding all the little bits that need smoothing off before the paint goes on for good

Because this is the hard-edged version of the camouflage pattern, it's quick and easy to do. Note the slight variation in shade of paint on some of the smaller panels

The underside gets exactly the same treatment, even though much of it is going to be covered in stripes and the rest is going to be mucky!

Pastel dust in place as well as a few paint chips and extra mucky bits around the wing roots

The gun bays, with a black oil wash look half decent, although nothing like the 1/24th version, of course

I left them completely untouched overnight and just let then get on with it. Come the morning light I was utterly gob-smacked to see that not only had they almost completely flattened out but that they had settled down into all the nooks and crannies and looked gorgeous! There were a couple of air bubbles and tiny wrinkles left but with a careful slice or two of a sharp knife and a drop more softening solution they literally moulded themselves into shape right before my eyes. Even the yellow leading edge identification stripes worked well enough and I had them pegged to be a complete disaster, so I am delighted to be able to heartily recommend the Airfix decals when used with the Microscale setting and softening solutions. I used a little pastel dust and Tamiya Smoke to fade them in a little and when they were sealed in with a quick coat of Klear they looked really good.

These are a mixed bag of good and not so good. The undercarriage units are neatly moulded, and although they are a little delicate they look good, especially as they come with weighted wheels as standard. The undercarriage doors are the right size and shape and the outer doors also act as supports for the flimsy legs, so that all works out rather well. The open gun bay in the wing with its separate doors also looks the part and the rockets and rails make it all look suitably 'butch'. The bad parts are the boarding step and IFF rod under the fuselage, which are hugely over-scale and the exhaust stacks, which are under-scale, so it's not all smiley faces. The propeller and spinner look good but are a little wobbly once fitted so I packed the rear of the connecting pin with a little White-tac to hold it more firmly in place, crude but effective.

The final finish for this one was Xtracolor XDFF flat varnish, which worked wonders at binding it all together and with the little pig-tails for the rockets made from fuse wire and popped into place, all that was left was unmasking the canopy and setting it into place. Job done.

Building a Selection 81

The rockets are an integral part of the whole look of the Typhoon, so it's a good job that Airfix have taken the time to get it right, note the wire pigtails with little blobs of superglue on the ends for the connectors

Verdict
Brilliant stuff from Airfix. It's not perfect by any means but it is easy to build and well detailed. It had some fine points like the thin trailing edges of the wings and the overall levels of detail both inside and out. Along with the neat options of bombs or rockets and the open gun bays, this makes the money spent well worth it. In the 'Dogfight Double' you get a first-class set of markings and they work superbly, as well as a little stand to pose your Typhoon and Focke-Wulf on, so what's not to love?

Airfix are making an excellent revival and products like these new ranges of 1/72nd kits are going to do them the world of good. Let's hope it's a permanent recovery this time?

Building a Selection

Brengun 1/72nd
Typhoon Mk Ib (Late Production)

by Steve A. Evans

With the Hawker Typhoon being such a popular type, it was sure to get a whole bunch of kits made of it. This offering from Brengun is just a little different, though. While most other 1/72nd versions are simple, straightforward kits, this one has gone for detail above all other considerations.

This Czech company hasn't been around that long and this is only their fourth kit in this scale, but they make some fine looking plastic. In the end-opening box, you get two big sprues of tan-coloured plastic and a single transparent one. All the plastic is very well done, with only tiny sink marks to deal with, although almost all of it has some form of flash or mould lines. This isn't much of a problem as it's not that bad but it does get a bit tedious cleaning up everything. The box itself has some decent art on the top and on the back are the 4 options on the small single decal sheet. There is also a very small, etched fret with seat belts and boarding step and a single A4 instruction sheet, divided into four pages. Right, it looks good but let's get the problem stuff out of the way first, shall we? The instructions are a generic type and give no indication that for the versions on offer, you have to chop the tail off and replace it with the 'Tempest' tail, supplied on the sprue that contains the wing parts. There are no reinforcing plates around this joint either, so you'll have to make your own. The panel lines, beautifully done for the most part, have lots of areas that have been clogged up, either by being damaged in the moulds or removed too early with the plastic still soft, so these will need re-scribing and there's a lot of it. Lastly and by no means least, is the dreadful mess Brengun have made of the markings. There are four versions in the kit but only one of them is a rocket-equipped Typhoon, two of the others are bomb carriers and the last version (Wg Cdr J.C. Button) carried neither. The serial numbers on option A and C are wrong

The box has some neat art on the top while the plastic looks very well detailed. With the addition of the tiny etched fret this seems to be pretty good at first glance

Building a Selection   83

The cockpit is excellent, with good detail throughout, apart from the missing gunsight

Chopping the tail off is easy enough, but not mentioned at all in the instructions

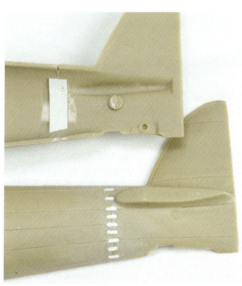

The plastic card butt strap keeps the new bit aligned, while the little reinforcing plates will need to be made from something very thin; tape, or even decal film might do

Building a Selection

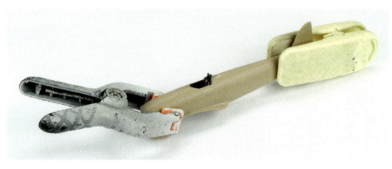

The fuselage joint is tidy enough but even at this size, clamps are a must

Stunning injected detail is what this kit is all about, and in this scale it doesn't get any better than this

and the 'Pulverizer II' scoreboard markings are completely fictitious! Considering that all the information about these aircraft is readily available, this is a serious disappointment.

Anyway, enough bad stuff, let's show some of the good bits. The plastic details are lovely, especially the cockpit and wheel wells, which have some of the best injected detail I have ever seen on a 1/72nd kit. For the most part, the build is pretty straightforward with a neat cockpit, complete with tubular structure and detailed instrument panel. You will need to create a gunsight for it, though, as there is nothing but the support arm in the kit. The parts on the sprue are fully generic between the various models as well, so you get the car door canopy and three-bladed prop and unshrouded cannon barrels, all

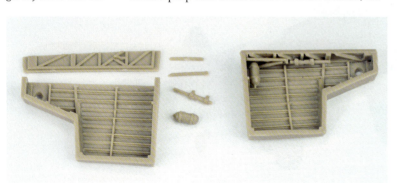

of which are heading for the bin with this one. Chopping the tail off is no big problem either, as it follows the panel line joint on the fuselage. A few scores with a sharp knife and it snaps cleanly off. The replacement item slots into place and I opted to fit a butt strap on the inside to keep it all aligned properly. Then it was sorting out the little fish-plates that reinforce the joint on the real thing to stop the tail falling off at inopportune moments. I used 0.050in. plasticard here, cut to shape and carefully glued on. Once dry these were lightly sanded down and will fade in quite nicely under the paint. The undercarriage bays, beautifully moulded, are a multi-part assembly and these lock into position in the wings, which need careful alignment with the fuselage to prevent any big gaps and get the characteristic anhedral/dihedral right. The wing trailing edges are a little on the thick side too, so I suggest thinning them out before sticking them in place. As you can imagine, as this is a short-run style project, there are no locating pins and the joints are a little clumsy, but with some filler it's not too much of a problem. In fact the only bad joint was on the left-hand horizontal tail, no idea why but it just wasn't pretty. Talking of clumsy bits, the cannon barrels are moulded onto the upper wing sections and to be honest these are rubbish. I would suggest cutting them from the wing, tidying the joint area and then sticking them back on as separate items.

The Typhoon is never going to have the most exciting of colour schemes because basically they're all the same. It's just the detail stuff that makes them a bit different. As all of the versions here are late-war ones, the invasion stripes had all but disappeared and the new regulations on markings were spectacularly dull. From September 1944 the Black and White invasion stripes were removed from wings and upper fuselage and from January 1945 the Sky band was off, as were the individual flight colours for the spinners, which were now supposed to be plain black. As you can imagine, the front-line squadrons often ignored the last bit of the rules (thankfully) and aircraft continued to have bright spinners. For the kit choices, because of the mix-up in serial numbers and problems with the 'Pulverizer II' markings, the only real option for one fully loaded with rockets, is HH•T, No.175 Sqn, 1945. This is of course in the standard day fighter scheme of Dark Green/Ocean Grey/Medium Sea Grey. All supplied by Humbrol enamels in this case. Usually I would opt for White Ensign enamels but as they were no more at the time of building, it was back to good old Humbrol.

Primer first for checking the surface and setting it up for the real colours. The lower surface is 165 Medium Sea Grey, with a few panels picked out in a lighter shade to give some variation. The first upper colour is the Dark Green 116, there is lots of discussion about which one of the Humbrol green shades is the best for this, but as I didn't have the proper 163 to hand, this one would do. This was then lightened with a drybrush of 102 Army Green, which makes it look a little faded and tired. Masking a slightly soft demarcation line is easy with some thin rolls of White-tack (like Blu Tack but slightly less sticky) and Mr Neo masking fluid to fill in the gaps. The Ocean Grey (106) was next, drybrushed with 127 Light Ghost Grey. Both upper colours also had some panels picked out with lighter shades and once fully dry, weathered with pastel dust, Tamiya Smoke along the panel lines and a few chips of soft silver pencil. As usual, it wasn't all plain sailing, as there is the disagreement with the instructions about the yellow leading edges and black anti-slip panels on the wings. Neither of these are on the painting guide but looking at pictures of these aircraft it seems that some had them and some didn't, no rhyme or reason to it and apparently random, so the choice is yours, just follow your reference material.

Sealed in under some clear, the paint looked good so it was time for the decals. Notwithstanding the mistakes, the decals are lovely. Very neatly printed, with sharp detail, good colour density and perfect register. In use they are close to being perfect, settling down with some Microscale setting solutions very nicely. The only thing to watch is that they can be very 'grabby', once on the kit they were very difficult to move about but apart from that, once dry, they look great.

A quick dust of pastels to fade them in for a more natural look and it's on to the last bits.

I know I said last bits, but to be honest there's still about 30% of the kit left to do. Undercarriage units are first up and they are nice, but delicate. The plastic in this scale looks good, very well moulded at least but be careful of the little struts, as they are all too easy to

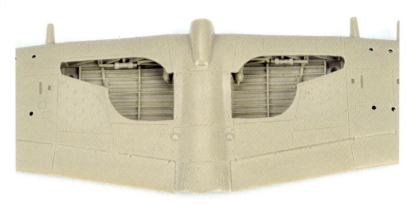

Once in place it all looks gorgeous and with careful painting will make you wish you could display this model upside down

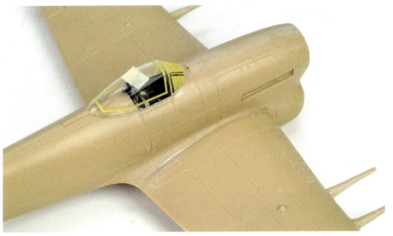

The main components fit together reasonably well, and although filler is used at just about every joint it's never too bad

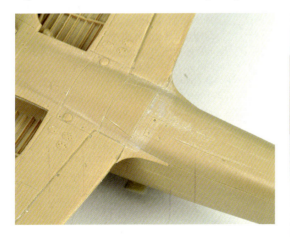

This spot is the worst of the main joints to deal with, especially as this needs to be a smooth, uninterrupted curve from nose to tail

No idea why this particular joint is so bad, for some reason the moulded parts just don't want to line up

86 Building a Selection

Primer Grey, Halfords of course, highlights the bits to be smoothed off and makes a fine surface for the following colours

Humbrol enamels throughout on this one, 165 Medium Sea Grey is the first to be applied. Note the lighter panels for effect

Humbrol 116 is pretty close if you haven't got the right Dark Green paint to hand (163). It looks a bit on the dark side but that'll be sorted by the following weathering

White-tack rolls and masking fluid make for some very nice soft edges to the demarcation lines. The fatter the rolls, the softer the edges

Humbrol 106 Ocean Grey makes for the classic RAF scheme. It's a pity that you can't have the Sky band and invasion stripes but this will still look good

break. The doors are also well moulded, the detail is really good throughout this kit, the only additional bits from me at this point were the brake lines on each leg made from little bits of fuse wire. You're going to need the rockets of course, why wouldn't you? They are supplied separate from the rails, which is good but also separate from their tails, which is a pain as they take ages to clean up and properly align. Painted various shades of dark green and with little pigtails made from fishing line they do look nice when they're in place.

You get two versions of the exhaust stacks but none of the four options kept the shrouded version. Even if they were built with the shrouds in place, the groundcrews in service almost always removed them, because they just got in the way! The only big bit left was the spinner and propeller and despite the regulations saying it should be black, No.175 Sqn kept the flight colours in place so this is a nice bright red. The propeller blades are the right diameter and not too bad in profile but are just a little skinny. It does rather set the aggressive tone of this machine when it's in place, though.

After that it was a single heavy coat of Xtra-color XDFF flat varnish for a really matt surface finish and it was time for the last few bits. These were the radio whip aerial on the spine and the IFF rod aerial underneath, the pitot tube under the left wing and de-masking the canopy and positioning it in the open position. One tiny little thing to mention is the upward identification light that sits behind the pilot's head. This is supplied in the kit but it's not necessarily fitted to all the options. Once again this bit seems to have no rhyme or reason to which aircraft they are fitted to, as they appear on some late model Typhoon and not others, so please check your references.

There's a lot to do here, considering that the rockets and rails make up 32 parts when fitted with the pigtails. One thing to note here is that the upper wing roundel should probably be the Type C1 with the thin white ring but once again, there are a huge number of variations in service

88 Building a Selection

Verdict
Brengun must be cursing Airfix because without the new Typhoon in this scale from them, this offering would easily be the king of the pile. As it is, it trumps the Airfix version on detail quite easily but it's going to be nowhere near as easy to build. It's a pity that the markings are so messed up and with the generic instructions it seems to be a half-hearted effort, which it obviously isn't but that's the impression you get. If you have a little experience under your belt and don't mind the more challenging nature of this one, then the detail will delight you and it'll be worth every penny. For the rest of us, the real problem is that you could have two Airfix Typhoons for the price of this one…ouch!

The decals, although wrong on so many points, get it spot-on with how well they work: faultlessly

CzechMaster Resin 1/72
Typhoon Prototype/Mk Ia

by Libor Jekl

While Typhoon late versions are pretty well covered in all the major scales, the very early versions do not exist in injected plastic. Fortunately there are resin kit manufacturers and one of them, CzechMaster Resin, offers the complete range of early Typhoon versions including the prototype. The kit of the Mk Ia is packed in a hard cardboard box with a colour profile on the top. The resin parts are bagged separately to minimize the risk of damage during transit. Quality of the parts is exceptional; they are cast almost flawlessly with only minor flash to clean up and with delicate panel lines and surface details. The kit also includes pre-painted etched brass from Eduard, die-cut canopy masks made of yellow Kabuki tape, four vacformed canopies (two per type) and a decal sheet offering seven options in total – two for the prototype and five operational machines. The propeller unit and the wheels are cast from darker resin and are in a separate bag within the main package and these were sourced from another company, Resin Art, as they offer more detail than the original CMR parts used in older issues – nice touch! The optional parts include a set of underwing stores (250lb, 500lb and 1,000lb bombs), external fuel tanks used on early versions, optionally positioned door cast from clear resin as well as, naturally, the parts necessary for the prototype - different style of rudder and exhaust stacks.

Not surprisingly the build commences with the cockpit. The hollowed fuselage halves featured some sidewall details that can be further

enhanced with the pre-painted photo-etched bits. The floor and the instrument panel needed a little adjustment to fit properly between the fuselage halves. The cockpit was sprayed in Interior Grey/Green and the details picked out in corresponding colours before the whole lot was given a light black-brown oil wash. As the cockpit is very well detailed I decided to open the door, so in preparation I cut out the door upper part from the vacformed canopy that would be installed later in the build. Some attention was needed at the fuselage front part, where the huge radiator goes. Its fit to the fuselage was not fully satisfactory, so some sanding and dry fitting

The cockpit interior combines resin and pre-painted photo-etched and is well detailed

right: Assembly is straightforward and relatively quick

far right: As you can see there is little need for any filler on this kit

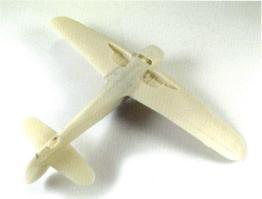

was necessary to get a acceptable fit. Despite that, the intake must be filled in all round and sanded smooth after closing the fuselage halves. The wings are a nice example of CMR's excellent craftsmanship, with delicate trailing edges and nice rib details in the wheel wells. However, to get the wing halves to fit to the fuselage needs patience and careful dry-fitting. Some superfluous material must be sanded off the joining surfaces and I also enlarged the openings in the wheel wells where the wing protrudes into the fuselage. Eventually all joints were filled with two-part epoxy putty, sanded, polished and the damaged panel lines rescribed. Now I could glue on the canopy, which was previously dipped in the Johnson's Klear (Future) to prevent fogging from the superglue. The fit was pretty good but still a little putty was needed to blend all the seams in. Assembly and attachment of the tailplanes was straightforward and free from any problems, so I could quickly pass on to painting.

I opted for R7580, freshly delivered to No.56 Squadron at Duxford in September 1941 wearing the Temperate Land scheme, as this together with the early style canopy gives the kit an unusual and rather "Hurricane-like" look to it. Anyway, the kit was primed first using Mr Surfacer 1000, sanded and polished. The kit instructions refer only to Federal Standard approximations, but it should not be difficult to locate appropri-

Building a Selection 91

left: The overall scheme starting to be applied after the post-shading, with the camouflage masked with a combination of tape and White-Tac Body Main

far left: The model primed and with a little sanding done to smooth out the centre seam and around the radiator unit

ate shades of your favourite hobby paints. I went for Gunze-Sangyo Aqueous paints mixed with a drop of white to give them a lighter tone for scale effect. The gloss and semi-matt varnishes also come from Gunze-Sangyo, but this time from the Mr Color range. The decal sheet is printed by MPD and is of good quality, with acceptable register (except the fuselage roundels) and colours. They responded well to Gunze-Sangyo Mr Mark Softer decal solution and settled down nicely into the panel lines.

At the very end I attach the remaining bits - the starboard door was glued in place, the aerial and IFF aerials were added from a length of black fishing wire, and the blue identification light on the fuselage was sourced from a CMK set.

Verdict

It is true that this is not the easiest of kits to build, needing careful dry-fitting and some filler, but it does fill the gap in a collection as far as a car-door example goes. The quality of the casting and the inclusion of the photo-etched, masks and detailed parts from Resin Art make this is superb kit for the experienced modeller.

Building a Selection

Hasegawa 1/48
Typhoon Mk Ib

by Steve A. Evans

This particular Hasegawa boxing of the Hawker Typhoon is the '137 Squadron' limited edition and dates back to 2001 but is of course their generic moulding of the two Typhoon types. The box has some good art on the lid and the plastic inside is well up to the usual standard for Hasegawa. It comprises 104 parts in medium grey-coloured plastic, including all the rockets and rails as well as the alternative bombs and racks. There's a little bit of flash on the smaller parts but everything is perfectly formed. You also get weighted wheels and the option of a decal or paint for the main instrument panel. The panels themselves are very neatly moulded with good, accurate detail so painting is the obvious choice.

Construction is perfectly straightforward with very clear and concise instructions, as always they are well drawn and easy to follow. Even though the interior is a little bit plain, the detail that's present is perfectly moulded and to be honest there's not going to be too much on show through the very small cockpit opening anyway. The tubular framework for the seat and floor panel support fits together very well and with

the addition of some etched fret or painted tape seat belts it looks just fine. Location of the parts within the fuselage is excellent and no trimming is required to get everything into place. The inserts for the cockpit upper decking, which makes the bubbletop Mk Ib, are a bit of a pain to get lined up properly and the one on the right-hand half is a little out of shape compared to the profile of the fuselage. This means some careful cutting and trimming to get the best possible fit and then sanding down later. The joint lines for

Set on the R.J. Caruana plans, you can see that the wing is about 1.5mm short on either side and it's all outboard of the cannon barrels

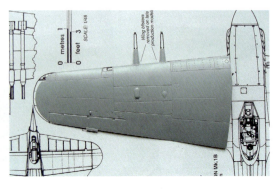

The length is off by nearly 3mm and this time it's all in the vertical fin, the easiest fix for this would be a fuselage 'plug' just aft of the strengthening plates

Building a Selection 93

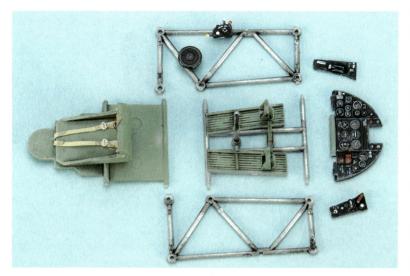
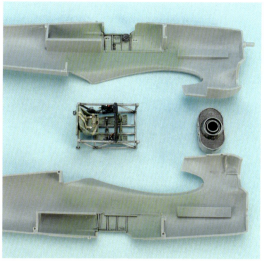

these pieces are going to need some filling and blending but thankfully it's not too bad and a quick dab of correction fluid is all that's needed.

Sub-assembly of the wings is pretty straightforward as well, with only the flashed-over holes for either rocket or bomb armament to take care of, before they are sandwiched together and slotted into place on the fuselage. It's at this point that the worst joints on the whole kit become apparent and that's at the wing roots. If the wing is held at somewhere near the right angle you get a considerable gap between the wing and the fuselage root fairings. It's more noticeable on the right hand side as well so there's obviously something not quite right here. The wing dihedral/anhedral is important to how it all looks, so filling that gap is an important job. It's plasticard to the rescue and a slice of 0.015in. card on the left and 0.025in. card on the right will just about do the job in this case. Trimmed and smoothed down you won't even notice these pieces are in there and they also make a sturdy joint when the Liquid Poly cement has set.

Colour schemes are a bit limited for the Tiffie and the ones in the box are pretty typical, although option #2 is remarkably boring; I don't think I've ever seen such a plain-Jane machine. Luckily option #1 is far better, with some neat invasion stripes as well as the classic RAF camouflage and identification markings of the time.

above: Fit of the internal parts is just about perfect with no trimming required

above left: Cockpit interior is pretty good with some excellent detail on the instrument panels

94 Building a Selection

The inserts on the rear fuselage aren't too bad with a bit of sanding down and filling they'll be all but invisible

The decals are worthy of note, however, as the serial number for #1 is incorrect, it should read MN980 and not MN680. Not a big problem as all you have to do is cut out the 6 and flip it over! Also on the decal sheet is a reasonable amount of stencilling but almost no indication in the instructions of where it should go. Again, not really much of a problem as most of the Typhoons appeared to be pretty short on any kind of stencils so just a couple in place will do to set the scene. The decals work very well but definitely need the help of setting and softening solutions to get them to fully conform to all the detail. They have very good colours and

density and as usual for Hasegawa, they are in perfect register but they are a little brittle, and if you've applied softening solution then DO NOT TOUCH them as they will come apart.

Finishing off is easy enough as well with very positive location of the undercarriage units although the hole in the wheel is too big for the oleo leg stub-axle, which makes it a job that has you wishing for that extra arm with the two hands and six opposable thumbs! The rockets and rails are reasonably accurate in shape and size but once again, good, positive location makes fitting them simple enough, even though there are eight sets to make, which is a bit tedious. The big, four-blade propeller is spot-on for size and shape and the aggressive 'roman-nose' spinner looks good too. As does the shape and size of the two-part canopy; the transparent parts fit neatly and you have the option of open or closed in the box so you do get to see in there a little bit. Accuracy-wise the kit is a couple of

The poorest joint - getting the anhedral right on the wing means you have a gap to fill at both wing-root joints

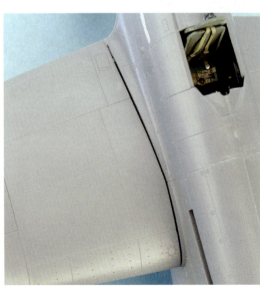

mm short on span, nearly all in the wingtips, and the length is about 3mm short, all in the vertical tail, especially aft of the rudder post. Neither of those facts can detract from the overall shape and stance of the kit as it is suitably aggressive looking and every inch the Typhoon.

Verdict

The Hasegawa range of Typhoons is just marvellous as it represents a real icon of the later years of the air war. It's long been recognised as one of the finest ground-attack aircraft and loaded up with those rockets you can see why. It's brutish and ungainly from some angles but that's all part of its charm and that's a lot of firepower it's carrying! Hasegawa have successfully captured that attacking posture and both versions of the kit that they produce (even with the inserts made necessary by the different versions) are not difficult kits to build at all. They have a couple of minor fit problems but these are easily outweighed by the excellent mouldings. The plastic parts are very good indeed and it's a pity about the dull markings in this particular release, but there are a whole host of wonderful looking machines out there to choose from.

above: It always looks good in stripes and that undercarriage has very positive location to make a sturdy model

above left: Camouflage demarcation, the Blu-Tack and masking fluid method

MDC 1/32
Typhoon Mk Ib

by Steve A. Evans

We've had plenty of kits of the amazing Typhoon before but as far as I know, there was only one in this scale and that's the venerable old Revell Mk Ib. Model Design Construction took the plunge in 2006 and thankfully gave us the bubbletop Mk Ib as opposed to the more old-fashioned looking car-door type. With such a limited choice in the bigger scale you are never going to have an easy time of it, either having to rescribe and detail old plastic or struggle with resin and the problems that go with this medium. The resin pieces in the MDC box are cast in various tones of medium grey and are, for the most part, well done. There is some flash on the parts, especially around the tubular framework of the cockpit. There is also a fair number or mould lines and mis-shaped parts, indeed, a large number of the cockpit pieces were warped and out of shape in my particular example. Most of this can be easily addressed by holding the parts in very hot water for a minute and then straightening them out, but they never look quite right again [MDC will replace any badly warped components if you just contact them, though]. You also get some very large single-piece castings for the wings and fuselage halves. These items are a mixed bag of good and bad, the good being the internal detail of the wheel wells and the external engraved panel lines on the wings, while the bad bits are the fuselage panel lines of varying depth and straightness and some casting irregularities along the bottom edge of the fuselage halves. There are some neat touches with location pins and bars, plus a through spar for the heavy wings and metal undercarriage legs to support the substantial weight of the model. You also get a little etched fret for the Sutton harness seat belts, with the option of using the full etched fret or just the buckles if you want to make your own webbing belts, plus an etched template for the landing light (clear) cover. The decal sheets are printed by Fantasy Printshop and sadly on my example the roundels

Cockpit components need careful trimming of flash and mould lines but the instrument panel is the star of the show

were a little bit out of register, which is really unusual for this decal manufacturer [Again, a call to MDC will quickly correct any such problem parts]. Thankfully they are thin and have good colours and shapes with the sky lettering being just about the perfect shade.

Construction begins with that tubular framework for the cockpit and the various bits and pieces that go in there, all in resin with plenty of scope for adding as much detail as you like. Most of the parts fit pretty neatly but as with all limited-run items you have to do plenty of trial fits and trimming as you go. One serious hindrance here are the instructions, which to me seemed vague, with lack of clarity in the photograph due to the poor quality of the reproduction and out of sequence events that require a lot of studying and relating to the actual resin pieces before it becomes clear. Basically this is not for beginners, simple as that. The star of the internal show is the main instrument panel, which is very neatly cast with fine and accurate raised detail, finished off with the superb instrument dial decals. Fitting the cockpit into the fuselage is very neat with positive location for the front and rear bulkheads, while the fuselage halves themselves close easily enough, without too much hassle. The centre-line joint is very good on the upper surface but along the rear fuselage on the underside it suffers with casting irregularities in the form of ridges and dips that will have to be taken care of. My preferred filler medium for this kind

Built up the framework is just the start for additional detail, if you so desire

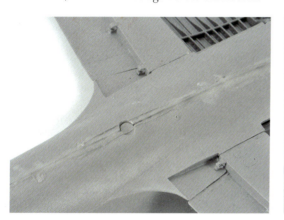

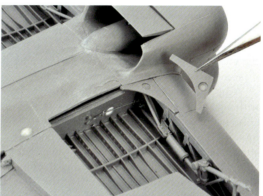

left: More tricky parts with little inserts around the wheel wells and some very delicate resin bits (note the broken edge)

far left: The hideous lower fuselage joint with massive mould creases and air bubbles…time for superglue!

of thing is cyanoacrylate mixed with talcum powder as it gives a dual effect of filling and bonding all in one go. Use slow-setting glue and you'll get the minimum of air bubbles in the surface and it's easy to sand down into a smooth shape.

Wing and tail connection is simplicity itself with a good set of locating tabs and spars, although once again, trial fits and trims are the order of the day. All of this is supported on the sturdy metal undercarriage legs and the rather complicated but well cast actuation gear. You also get the choice in the kit of either the 3- or 4-blade propellers, which is a good alternative but you get no help as to which one goes with which marking option. The cockpit canopy is next to go on and I opted to leave it closed. This is supplied as a vacform item (with spare) so very careful trimming is required, especially as the framework detail isn't very prominent. It will need a bit of blending in but with care and attention it eventually fits well enough.

Colouring in the 'Tiffie' is a fairly standard affair with only one colour scheme available and that's the day-fighter scheme of Dark Green and Ocean Grey over Medium Sea Grey undersides. The five options in the kit are pretty typical of the breed with two of them having invasion stripes to liven them up a bit. Sadly the marking guide is another poor effort as there is no information about whether the stripes are full wrap-around ones or just underside versions. There is also no indication at all about what, where or who the aircraft belonged to, so once again it's time to hit the reference books. Also on the marking guide, even though the national markings are shown, no other stencilling data is even hinted at so those reference pictures you find are going to be of vital importance when it comes to the decals. As a quick side-note here, if you choose to do BR•M (serial RB382) the upper wing roundel should be the Type C1, which is on the decal sheet but not indicated in the instructions. The camouflage pattern is easily applied with either paper masks or Blu-Tack rolls to create a slightly feathered edge at the demarcation lines. Lots of masking is needed for the stripes but there are plenty of available drawings and pictures to work from so it's not too difficult. I opted for MR•?, option 1 on the sheet, and even though it should probably have a spiral on the spinner I went for the classic look of blue and white bands purely because it looks so much better. I also opted for full invasion stripes and not just the underside versions, although there seems to be a lot of debate about just what the real aircraft had painted on it. Weathering was pretty harsh for this one as it worked in a tough

Fit of the cockpit into the fuselage is faultless and here you can also see the radiator unit and the main spar for the wing attachment

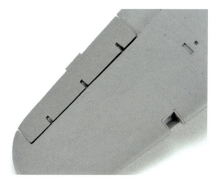  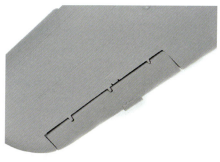

More gaps to take care of, this time on the ailerons

Plasticard, cut to size and shape will take care of the spaces

Luckily the upper surface of the hinge line is perfect

environment, with lots of paint chipping and grubby panel lines making it look thoroughly 'tired'. Pastel dust and Tamiya X-19 Smoke are the main weathering mediums, sealed in with Johnson's Klear, ready for decal application. The decal sheets contain the full set of markings for all five versions on offer, as well as one set of national markings and stencil data. As mentioned, mine had a slight misregister on the roundels but apart from that they are very good indeed. The colours are right and the printing is excellent with good density and no ragged edges. The tricky 'Sky' colour is also very nice, although it initially looks a little dark on the sheet that is really just an optical illusion due to the contrast between the decals and the backing paper. Once on the model the colour is perfect. In use the decals release from the backing paper quickly in warm water and they are thin but not too brittle and are easy enough to move around on the model. They need some help from setting and softening solutions to fully conform to the details and they are prone to a little silvering, so some care is needed.

Care is also needed with the finishing process for this kit and the choices of how much additional detail you wish to add. Right from the beginning of the build it's obvious that, in this scale, there is so much more that could be done. Two obvious additions that are necessary are the brake lines and the oxygen bottles, one in each of the main wheel bays. I've no idea why these last two items were not included in the kit as they are a prominent feature of the Typhoon and will definitely need to be added. The rockets and their associated rails need to be fitted now and it was a serious disappointment to find that there is no such armament in the box. The box-top art has the Typhoon typically loaded up for an attack mission with a full set of rocket rails

100 Building a Selection

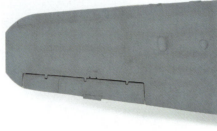

The lower surface Medium Sea Grey has almost zero contrast with the grey primer so it'll be down to post-shading to make it look more realistic

The upper surface Ocean Grey is a touch darker than the primer so you can get a bit more life to the colour straight away

The oldest technique in the book; paper masks for the camouflage, the bigger the gap between the mask and surface, the softer the edge feathering

First of the masks, ready for the white

Stripes applied and paint chips in place courtesy of some strategically placed Maskol masking fluid

The lower surface with patchy stripes and a bit of Tamiya Smoke and pastel dust to sort out the weathering

Weathering complete and Klear coat on just waiting for the decals

The decals need a little help from the solutions but they look great with wonderful colours

and I would expect to be able to make the kit as it's shown on the box; that's not unreasonable is it? Anyway, the rockets are available to buy separately but be warned, they are also cast resin items and every single rocket and rail in my set needed to be heated and straightened [Please note that MDC now produce various sets from the Mk 1 through to the light-weight Mk 3 rails, which is why these rockets are sold separately]. They come as a multi-media product with resin main structures, photo-etched tail fins and soft vinyl electrical connections. All of these parts need careful preparations before construction; straightening the resin being the main job. The little 'pig-tail' connectors though refuse to do anything but what they wants to, and no amount of heat application or teasing would change their shapes to something more natural. I may have to replace them later but for now they will have to do. Final surface finish is Xtracolor XDFF flat varnish and with the little whip aerial added to the upper fuselage and a light spray of very dark brown enamel for the exhaust staining, that's this big scale Typhoon finished.

Verdict

Not for a beginner or those with a frail constitution. This fine looking Typhoon from MDC is a lot of work and you need a certain amount of experience with resin and multi-media style limited-run kits to get the most from what's in the box. There are areas that I felt were disappointing, namely the instructions and some of the casting, but with care and attention you do get an impressive model to sit on the shelf.

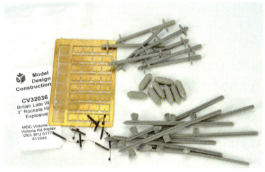

The additional set of 60lb rockets, all trimmed and straightened ready for assembly. It's a pity these aren't included in the kit, though

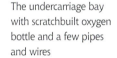

The undercarriage bay with scratchbuilt oxygen bottle and a few pipes and wires

Airfix 1/24th
Typhoon Mk Ib

by Dani Zamarbide

The first thing that strikes you when you get this kit is the size, not just the scale, but the fact that the Hawker Typhoon was a large aircraft. What also impressed me upon opening the box was just how much is inside it, you can't see the bottom.

Interior

This can be divided into three parts, the cockpit, engine and cannon bays. I actually started with the element I thought would be the most complex, the engine. Because of its complex nature you have to follow the instructions faithfully and some of the joints required filler to deal with unsightly gaps. I added detail, so with images of a real engine to hand I added various cables from tin and copper wires. The engine was painted with a base coat of matt black and then with different shades of grey to give interest, with highlights done with lighter grey and shadowy areas with dark grey. It then had a coat of gloss varnish to allow a series of washes to be applied as these give the appearance of dirt, and were followed by similar washes using oil paints to give the appearance of grime. The huge radiator was painted Dark Aluminium (AK Interactive Xtreme Metal), then a dark brown wash was applied and the engine was then ready to be installed.

For me the internal structure and engine mount are the most amazing parts of this kit. The first task is a very tedious, though, because you need to remove all the mould lines from the tubular structure. After hours of eliminating these steps and refining all the pieces I started assembling all of them, carefully following the instructions. This assembly can be painted in one of three colours, silver, black or Interior

Here you can see the kit instrument panel during detail painting, with contrasting greys used to highlight raised areas and to get away from an all-black panel

Green. I chose the former, simply because I like it and it gives more options as far as the painting and weathering go. I applied a base coat of silver (Tamiya enamel X-11), then with Vallejo black acrylic I brush-painted the engine bulkhead and the armour plates behind the pilot.

The cockpit interior is one of the most outstanding parts of this model, especially the detailed instrument panel and side consoles. The seat is well detailed and even has the harness but I decided to use the resin seat with moulded harness from BarracudaCast. Once I had painted and weathered the seat I turned my attention to the instrument panel. The panel itself is moulded in grey-coloured plastic while the 'dials' are done in clear plastic. Once I had assembled and painted this I could set to work actually adding the dials. I must say that in the past I have always painted dials using a fine brush, but in 1/32nd and 1/24th scales you need to use decals. Airscale has a specific decal sheet for the instrument dials in the Typhoon and I utilised it here. The sheet actually has the option of a complete decal that goes behind the clear element, or each individual dial face. For me, I felt that the more realistic option was to go with the individual decals. The side consoles received the same treatment as the instrument panel, except the throttles were replaced with pieces of copper rod with small drops of white glue on the tip to create the knob. All the other elements are fine as supplied, just remember to follow the instructions, as I did not a couple of times and the parts simply would not fit at a later stage. The last task for the interior was to paint and fit the fuel tank between the engine and cockpit.

Cannon

The cannon bays in the kit are great, these being built up in between the wing spars and outboard of the undercarriage bays. The kit guns look good but lack real detail, so you can either add the missing detail from scratch or, like me, buy the Brassin resin set that comprises the guns and their ammunition boxes. The resin cannon are of the highest quality but remove the locating pins underneath them and position each so that they line up with their ammunition boxes, otherwise it will all be out of line. The rest of the assembly of the gun bays went without a hitch.

Undercarriage Bays

Theses are wonderful from an engineering point of view and you just have to assemble and paint them because all the cabling and pipework is there, nothing needs to be added from scratch. The remainder of the wing internal components, the gun bays, fuel tanks and the undercarriage bays themselves are all assembled and painted separately. Their final assembly was the only stage in which I did not follow the prescribed method in the instructions, as I felt by adding all the various elements from above, then turning the whole thing over, everything was in the correct place.

The completed panel, with the individual dials from the Airscale sheet

Assembly

The main assembly is one of the big surprises of this kit because you would think with such large pieces there would be problems, but the fit is perfect. The assembly has several stages, first you glue the bottom halves of the wings to the interior structure, because it reinforces the whole assembly, then once the glue is dry, the upper halves of the wings can be attached. When the wings are firmly together the most delicate moment of the assembly process begins, fitting the fuselage onto the wings. To do this, work from the front backwards, sticking the root fillet

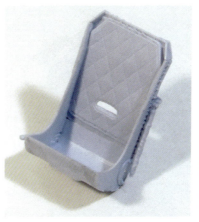 

The BarracudaCast (right) is far better than the kit version (left)

The completed seat after all the painting and weathering stages

104 Building a Selection

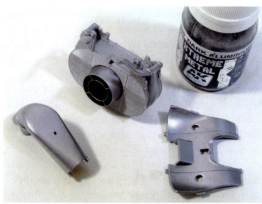

The radiator unit, complete with the revised intake from the BarracudaCast range, seen after painting and weathering

The complex main internal structure received an overall coat of Tamiya silver enamel (X-11)

The completed engine with the suitably weathered exhaust stacks fitted

The completed interior structure with all the cockpit and engine elements added

in stages to ensure perfect alignment and you should find that no filler is necessary. Depending on how you want to display your model, at Stage 147 in the instructions it shows you how to remove the forward cowls if, like me, you want the entire engine exposed; you have the option of all cowls off, the side panels still on, or all the cowls in place. Once the fuselage is attached to the wings, you can complete the rest of the assembly with the separate bottom section and, finally, the vertical fin and tailplanes; these latter items depend on the option you are building, as options A, C & D have the wider 'Tempest' tailplanes (#L01 to L04), whilst Option B has the original narrower version (#L14 to L17). Finally the elevators and rudder can be installed and the aircraft is now fully assembled.

Paint

This phase is perhaps, for me, the one I like the most because it is when the model acquires a personality. I always start by applying the colour that will be visible inside the cockpit canopy, in this case black. Next comes the first camouflage colour, following the pattern of Dark Green and Ocean Grey over Medium Sea Grey. I started with the lightest colour, and once the underside Medium Sea Grey was dry, I added a little white and highlighted all the rivets and panels. Then with heavily diluted (almost transparent) paint I applied layers around the wheel wells and tailwheel to create the effect of dust. With an earth colour, again heavily diluted, and using the same technique, I created a more marked effect along the axis of the aircraft and on the borders of the wheel wells, creating the look of dirt. I masked off the underside and turned my attention to the upper camouflage. It is always best to paint from the lightest to the darkest, so I began with the Ocean Grey. I applied the colour as defined by the pattern I had marked with a soft pencil then I did the same with the green. Once done I could deal with the huge invasion stripes, and in the option I had chosen one of the squadron characters and the serial number are within the stripes, so this had to be taken into account. The stripes also partially cover the Sky tail band, so this band had to go on first. Once the Sky band was applied, a little white was mixed in with some Sky so that I could add some highlights. Although the instructions give the total width, I like to mark each band to ensure the overall length is correct and once this is done and the rest of the airframe protected, the white can be applied. Once dry I marked out with a pencil the five divisions, taking my time to ensure the lines were perfectly straight and parallel. The matt black was applied and once it was all fully dry, the masking could be removed.

Now we come to a crucial point in the painting, the roundels and other markings. Miracle Masks offers a set of masks for the Typhoon and by carefully following the instructions you can paint on all the national markings, even the fuselage ones with the thin outer yellow band. I also took the time to paint on the walkways and the yellow wing leading edge bands.

Weathering

The first weathering stage was to repeat the same processes that I used on the underside, namely to highlight the rivets and panels with a grey colour mixed with white on the Ocean Grey areas and repeat using green mixed with a buff shade for the Dark Green areas. To create wear I used a grey or greenish tone on the Dark Green and a neutral or light grey on the Ocean Grey areas.

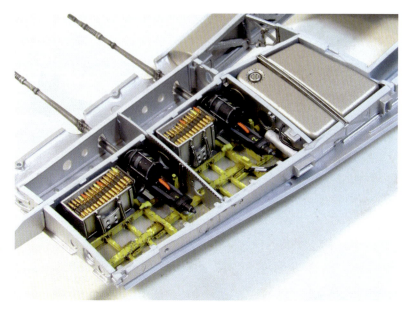

The cannon bay with the excellent Brassin resin cannon in place and everything painted and weathered. The fuel tanks are also in place at this point

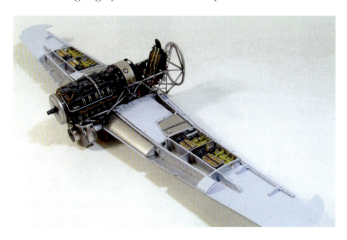

The wing panels being added

The fuselage sections can all now be fitted

The kit rocket (top) is no match for the superb Master example (bottom)

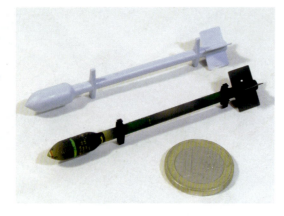

The propeller blades once painted, receive chips created with a watercolour pencil

Dots of oil paint are blended in with Humbrol enamel thinners

The spinner is painted and weathered in a similar manner to the blades, then the whole unit can be assembled

Pigments from the MIG Production range are added to the tyre sidewalls (left) and then blended together with pigment fixer (right). This was a test using the kit wheels

The completed resin wheels, which received the same pigments and washes as first tested on the kit tyre

The tailwheel is painted in a similar manner to the main wheels, with the detail picked out with a dark brown wash

The underside after all the paint effects are completed

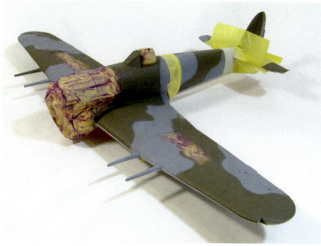
The upper surfaces with the basic main camouflage colours applied

The invasion stripes applied

With all the main colours on, the markings could be painted on using self-adhesive vinyl masks

The panel wash was applied, left for 20 minutes, then the excess removed

Once finished I could do the paint chipping, which was achieved with a silver watercolour pencil and applied along the edges and joints of the panel lines and in the walkway areas. We were still only halfway through the entire process and what followed was the application of a coat of gloss varnish prior to applying the decals. Airfix's decals in recent years have been of very good quality and these are no exception, as they went on without any complications, despite their size. Once the decals were all on and dried, I applied another coat of gloss varnish but this time just around the newly applied decals, then left it for 12 hours to dry before I proceeded to highlight all the rivets and panels with a dark brown wash. After twenty minutes the excess wash was removed with a cloth in the direction of the airflow. It now only remained for the final detail, which means oil paints applied to create variations in the volume of the colours. To do this, for the Ocean Grey areas I used a light grey colour, applying it to all vertical panels in the upper left corner and in the horizontal panels at the front edge. After a couple of minutes, I blended the oil in the direction of the airflow to lighten each panel. I performed the same operation with the Dark Green areas, but this time using a Yellow Ochre colour. Having created 'light' effects, I now needed to make the shadows and for this I used a very dark brown (almost black) that was applied in the right lower corner in the vertical panels and the rear areas of the horizontal panels. These were then blended in using the same method as I did with the lighter colours. I finished the whole process of painting with a coat of matt varnish to protect all the work done thus far.

Weathering to the wing leading edges was done with three earth-tone watercolour pencils, then paint applied lightly with a piece of sponge

Propeller

The propeller is an element that needs a little care in terms of effects because it is a focal point on the completed model. The Typhoon propeller is huge, and in the kit you have the option of a three- or four-blade unit. The blades are individually moulded and this allows you some flexibility as far as their painting goes. Black is the base colour, for both blades and hub, then working from the tips down each blade, I applied tonal graduation with NATO Black, as this is less dense than the base black and gives an aspect of wear. Then, with the paint dry, I added paint chips to the edges of each blade with a watercolour pencil making little chips at the base of the blades and somewhat larger ones towards the ends (which were previously painted a dull yellow). Next the gloss varnish could be applied and once dry, oil paints in grey and earth tones were added to look like accumulated dirt and grime before the whole unit was sealed with a coat of matt varnish.

Wheels

This is one of the weakest aspects of the kit, and although of great proportions, the overall detail is less when compared with the replacements offered in resin by BarracudaCast (thanks, Roy!). I wanted to give an appearance of dust and dirt on the wheels because they operated from temporary landing strips etc. After several processes, which you can see in the accompanying images, I successfully completed the wheels, although I had to open up the hole in the centre for the axle, as it's too small to accept the stub on the oleo leg otherwise.

Rockets

This is another element in the model that has little real detail. The kit does give you the option of two types of rocket rails, and I went with the wider style. The rails were painted with the same colour as the underside except where the missile saddles sat, and these were silver. As for the rockets, fortunately Master Models of Poland produce rockets suitable for the Typhoon, which are wonderful turned metal and brass with a variety of warhead types. Thanks to the advice of Bogusław Słotwinski at Master, I used a mixture of war-

head types to give more originality to the model, and to be more in keeping with period images of Typhoons around D-Day. Each rocket consists of eleven pieces, combining aluminium, brass, photo-etched and plastic, and they are simply wonderful. Painting them could not be easier, the base colour in a deep olive green and then I applied the same oil paint effects that I used on the camouflage Dark Green of the airframe. Each rocket has a decal for the various stencils so that once they are completed and added to the rails they look stunning; you even get the 'pigtail' arming wires as well in the Master set.

Final Assembly

Now we only had the minor parts left such as the undercarriage doors and cannon bay access covers, all of which had the same paint treatment as used on the rest of the model. Once all these parts are completed, you need to attach them in an orderly manner and to do this I started by installing the landing gear and tailwheel and when the glue was dry enough, I attached the wheels, ensuring that they sat correctly on the ground to give the right 'feel' of weight to the fully-loaded model. After removing all the masking, and with any retouching done with a fine brush, the cockpit windshield was installed, and with the model on its own wheels I could now ensure that each and every rocket/rail was perfectly perpendicular to the ground. I completed the assembly with the fitment of the lights, both upper and lower antennas, and cockpit canopy in the open position.

All the various sub-assembles and components waiting to be installed at the very end of the build

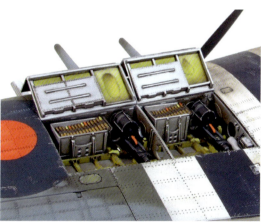

Verdict

Certainly, I feel that I have done one of my best models of recent years largely due to the high quality of the Airfix kit. They have been improving their quality over the years and I think the Hawker Typhoon is their finest to date, with exquisite detail, fine shapes and rivets in both positive and negative form. The fact they you have options for a variety of elements and the options of rockets, bombs or drop tanks just adds to the overall product. The kit is perfection in terms of assembly and the high quality of its decals make this model a work of art.

I recommend if you have the opportunity, and the space to display it once completed, that you make this wonderful model of the all-powerful Hawker Typhoon.

Chapter 9: Building a Collection

With so many versions of the Tornado & Typhoon as potential modelling subjects we thought it would be useful to show you the difference between all these machines to assist you in making them.

All artwork ©Jacek Jackiewicz 2011

Tornado P5219 - First prototype in its initial form, October 1939

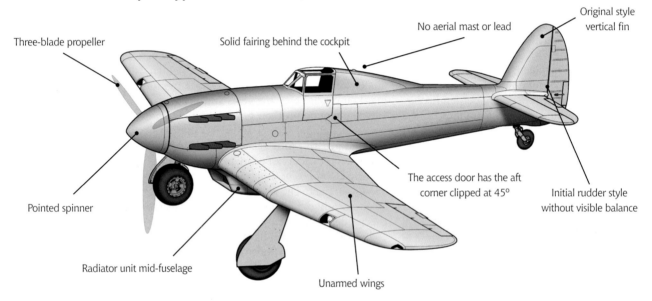

Tornado P5224 - Second prototype, December 1940

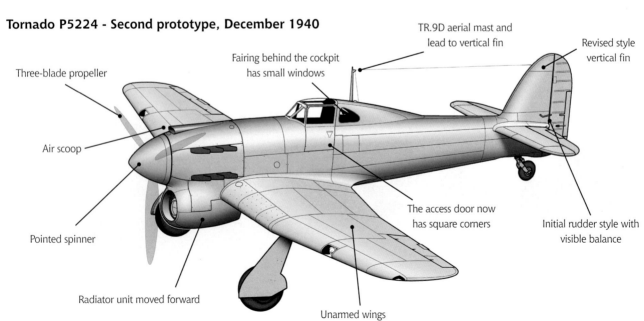

Tornado R7936 - Third prototype used as propeller test-bed, 1943

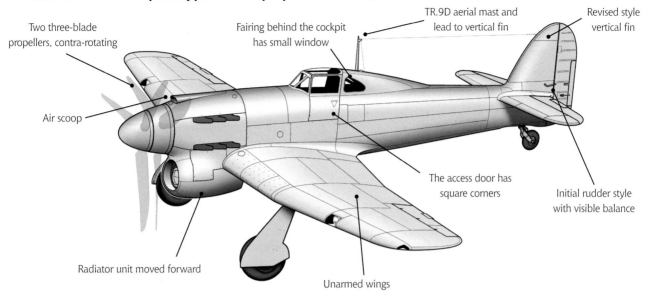

Tornado HG641 - Test-bed for Centaurus IV, October 1943

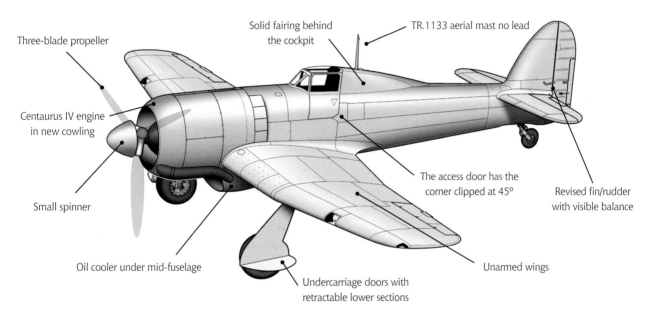

Tornado HG641 - Test-bed for Centaurus IV, November 1943

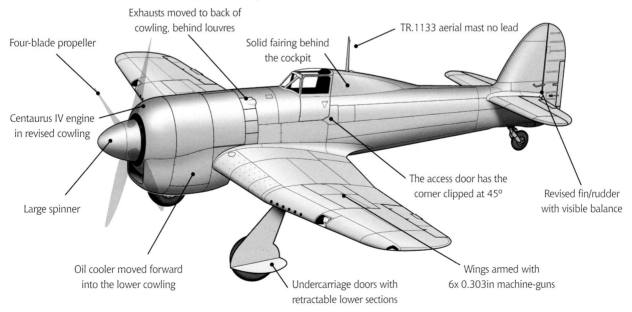

Typhoon P5212 - First prototype in its initial form, April 1940

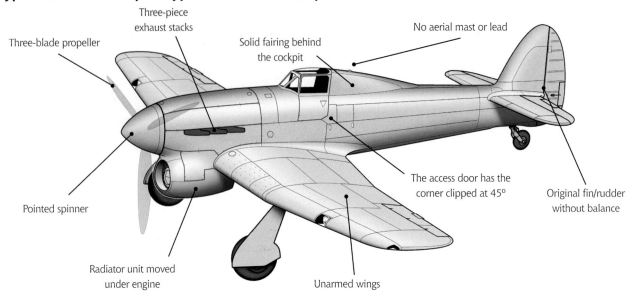

Typhoon P5212 - First prototype in its revised form, early 1941

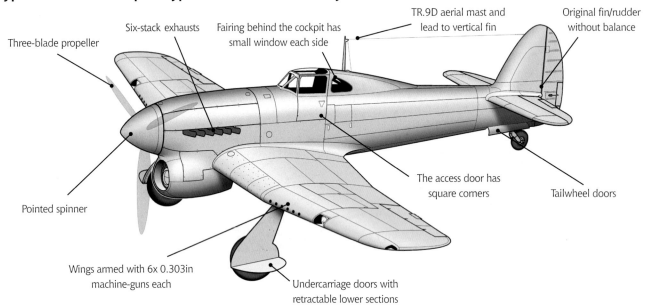

Typhoon P5216 - Second prototype in its initial form, May 1941

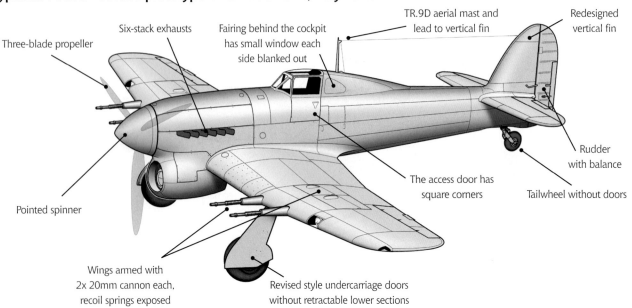

Typhoon Mk Ia - Production version

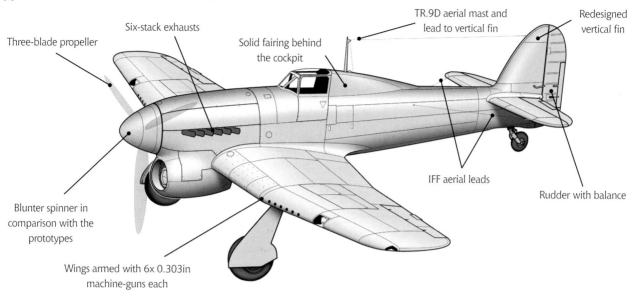

Typhoon Mk Ib - First Production Batch

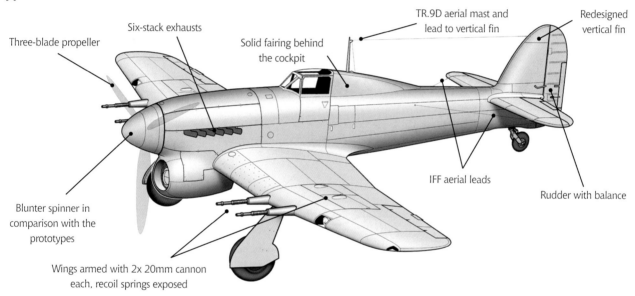

Typhoon Mk Ib - Early Production Batch
Same as the Mk Ib First Production Batch except:

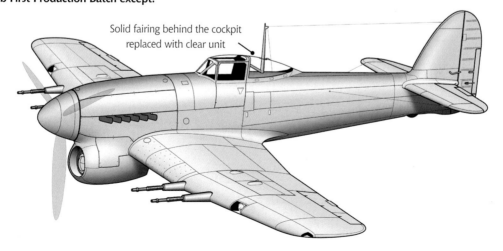

Typhoon Mk Ib - 2nd Early Production Batch
Same as the Mk Ib Early Production Batch except:

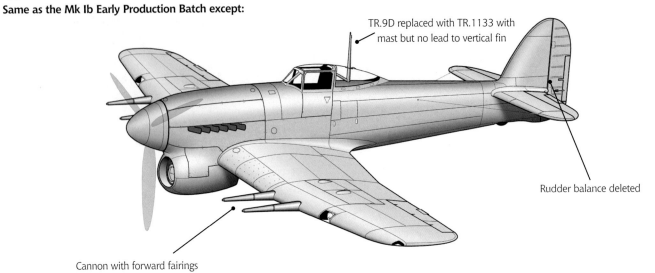

TR.9D replaced with TR.1133 with mast but no lead to vertical fin

Rudder balance deleted

Cannon with forward fairings

Typhoon Mk Ib - Early-Mid Production Batches, Spring 1943
Same as the Mk Ib 2nd Early Production Batch except:

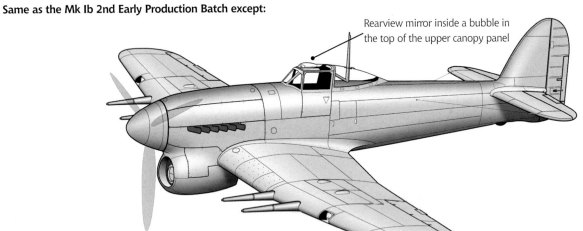

Rearview mirror inside a bubble in the top of the upper canopy panel

Typhoon Mk Ib - Mid-Production Batches
Same as the Mk Ib Early-Mid Production Batches except:

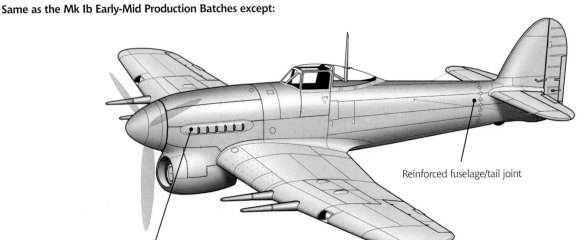

Reinforced fuselage/tail joint

Shrouds fitted to exhausts (usually removed in service)

Typhoon Mk Ib - R8694 Annual Cowling, 1943

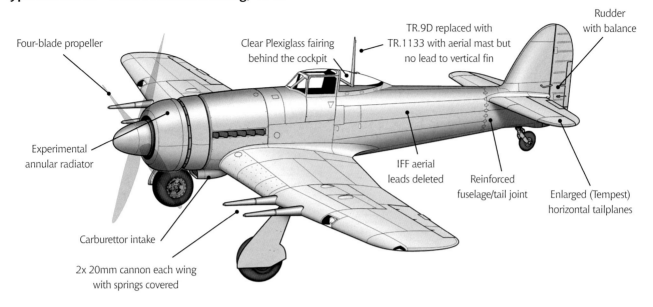

Typhoon Mk Ib - Mid-Production (Last with Car Door)
Same as the Mk Ib Mid-Production Batches except:

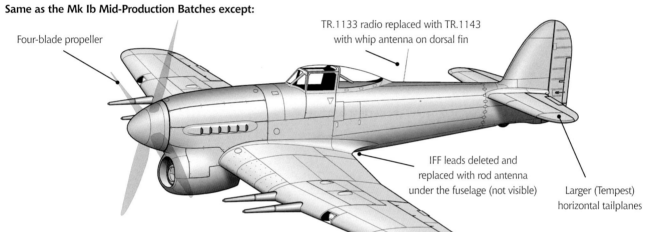

Typhoon NF Mk Ib - R7881 Prototype, March 1943
Same as the Mk Ib Mid-Production Batches except:

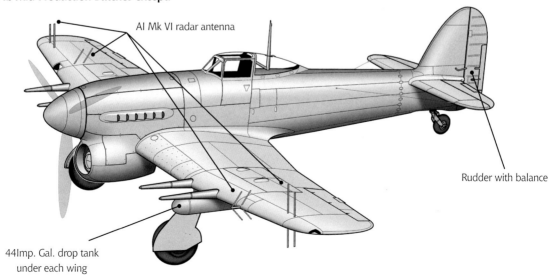

Sea Typhoon - Project P.1009 for carrier fighter

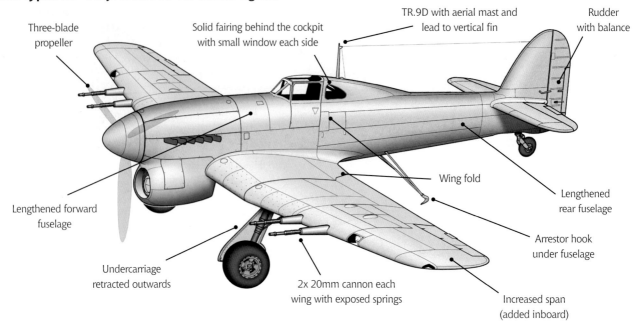

Typhoon FR Mk Ib
Converted from bubble canopy machines of different production batches

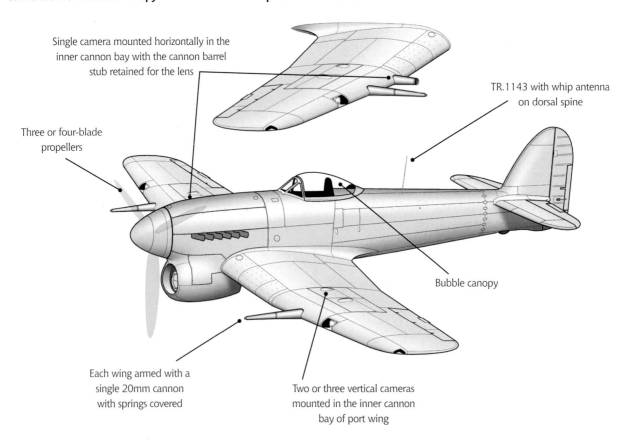

Typhoon Mk Ib - Mid-production (first with bubble canopy)

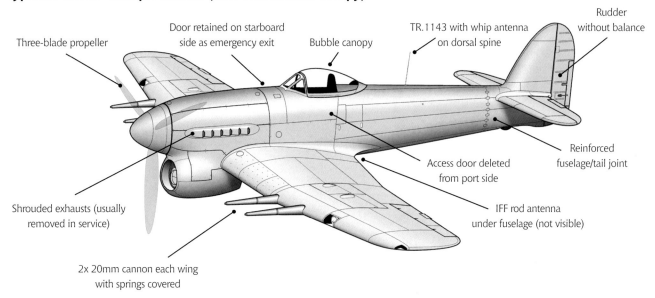

Typhoon Mk Ib - Late Production (first with bubble canopy)
Same as the Mk Ib - Mid Production (first with bubble canopy) except:

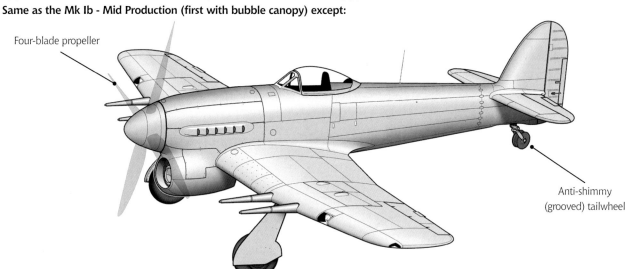

Typhoon Mk Ib - Last Production Batches
Same as the Mk Ib - Late Production (first with bubble canopy) except:

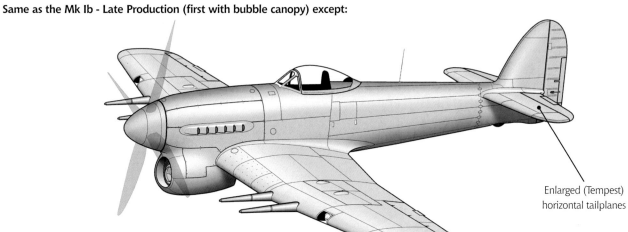

Typhoon Mk II - HM595 Prototype for Tempest V in initial form, September 1942

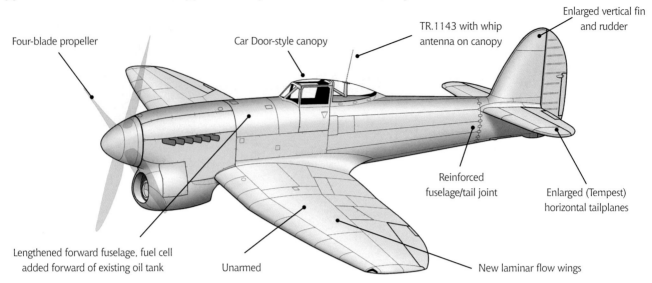

- Four-blade propeller
- Car Door-style canopy
- TR.1143 with whip antenna on canopy
- Enlarged vertical fin and rudder
- Reinforced fuselage/tail joint
- Enlarged (Tempest) horizontal tailplanes
- Lengthened forward fuselage, fuel cell added forward of existing oil tank
- Unarmed
- New laminar flow wings

Typhoon Mk II - HM595 Prototype for Tempest V in later form, early 1943
Same as Typhoon Mk II - HM595 Prototype for Tempest V in initial form, September 1942 except:

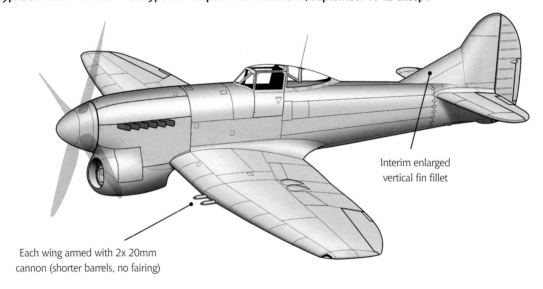

- Interim enlarged vertical fin fillet
- Each wing armed with 2x 20mm cannon (shorter barrels, no fairing)

Typhoon Mk II - HM599 Prototype for Tempest I in initial form, February 1943

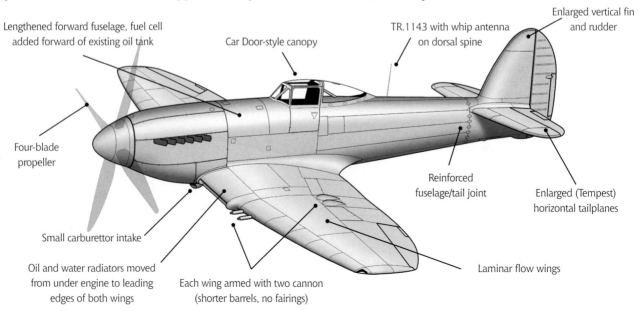

- Lengthened forward fuselage, fuel cell added forward of existing oil tank
- Car Door-style canopy
- TR.1143 with whip antenna on dorsal spine
- Enlarged vertical fin and rudder
- Four-blade propeller
- Reinforced fuselage/tail joint
- Enlarged (Tempest) horizontal tailplanes
- Small carburettor intake
- Oil and water radiators moved from under engine to leading edges of both wings
- Each wing armed with two cannon (shorter barrels, no fairings)
- Laminar flow wings

Typhoon Mk II - HM599 Prototype for Tempest I in later form, February 1943
Same as Typhoon Mk II - HM599. Prototype for Tempest I in initial form, February 1943 except:

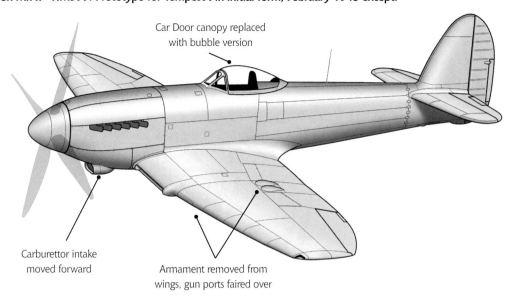

Car Door canopy replaced with bubble version

Carburettor intake moved forward

Armament removed from wings, gun ports faired over

Typhoon TT Mk I - Converted from various production versions
Same as the Mk Ib Mid-Production Batches except:

Four-blade propeller

Wires around vertical fin and rudder to protect it from fouling with towing wire

Target tug equipment installed under rear fuselage - various systems were used so the one shown is illustrative only

Cannon deleted from wings, ports in wing leading edges covered

Car-door Typhoon DN340 is seen here during performance and acceptance trials with two 1,000lb bombs under the wings in June 1943. The aircraft is a very late production car-door version, as it has faired cannon barrels, the anti-shimmy tailwheel and a four-blade propeller
(©A&AEE/crown Copyright)

120 **In Detail**

Typhoon Mk Ib cutaway from the official service manual (©*Crown Copyright*)

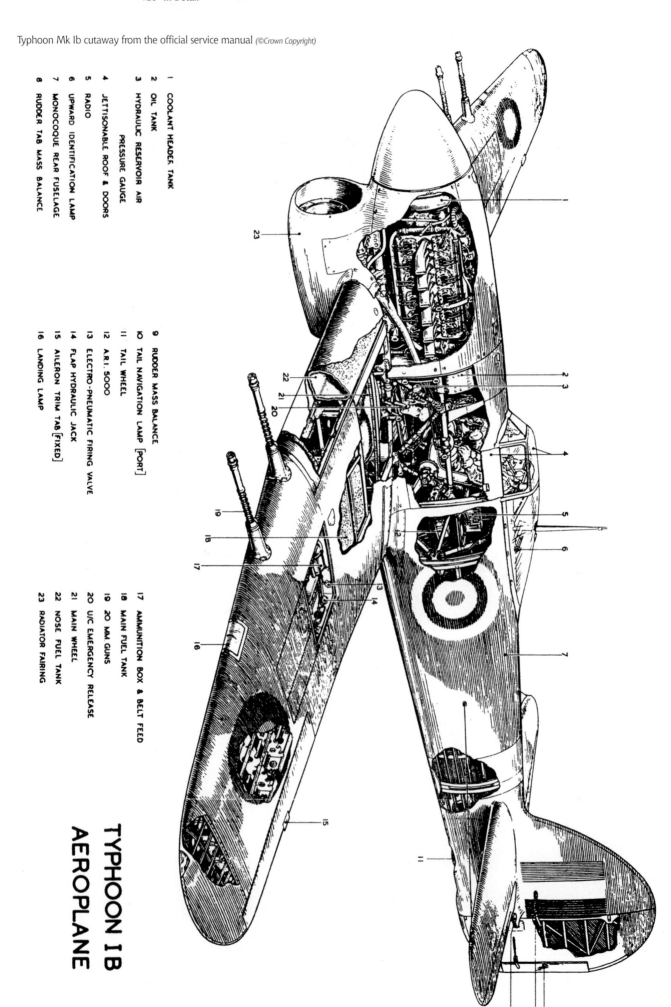

1 COOLANT HEADER TANK
2 OIL TANK
3 HYDRAULIC RESERVOIR AIR PRESSURE GAUGE
4 JETTISONABLE ROOF & DOORS
5 RADIO
6 UPWARD IDENTIFICATION LAMP
7 MONOCOQUE REAR FUSELAGE
8 RUDDER TAB MASS BALANCE
9 RUDDER MASS BALANCE
10 TAIL NAVIGATION LAMP [PORT]
11 TAIL WHEEL
12 A.R.I. 5000
13 ELECTRO-PNEUMATIC FIRING VALVE
14 FLAP HYDRAULIC JACK
15 AILERON TRIM TAB [FIXED]
16 LANDING LAMP
17 AMMUNITION BOX & BELT FEED
18 MAIN FUEL TANK
19 20 MM GUNS
20 U/C EMERGENCY RELEASE
21 MAIN WHEEL
22 NOSE FUEL TANK
23 RADIATOR FAIRING

TYPHOON IB AEROPLANE

Chapter 10: In Detail

What follows is an extensive selection of images and diagrams that will help you understand the physical nature of the Typhoon

All images © Richard A. Franks unless otherwise noted

Cockpit & Canopy

This car door-style canopy used on the Mk Ia and initial production of the Mk Ib
(©British Aerospace)

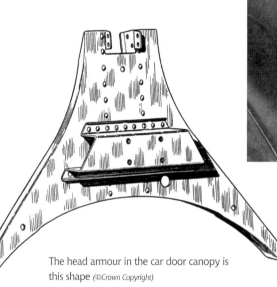

The head armour in the car door canopy is this shape (©Crown Copyright)

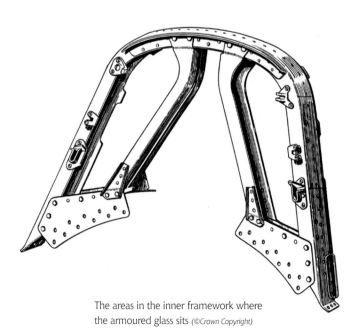

The areas in the inner framework where the armoured glass sits (©Crown Copyright)

There is much debate about the fitment of armoured glass in the mid-section on the car door examples, many personal accounts dispute it while photos confirm it; this close-up clearly shows the distortion caused by thick glass in this area of an in-service machine
(©British Official/Crown Copyright)

122 In Detail - Cockpit & Canopy

This period image shows the cockpit of the Tornado prototype P5224, taken from the starboard side door *(©Hawker Aircraft Ltd)*

Few images inside an early Mk Ia exist, this one shows the port side as viewed from the starboard door *(©Hawker Aircraft Ltd)*

In Detail - Cockpit & Canopy 123

In this close-up from a wartime shot it looks as if no armoured glass is fitted in the mid-section. The light, electrical lead and aerial mast in the back section are noteworthy
(©British Official/Crown Copyright)

This is the main instrument panel of the Centaurus-powered Tornado prototype HG641. Note the four cylinder temperature gauges above the blind flying panel
(©Hawker Aircraft Ltd)

This diagram from the parts manual shows the aerial mast for the car door canopy *(©Crown Copyright)*

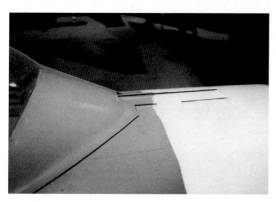

When the bubble canopy is closed this section of the canopy rail can be seen on the upper decking

A good overall view of the bubbletop clear canopy fitted to mid- and late-production Mk Ibs *(©British Aerospace)*

124 In Detail - Cockpit & Canopy

The upper section of the instrument panel and Type I Mk III Projector Sight in the cockpit section at Duxford *(©Alan Bottoms)*

This is the port sidewall of the cockpit section at the IWM, Duxford *(©Alan Bottoms)*

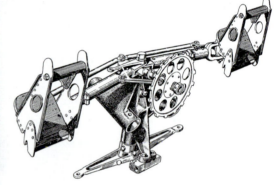

The rudder pedals, a diagram from the parts manual *(©Crown Copyright)*

This is the starboard sidewall of the cockpit section at the IWM, Duxford *(©Alan Bottoms)*

Overall view of the instrument panels in the cockpit section at IWN Duxford *(©Steve A. Evans)*

In Detail - Cockpit & Canopy 125

This is the starboard corner of the instrument panel in MN235

The port corner of the instrument panel in MN235, showing such things as the rudder pedals and compass

126 In Detail - Cockpit & Canopy

Looking straight down from the starboard side of MN235 you can see the seat pan, floor kick plates and control column

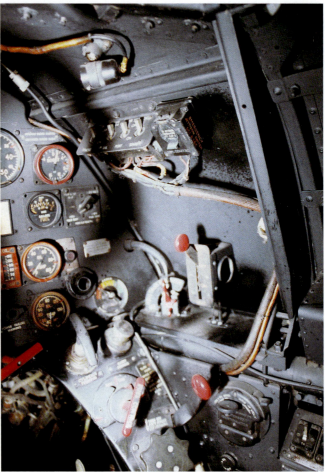

In the fuselage side by the starboard edge of the instrument panel you have the bomb fusing switches, IFF push-button, cockpit heating control (lever) and signalling switchbox

The port sidewall of MN235, showing that the upper section is black, while the lower panels are grey/green. Later in Tempest production the 'black' was in fact a blue/black coating

In Detail - Cockpit & Canopy 127

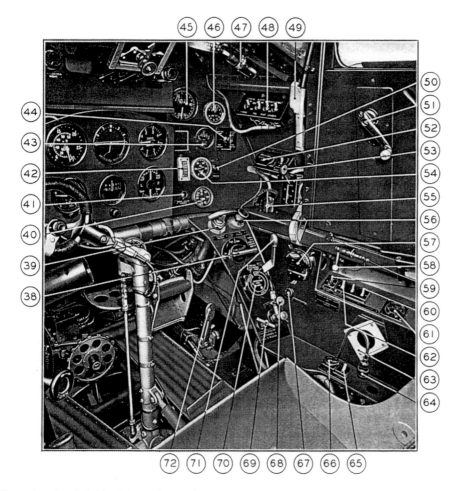

KEY TO *Fig. 3*
COCKPIT—STARBOARD SIDE

38. Fuel cock control.
39. Cylinder priming pump.
40. Radiator temperature gauge.
41. Power failure warning light.
42. Oil pressure gauge.
43. Fuel contents gauge.
44. Fuel contents gauge selector switch.
45. Engine speed indicator.
46. Boost gauge.
47. Starboard cockpit lamp.
48. Bomb fusing and selector switches.
49. Starboard door jettison lever.
50. Fuel pressure warning light.
51. Starboard window winding handle.
52. I.F.F. pushbuttons and switch.
53. Cockpit heating control.
54. Oil temperature gauge.
55. Fuel tank pressurising control.
56. Carburettor priming pump.
57. Signalling switchbox.
58. Sutton harness release.
59. Pressure-head heater switch.
60. Navigation lights switch.
61. Voltmeter.
62. Radio contactor heater switch.
63. Wedge plate for camera gun footage indicator.
64. Socket for footage indicator plug.
65. Camera gun master switch.
66. Oil dilution pushbutton.
67. Switch for panel light.
68. Windscreen de-icing pump and needle valve.
69. Engine starter reloading control.
70. Drop tank cock control.
71. Drop tank jettison control.
72. Undercarriage emergency release pedal.

The starboard cockpit side of the car-door version *(©Crown Copyright)*

KEY TO *Fig. 2*
COCKPIT—PORT SIDE

1. Hydraulic handpump.
2. Landing lights lever.
3. Friction adjuster.
4. Supercharger control lever.
5. Friction adjuster.
6. Propeller control lever.
7. Throttle lever (bomb release pushbutton incorporated).
8. Mixture control lever.
9. Undercarriage indicator switch.
10. Ignition switches.
11. Buzzer indicator light.
12. Radio controller.
13. Port door jettison lever.
14. Port cockpit lamp.
15. Undercarriage indicator.
16. W/T contactor master switch.
17. W/T contactor.
18. Undercarriage buzzer test pushbutton.
19. Reflector sight dimmer switch.
20. Compass light dimmer switch.
21. Flap indicator.
22. Booster-coil pushbutton.
23. Engine starter pushbutton.
24. Instrument flying panel.
25. Oxygen regulator.
26. Gun-firing pushbutton.
27. Pneumatic pressure gauge.
28. Camera gun pushbutton.
29. Rudder pedals adjustment wheel.
30. Starting and slow-running cut-out control.
31. Trimming tab lamp dimmer switch.
32. Landing lights switch.
33. Beam approach master switch.
34. Undercarriage emergency release pedal.
35. Undercarriage selector lever.
36. Flap selector lever.
37. Radiator flap selector lever.

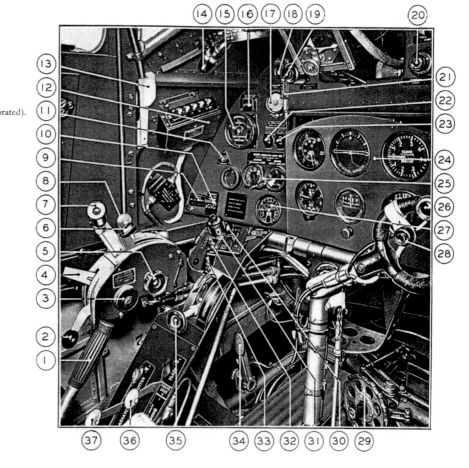

The port cockpit side of the car-door version *(©Crown Copyright)*

128 In Detail - Cockpit & Canopy

Overall view of the instrument panel in MN235 (bubbletop)

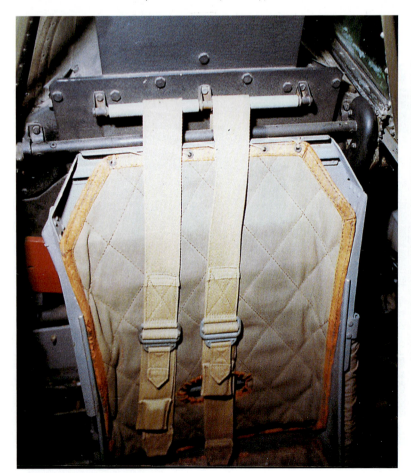

This is the top of the seat, seat belts and head armour on MN235, a bubbletop Mk Ib

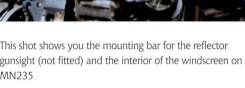

This shot shows you the mounting bar for the reflector gunsight (not fitted) and the interior of the windscreen on MN235

In Detail - Fuselage 129

This restoration seen at Fairford a few years ago does illustrate well how the tubular centre section and monocoque rear join together with the upper decking added over the centre *(©Steve A. Evans)*

Fuselage

The tubular centre section that is similar in construction to many previous Hawker designs and in modified forms would also be used in the Tempest
(©Crown Copyright)

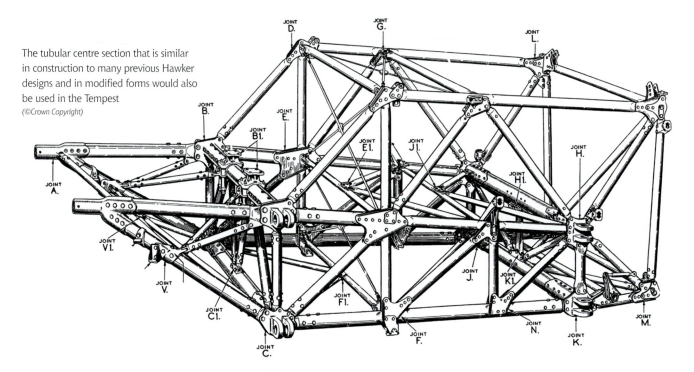

130 In Detail - Fuselage

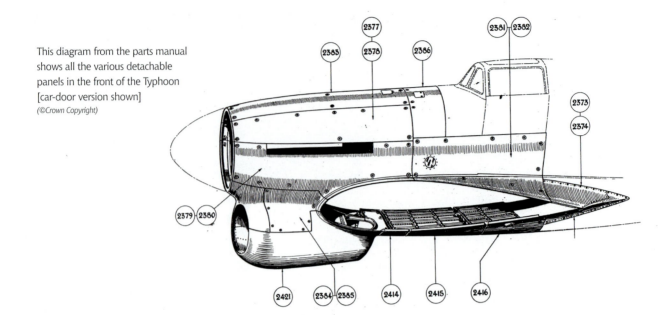

This diagram from the parts manual shows all the various detachable panels in the front of the Typhoon [car-door version shown]
(©Crown Copyright)

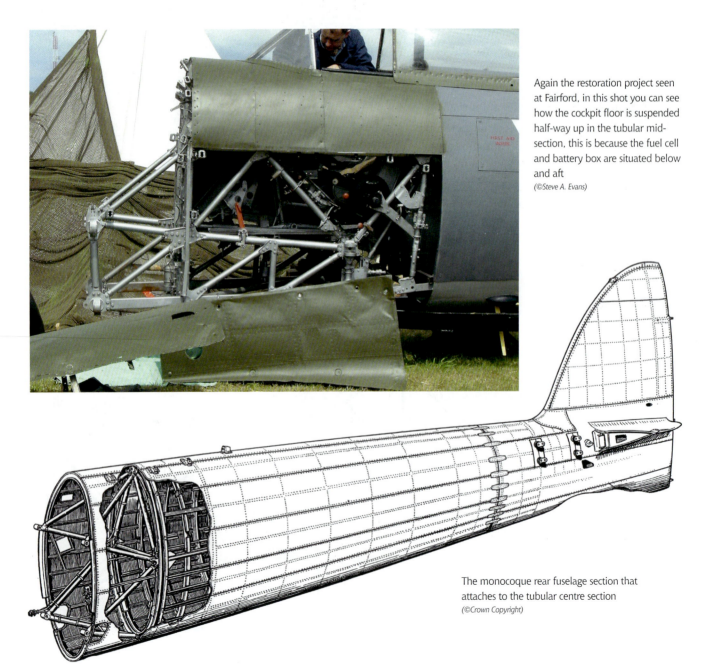

Again the restoration project seen at Fairford, in this shot you can see how the cockpit floor is suspended half-way up in the tubular mid-section, this is because the fuel cell and battery box are situated below and aft
(©Steve A. Evans)

The monocoque rear fuselage section that attaches to the tubular centre section
(©Crown Copyright)

This shot of the mid-port fuselage side shows the two vents there as well as the radio access cover *(©Steve A. Evans)*

This is the footstep extended, it is fitted only to the starboard side

The mid-starboard fuselage side contains various handholds and footsteps as well as another small vent *(©Steve A. Evans)*

Under the port fuselage, just aft of the wing trailing edge, are the IFF rod antennae and, in later production machines only, the 'boat antenna' (the black object)

This factory image shows the 4mm armour plates that were added to the cockpit side of the later Mk Ib [bubbletop] series. There are numerous test reports from Hawkers on the installation of such armour, but we cannot find any mention of it in the official RAF manuals, so it may have remained a test item, a modification that could be added as needed, or it may not have been adopted by the RAF (©Hawker Aircraft Ltd)

This close-up of the rear of MN235 at Hendon shows the fishplates added around the rear transit joint (©Alan Bottoms)

Up the front, this is the intake in MN235 at Hendon. Not much point taking any notice of the radiator, as it is a mock-up made from a cut-down Bedford lorry unit! (©Alan Bottoms)

What everyone calls the 'cuckoo doors', these replaced the Napier-designed dome from December 1944 as it allowed back-pressure in the carburettor air intake ('back-fire') without the risk of the filter flying off and injuring men or machines!

The gun camera in later models of the Typhoon was moved from the wing (inboard) leading edge to a mount on the starboard side of the engine, with this port visible in the cowling. The discoloured patch around it was caused by doped fabric that was applied when the aircraft was initially delivered to the MU, as it had no camera installed, but the overall paint scheme had been applied
(©Public Archive of Canada)

In Detail - Fuselage   133

This wartime shot shows you what the interior of the chin intake should look like - oil cooler element in the middle (round) and water cooler elements around the outside *(©Hawker-Siddeley Ltd)*

Various intake filters were used on the Typhoon, some field mods, other made by Napiers; this wartime image shows the domed filter designed and made by Napiers in a few days in June 1944 to combat the dust of operations in Europe immediately after D-Day *(©British Official/Crown Copyright)*

Some period images also show that basic wooden 'FOD guards' were made up to blank off the intake when the aircraft was on the ground, as seen here on JP963 on the continent just after D-Day. The simple wooden board is held in place by the length of wood that is jammed into the intake lip and it is there to stop mud and stones from other aircraft and even bomb blasts from getting into the intake *(©British Official)*

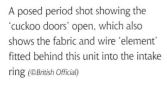

A posed period shot showing the 'cuckoo doors' open, which also shows the fabric and wire 'element' fitted behind this unit into the intake ring *(©British Official)*

This shot shows the mesh screens often installed in the intakes of Typhoons operating out of rough stripes in France during the hectic first few days after the initial landings on D-Day

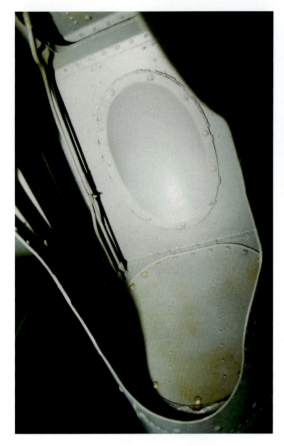

Once the chin cowl is fitted, this is what you can see when you look inside

A quick look up into the tailwheel housing, looking forward

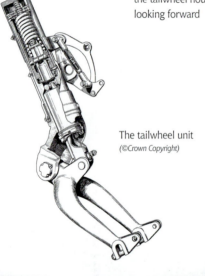

The tailwheel unit
(©Crown Copyright)

People probably want to know what is behind the radiator, hidden by the lower chin cowl, well the answer is this trunking, viewed here from the starboard side

You will never see it unless you open the access panel, but while it was out during checks in 1995, this is the R1143 radio unit used on late production Typhoons

This is the grooved anti-shimmy tailwheel tyre fitted to MN235 at Hendon. This type of tyre was usually only associated with mid- and late-production (bubbletop) machines

Propeller

The business end of the Tiffie, that huge propeller and the big chin intake - ignore the spinner, it is not original, being cut down and modified from a Hastings (four blade propeller) unit by No.27MU RAF Shawbury in the 1960s (©Steve A. Evans)

This wartime image of a pilot standing in front of the propeller on a Car Door Mk Ib in 1943 gives you an idea of the overall size and shape of the three-blade unit used on the type (British Official)

This close up of F/O A Côtés aircraft is interesting because it shows the larger and more bulbous spinner of the four-blade propeller (which effects the cowling as we will discuss elsewhere in this chapter) and the blade root cut-out shape, which remains the same as the three-blade version; the odd demarcation of the colour of the spinner is also of note and very unusual on the Typhoon (©Public Archive of Canada)

This is a four-blade unit that was fitted to Car Door Mk Ib DN430 during bomb trials in 1943. This de Havilland Hydromatic propeller was first tested on the prototype and then became standard at some stage in the final stages of production (the exact date is not determined). A Rotol unit was tested, but it was not adopted for production machines (©Air Ministry)

Cowling (debate)

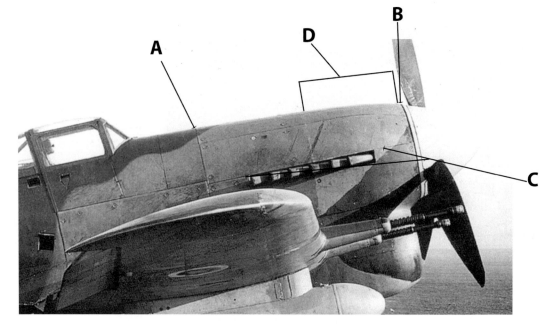

This is R8762 at Boscombe Down during drop tank trials in 1943, it was a Car Door Mk Ib with the three-blade propeller, note the curve of the uppermost seam on the cowl and the shape of the cowl above it (©Air Ministry)

Since originally writing this title, much has been said about the 'shape' of the Typhoon cowling, specifically those on the late production batches. It has been claimed that the upper cowling profile was revised and that some of the last production machines had the cowling seen on the Series I Tempest Mk V. If this is true, and it's still very much open to debate, there is little use using the cowls on the world's only example (MN235 owned by the RAF Museum) as an example, because nearly all the engine cowlings are replicas, fabricated at No.27 MU, RAF Shawbury in the late 1960s when this machine was restored (and probably using those from Tempest Mk V NV778 as patterns), because all (except the lower chin cowl) the originals were lost during its 23 years in the USA.

The accompanying images attempt to highlight what might be a revision, although I am still not 100% convinced because it will take photos taken from the same angle, at the same distance in exactly the same lighting conditions to ever really prove this by photos alone. If production drawings come to light then we may all see the changes, or via modification sheets for the Typhoon, but as yet, none of these exist as far as I know. To understand the thought behind this, we must consider the physical nature of that area of the Typhoon. The cowlings from the panels around the exhaust up are what are under scrutiny, these comprise a short panel on the port and starboards sides, with the main upper cowling on top. Three points must remain constant for either cowl type otherwise ALL of the engine cowlings would need to be changed, which is unlikely. These are the shape/height of the cowl at the engine bulkhead (A) and behind the spinner (B), because the spinner diameter did not change. The other factor that must remain constant is the line of the cowl above the exhaust stacks (C), otherwise nothing would line up. So, that really only leaves you with one area in which the cowl profile can change (D), unless the whole area from A to B is that which is in question, with it being curved instead of flat?

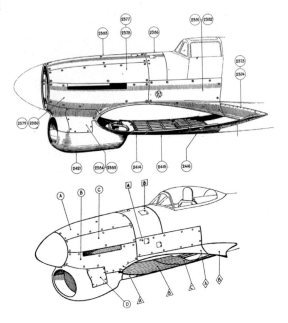

This diagram from the manual shows the Typhoon cowls on the top and the Tempest ones at the bottom. The extra fuel tank forward of the cockpit means the nose is longer on the Tempest, with the nose area ahead of the wing root leading edge projecting further forward as a result. This means the chin cowl and panels around the exhausts ('B') on a Tempest can't fit a Typhoon, but it is possible that the two above this ('A' and 'C') could, and therefore these may have been used on some late production Typhoons with 'A' having a 'revised' profile? Gloster Aircraft never made the Tempest, but they did build most Typhoons, including the last batches, so I really wonder why/how cowls produced at Langley for the Tempest ended up on Typhoons being built by Gloster, when Gloster Aircraft still had the jigs and tools to make the original Typhoon ones? (©Crown Copyright)

In Detail – Cowling 137

Here we have the cowl on FR Mk Ib EK427 in late 1944, which was a machine from the 2nd lot of the 3rd production batch built by Gloster Aircraft Co., Ltd from 09-43 to 04-44. These were all Mk IB 'bubbletops' with the four-blade propeller fitted. To my mind I can't see any great change because the area at the very front of the cowl (marked 'D' in the photo of R8762) looks the same, with the same curve to the panel line and the same hump to the top of the cowl. The spinner on the four-blade propeller is different, though, the backplate diameter must be the same as the three-blade, otherwise the whole front end profile would have to be changed along with all the cowls, but the spinner is longer and thus more bulbous *(©Hawker Aircraft Ltd)*

Now this is RB389, 'Pulverizer IV', which is a bubbletop Mk IB with four-blade propeller from the penultimate production contract built by Gloster Aircraft Co., Ltd from 06-44 to 01-45. Look at the top line of the cowl, the gap between the seam lines and the top at the back look similar to the previous two images. Does the profile of the top section of the cowl now follow the revised curve of the bigger, more bulbous spinner?

Maybe another late machine will help, this is SW494 from the very last production batch, built by Gloster Aircraft Co., Ltd from 01-45 to 11-45. Does that upper cowl profile look different, I am not 100% convinced by the theory or evidence? *(©Public Archive of Canada)*

The light on this shot of the nose of Tempest Mk VI, NX135, in early 1946 does help to highlight the two seams now visible in the mid-panel, where before there had only been one. Personally, I think it is more likely that the way the Tempest cowls as a whole were built is what changed on some of the last production Typhoons, and that the revision to the profile is an optical illusion caused by the more bulbous nature of the spinner for the four-blade propeller? Airfix of course muddy the waters still further, as their 1/24th scale kit includes two different size/shape spinners for the three-blade propeller, one of which is much longer/bulbous…!

If we look at the Tempest Mk V, Series I, in this instance JN729, you see that the top cowl profile is curved; look at the curve in the shadow of the propeller blade. This is almost certainly associated with the extra fuel tank in front of the cockpit in the Tempest and the manner in which all the engine cowls were revised as a result. However, there are no changes to the top profile of the Sabre

You make up your mind, because I have to say I can't find any real evidence that confirms a sufficiently revised profile in the front or upper part of the top engine cowling in the late production batches. Until more period evidence appears, I think this one has therefore to remain a point of contention and debate.

Engine

A brand new engine change unit (the original 'ECU') being lifted for fitment into a Typhoon
(©Public Archives of Canada)

Just to give you an idea of how complex these big piston engines were, this is all the ancillary equipment aft of the engine on the starboard side

A crane and lifting (spreader) bar are needed to remove the Typhoon's engine, as seen here in this wartime image. The whole engine, radiator, front plate and header tank all come off as one unit (©Public Archives of Canada)

Although a little grainy, this wartime image does show the radiator and all its associated pipework. The stencil on the side warns that the engine must not be supported with a trestle under this unit

In this wartime shot of a Typhoon with the upper cowling removed you can see all the ancillary equipment atop the engine (©Crown Copyright)

In Detail - Engine 139

It is a big and complex lump, the Sabre engine. In this instance this is the unit in the Tempest Mk V whilst being restored by the late Ian Mason at the, then, RAF Museum Restoration Facility at Cardington in Bedfordshire - the quality of the workmanship speaks volumes for Ian's skills, he is sadly missed

A nice shot of the side of the Sabre, showing the bearers underneath and six-stack exhausts that combine the gases from upper and lower cylinders in this 'H-Type' engine layout

Exhausts

The Typhoon also had a series of different exhausts fitted during its life; this is the three-stack unit used on the prototype P5212 *(©Air Ministry)*

This is prototype P5212 after various modifications, including the fitment of six-stack exhausts *(©British Aerospace)*

The production Mk Ia series also kept the same six-stack exhausts, as seen here on R7579 *(©British Aerospace)*

Here you can see the large shrouds that were the idea of an MU in an attempt to clean up the airflow over the stacks. The cover was not liked by groundcrew, as it made removing the cowls difficult, so they were usually taken off in service. This close-up is from a shot of Mk Ib, JR128, HF•L of No183 Sqn

This is a shot of the exhausts of Car Door Mk Ib EK286 in April 1943, note the prominent weld seams on each stack *(©Hawker-Siddeley)*

When the final style of shrouds were removed in service, they could result in unpainted areas being exposed, as seen in this close-up from a period image. The front fairing was obviously painted under first (or after removal), the rear one seems not to have been

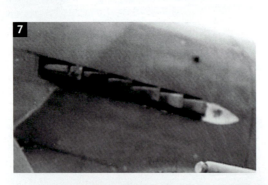

This is MN180, fresh from Glosters in January 1944, it was from the fifth production batch and you can see that it had aerodynamic blisters added fore and aft of the stacks plus individual shrouds over each unit, to try and 'clean up' the airflow over them, whilst not being as complex as the shroud devised by the RAF MU *(©Hawker-Siddeley)*

These are the shrouds on MN235 at Hendon (before it went to Canada on loan). Note the two small pipes coming out of the top of the cowling - there is a single one on the port side and another under the fuselage mid-section, off-set to port [battery drain probably]. You can't take much notice of any of the engine cowls on MN235, though, as these are all replica parts made at 27MU, RAF Shawbury during its restoration in the late 1960s, as all the originals were lost whilst it was in the USA. I suspect they were made by copying the only option at that time, Tempest Mk V, NV778, which was at Shawbury at the same time undergoing refurbishment for display before its eventual move to the RAFM with MN235 *(©Steve A. Evans)*

Wings

This is the foot-step built into the upper trailing edge of the starboard wing root. The unit is sprung-loaded so sits flush with the wing surface when not actually being used

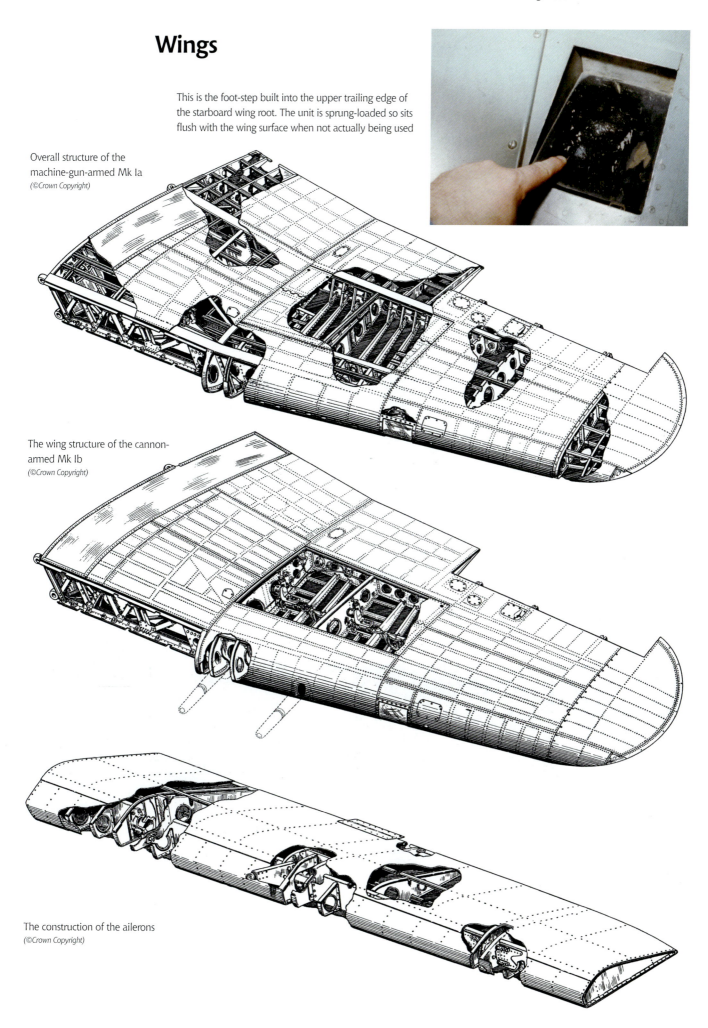

Overall structure of the machine-gun-armed Mk Ia
(©Crown Copyright)

The wing structure of the cannon-armed Mk Ib
(©Crown Copyright)

The construction of the ailerons
(©Crown Copyright)

142 In Detail - Wings

This is the six-gun wing of the F.18/37 prototype in a photo dated February 1940 and as adopted for the Mk Ia (©Hawker Aircraft Ltd)

Looking at R8884's wing from the tip inboard, you see the pronounced nature of the oblong bulge, but the smaller teardrop-shaped on inboard looks almost completely flat in profile (©British Official/Crown Copyright)

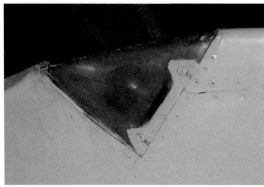

The tip lights have coloured bulbs and clear covers, even though the Perspex on those fitted to MN235 has degraded over time to this yellowy colour (©Alan Bottoms)

The pitot-static tube is the traditional 'L' shape and is located around mid-span under the port wing, as seen here on MN235 (©Alan Bottoms)

In previous photos you have seen the landing light in the starboard wing, well from early 1944 this was deleted and covered over. The type retained the unit in the port side, though, as seen here in a Car Door Mk Ib in 1943, although this too was often covered over by rocket-carrying machines from mid-1944 onwards as the rocket motor blast often broke the Perspex. Note the shape of the unit at the rear, it is not a squared-off back, it is angled in each corner (©Air Ministry/British Official)

In Detail - Wings 143

This period photo clearly shows how the combination of lowered step, wing-root foot-step and fuselage-side hand-holds are used to get into a Typhoon. The system remained the same on the bubbletop version [this is EK286, 'Fuji VI' by the way] (©Hawker Aircraft Ltd)

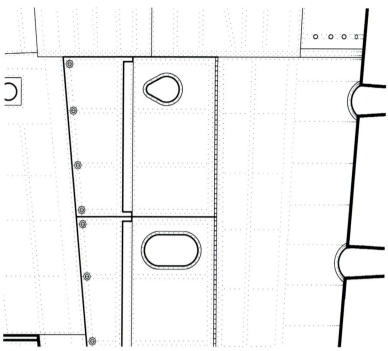

There seems much confusion on the inboard teardrop-shaped 'bulge' seen here in these scale plans. Due to the wing outer panel dihedral, the side views do not show the top skin of the wings in profile, so kit manufacturers are left wondering what shape this feature is?
(© Jacek Jackiewicz)

Just to confirm this, here is MN235 at Hendon today and as you can see, or should we say, not see, there is the prominent outer bulge, but inboard, well just the faintest hint of a bulge
(©Steve A. Evans)

The two sections of the trailing edge flaps on the Typhoon
(©Crown Copyright)

This shot from the back of R8884, HF•L of No.183 Sqn clearly shows, thanks to the shadows cast by the low sun, that the outer blister is indeed that, but inboard - well you can just make out a slight rise in the middle of the yellow ID band (©British Official/Crown Copyright)

When R8884's wing is viewed from the front and side you get a better idea of the profile of the bulge, as the yellow paint highlights it nicely - it is a very slight bump
(©British Official/Crown Copyright)

Undercarriage

Wartime shot up into the port undercarriage bay, you can just see the pouch for the control locks on the rear bulkhead

This is the pouch from the wheel wells that was used to safely store the u/c locks when the aircraft was in use
(©Crown Copyright)

In this shot of the starboard u/c unit you can see the towing eyelet and the route of the brake line

Lower down the oleo leg the brake cable is connected to a flexible tube that goes to the centre of the wheel hub

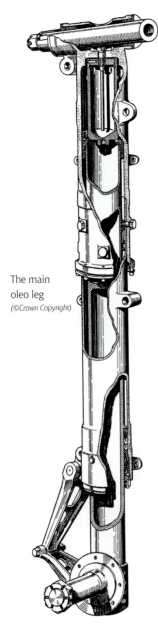

The main oleo leg
(©Crown Copyright)

The port undercarriage leg and wheel of MN235 at Hendon (©Steve A. Evans)

This wartime shot of an in-service Typhoon's starboard undercarriage unit clearly shows the later five-spoke wheel hubs and the radial rings moulded into the sidewall of the tyre; the tyre itself never had any treads on Typhoons (©British Official/Crown Copyright)

In Detail - Undercarriage 145

The inner u/c door on MN235, the L-shaped panel is a scuff plate that stoppped the wheel spinning when the leg was fully retracted, it was always unpainted

An excellent overall view of the port undercarriage bay on MN235. The light in the bay leading edge was only fitted to late-production (bubbletop) Typhoons, and there is another unit in the edge of the starboard bay [green lens]
(©Steve A. Evans)

The main undercarriage door assembly
(©Crown Copyright)

Looking forward and inboard in the port undercarriage bay you find the oxygen bottle that dominates this area and the back of the downward ident light; this latter item was only on late-production machines

Looking up into the roof of the main u/c bay - note the pouch for the u/c locks on the back bulkhead

This is the retraction jack and complex linkage framework inboard of the main oleo - this is the starboard unit

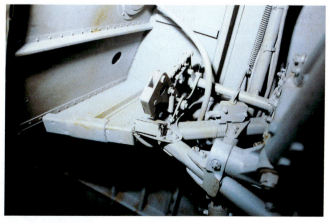

At the back of the framework behind the retraction jack is this complex assembly - the hook is the u/c 'up' lock, while the small oblong block in front is the switch that triggers the lights in the cockpit to tell the pilot if the wheels are up or down, the lead is the electrical cable for this circuit

146 In Detail - Undercarriage/Tail

This view up into the starboard wheel well of MN235 highlights the very small numbers of pipes etc. in this area. The bays are painted Medium Sea Grey here, but that is down to the restoration in the 1960s to afford the area some degree of protection *(©Alan Bottoms)*

A view up into the port undercarriage bay of MN235, you can see the hydraulic ram that operates the inner door, plus the pouch on the back wall (spar), which contained the undercarriage locks when not in use *(©Alan Bottoms)*

This Car Door Typhhon had its tail shot up by Flak over Dixmunde, but the photo does clearly show the external rudder and trim tab mass balance arms, as well as the stencils on fin and rudder, the small formation lights in the rear root fairings, the linkage arm for the trim tab and the clear panel in the bottom edge, behind which is the manufacturer's plate *(©Air Ministry/British Official)*

Tail

This diagram from the manual combines all the features of both early and late machines, in that the external mass balance arms seen either side of the fin ahead of the rudder, as well as the mass balance weights on the trim tab itself that are only applicable to the Mk Ia are shown, while the inset diagram on the top RH shows the in-built mass balance of the trim tab used on the Mk Ib; the rudder mass balance was integral of the fin on the Mk Ib *(©Crown Copyright)*

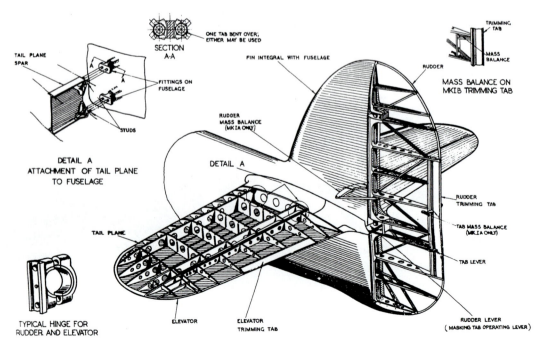

In Detail - Tail 147

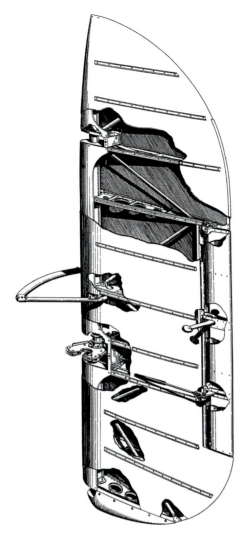

The rudder assembly of the early production machines. Note the balance horns that were deleted from mid- and late-production machines. The mass balance on the trim tab was also later deleted (©Crown Copyright)

The vertical fin and rudder of MN235 at Hendon, note the recognition light built into the trailing edge of each tailplane root/fillet (©Steve A. Evans)

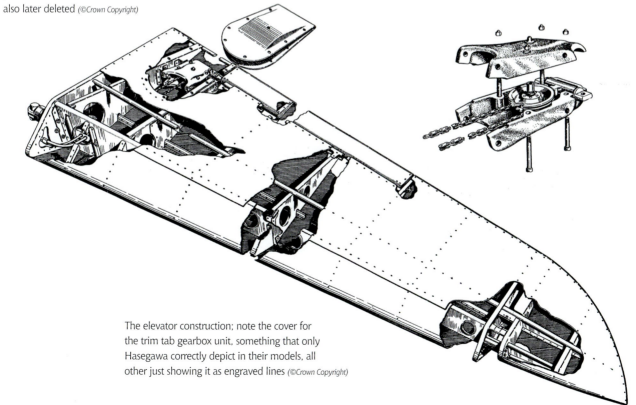

The elevator construction; note the cover for the trim tab gearbox unit, something that only Hasegawa correctly depict in their models, all other just showing it as engraved lines (©Crown Copyright)

Armament

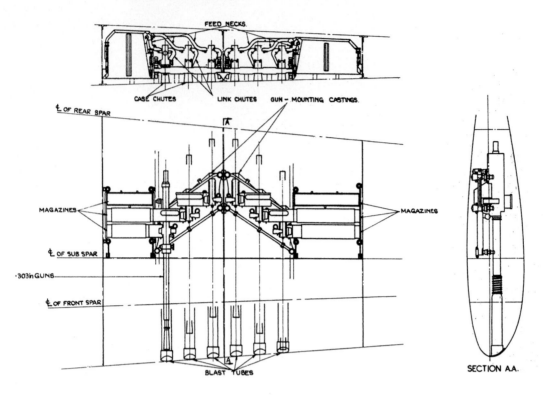

The gun and ammunition layout in the machine-gun-armed wing
(©Crown Copyright)

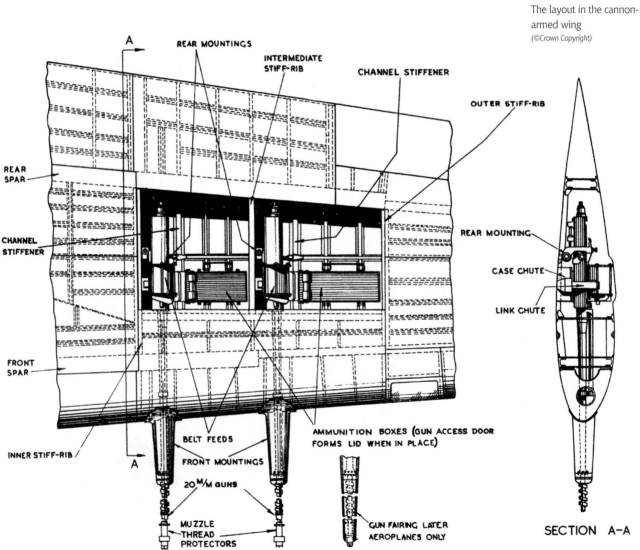

The layout in the cannon-armed wing
(©Crown Copyright)

In Detail - Armament 149

The cannon fairings on MN235 at Hendon are those that cover the entire barrel
(©Steve A. Evans)

The cannon fairings, showing the initial and later design of these items
(©Crown Copyright)

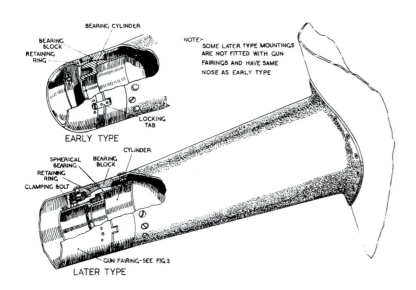

This is another early Mk Ib with the exposed cannon springs, but in this instance the spring cross-section is round
(©British Official)

This is an early Mk Ib in April 1943, with the exposed cannon springs that have a flat cross-section to them (©British Official)

This is a close-up of the base of the cannon barrels on MN235 (©Alan Bottoms)

In this photo of 'Car Door' Mk Ib, RB656, FM•L of N.257 Sqn in May 1943 you can see the ammo feed drum for the outboard cannon, which has been rotated to allow the ammo belts to be loaded, plus you can also see how the access doors opened/folded up. The big bulge in the main cover can easily be seen as a pronounced indentation, but the smaller teardrop-shaped is obscured by the groundcrewman *(©British Official)*

This close-up from a wartime photo taken around D-Day shows the later covers on the cannon, but this is a bomb-carrying Typhoon and the interesting thing is the raised lip to the cannon cartridge ejector port under the wing. See this 'deflector chute' associated with the bomb carrier, in the diagram on p154

The end of the barrel has this hexagonal nut shape to it; this covers the threaded end of the barrel on which some guns would have flash eliminators etc.

Armourers slide the rocket onto the rail - note that the saddle on the rocket has a 'T' to the top of it that slips between the two tubes on the rail, it is simple as that. The 'pig tail' electrical connectors can be seen hanging out of the back

This view up under the wing of MN235 does highlight the twin ports for each cannon, one for cartridge cases, the other for links, you can also just make out the two holes (front and back) for each of the rocket rail support struts *(©Alan Bottoms)*

In Detail - Armament 151

When pilots were training to do rocket attacks the rockets could be fitted with these 60lb concrete (inert) heads; note the rocket body, which is painted white, probably to aid visual tracking of the rocket *(©British Official)*

One installation that is unlikely to have been used operationally on the Typhoon is the double-stack Mk Ia system as seen here when it as tested at A&AEE. The rockets could not be fired independently of each other, although this would come post-war for other aircraft *(©British Official/Crown Copyright)*

Wartime image showing armourers fitting 60lb heads to Mk I rockets. The square fins denote the earliest form of 3in RP, but it is doubtful the Typhoon ever operated with the later style on the rockets they used *(©British Official/Crown Copyright)*

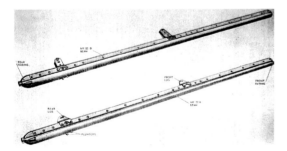

This official diagram, although not very clear, shows the Mk IIIA (bottom) and Mk IIIB (top) RP rails, the latter being applicable to the Typhoon *(©Crown Copyright)*

Posed, but nonetheless nice, this image of an 'Erk' fixing the cannon barrel cover screws on a Typhoon at B5 airfield in July 1944 does at least give you a clear shot of the tips of the Mk Ib rails with their twin guide tubes and riveted steel construction *(©British Official)*

152 In Detail - Armament

In this close-up of a Typhoon being inspected by HRH King George VI, you can see the style of the initial Mk Ib rail. The distinguishing features are the two tubes into which the saddle plate of the rocket fits, plus the lack of gap between the top of the rail and the stub support brackets
(©British Official/Crown Copyright)

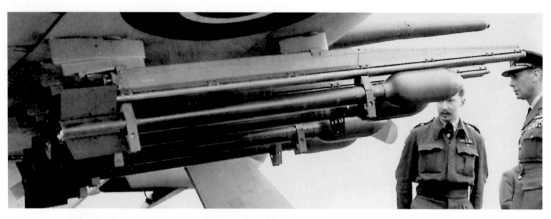

These armourers are sliding the saddle plate on 3in RPs into the two 'tubes' on the Mk Ib rail
(©British Official/Crown Copyright)

From late 1944 and into 1945 the Mk IIIa rail started to appear. This was known as the lightweight rail and is distinguished by the lack of the 'tubes' for the saddle plates and the spacer tube in the gap between the rail top and the support stub brackets front and rear. The type did not replace the Mk Ib during WWII so both types can be seen in use right up to May 1945 *(©British Official/Crown Copyright)*

At the back of each rocket is what is known as the 'pig tail' but officially was called the Weak Link Lead
(©British Official/Crown Copyright)

This diagram shows the construction of the Weak Link Lead. For single tiers this was 21.5in long, when double rockets were used [something the Typhoon did not do operationally] the lead was 34.5in long
(©Crown Copyright)

Rocket motor weak link lead

This close-up shows the saddle plate for the Mk Ib rail
(©British Official/Crown Copyright)

In Detail - Armament 153

Although grainy, this photo does show the installation of two-tier 60lb RPs on Mk I rails with No.8 saddles as tested by MN861 at Boscombe Down in August 1944. This is the same machine that is shown elsewhere with the similar installation, but with concrete heads on the RPs. The used of 'paired' rockets made no difference, so the installation was not adopted by the Typhoon (©Air Ministry)

Sometimes the Typhoon would be seen with fragmentation rounds, which are basically the SAP with its lower grade steel body and a fragmentation ring on the front to spread the blast effect. In this shot a mixed load of fragmentation and 60lb HE heads are being carried. These are carried on Mk III rails, which were made of aluminium, not steel as per the Mk Ib (©British Official/Crown Copyright)

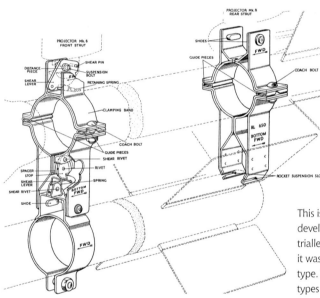

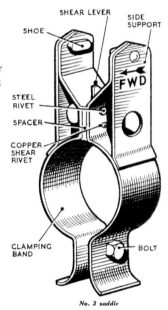

This is a diagram from the RP manual showing the No.3 Saddle used for single RPs on the Mk IIIB rails (©Crown Copyright)

This is the No.8 Mk 2 saddle, which was developed with the Typhoon when it trialled the two-tier RP fit, even though it was not adopted for service use by the type. This layout was later used on such types as the Hornet (©Crown Copyright)

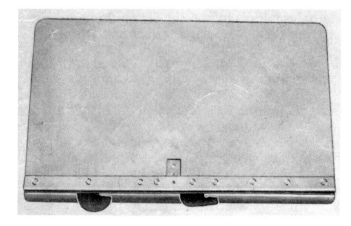

Fin, Mk. I

There are two types of fin applicable to the Typhoon's service, this is the Mk I, which ends flush with the end of the rocket motor body
(©British Official/Crown Copyright)

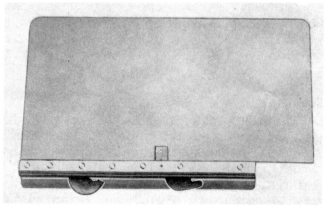

Fin, Mk. 2

This is the Mk 2 fin, which as you can see projects back past the end of the rocket motor body
(©British Official/Crown Copyright)

Ordnance

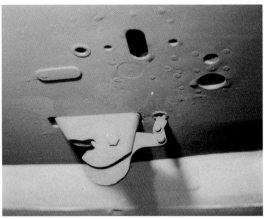

The bomb carrier was attached to the wing underside via two sets of hooks; this is the front (double) set and they have a sprung-loaded catch to retain the carrier

This is the single hook for the back of the bomb carrier

The Typhoon could also carry bombs or tanks; the former is seen here as a 1,000lb GP bomb is winched up onto the wing rack (©British Official)

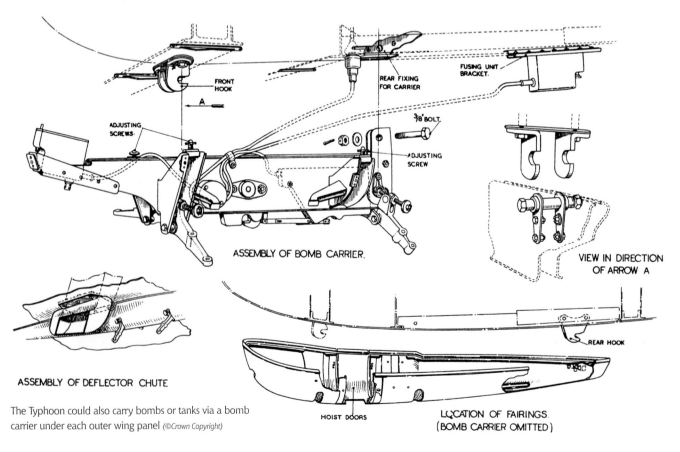

The Typhoon could also carry bombs or tanks via a bomb carrier under each outer wing panel (©Crown Copyright)

In Detail - Armament, Ordnance 155

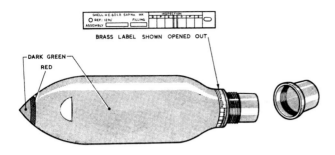

This is the 60lb HE head, which is the more usual RP head used by Typhoons
(©British Official/Crown Copyright)

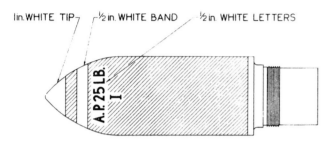

This is the 25lb Armour-Piercing (AP) head, which was also used by the Typhoon either as the only type, or mixed 50/50 with 60lb HE head rounds
(©British Official/Crown Copyright)

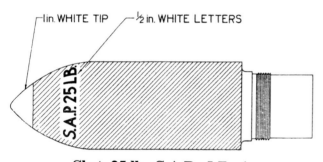

Probably the least common head type for the Typhoons RPs was the Semi-Armour-Piercing (SAP) 25lb version
(©British Official/Crown Copyright)

F/O C. LeBert Burgess of No.439 Sqn, alongside a 500lb bomb under the wing of his Typhoon *(©Public Archive of Canada)*

This image of DN340 at Boscombe Down in June 1943 clearly shows the bomb racks fitted to the Typhoon, which here are shown with a 500lb GP bomb attached *(©Air Ministry/A&AEE)*

In this close-up of RB389, 'Pulverizer IV' you can see the 500lb bomb, but you can probably just make out the arming wires from the wing to the bomb and the fact these bombs were tail fuzed, i.e.. the arming vane is at the back of the tail, not in the nose

A close-up of the 900lb bomb canisters under the wing of a No.143 Squadron machine in Germany in 1945

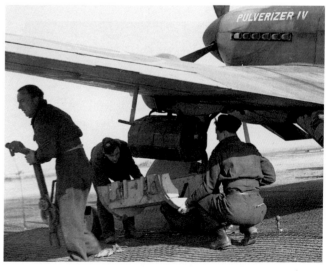

The Typhoon could also carry 900lb anti-personnel bomb canisters, as seen here being put under the well-known 'Pulverizer IV from No.440 Sqn *(©Public Archive of Canada)*

Sighting

Here you can see a Mk II* sight modified without the lens to make a simple projector unit that puts the ring on the windscreen (©British Official)

Initially the Typhoon used the Mk II* gunsight, as seen here in a Car Door machine operated by No.257 Squadron at RAF Warmwell in May 1943 (©British Official)

Here is a close-up of the Mk II* gunsight, viewed from the starboard side

Here the diagram of the Mk II* gunsight from the manual (©Crown Copyright)

Some ground-attack squadrons used a modified Mk II* with the screen removed and the graticule modified to a plain 100mph ring and dot. This became the Type I Mk III Projector Sight as seen in this diagram from the manual (©Crown Copyright)

Here you can see the modified Mk II* in the cockpit section at the IWM, Duxford (©Alan Bottoms)

The mounting bars for the Mk II* were simply reversed to protect the new Type I Mk III projector, as seen here in the cockpit of the RAFM example (albeit the gunsight is not fitted to this machine). The adoption of the Grade A armoured glass made this type of projector sight much more efficient, as the previous type of glass caused optical distortion

Drop Tanks

In the field the fitment of tanks resulted in a reduction from four to two 3in RPs per wing, as seen here on this 2nd TAF aircraft on the continent, post D-Day *(©British Official)*

The Typhoon underwent drop tank trials in early 1943, as seen here with R8762 at Boscombe Down. The tanks were standard Hurricane items, which some list as 44 Imp. Gal. and others 45 Imp. Gal. *(©Air Ministry)*

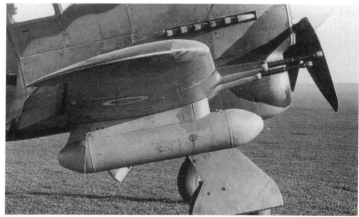

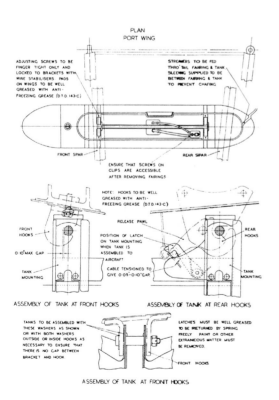

Diagram showing the attachment of the drop tanks *(©Crown Copyright)*

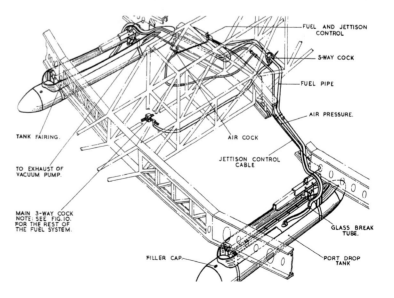

Diagram of fuel system with drop tanks fitted *(©Crown Copyright)*

Miscellaneous

JR307 was used to test the American M10 smoke tanks to discharge gas, but they were found to strike the aircraft when jettisoned. JR307 was sadly lost in a fatal crash in March 1944 during bombing trials. The M10 was also tested on bubbletop Mk Ib MN519
(©Air Ministry/A&AEE)

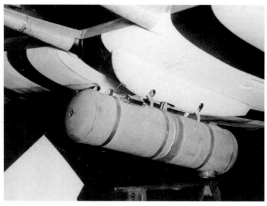

The Typhoon tested various 'SC' (smoke curtain) tanks, this is one of the earliest version seen during test in 1944
(©British Official)

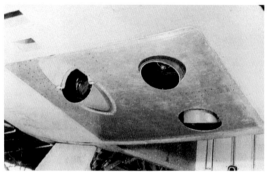

This is the view of the camera underneath the port wing, with the long-focus, high-speed oblique in the front and the two split obliques at the rear. The ejector ports for the outboard cannon can been seen on the top left, with the top of the undercarriage door at bottom left and the space for the fuel tanks at bottom right (©Hawker Aircraft Ltd)

The Typhoon was also used in the photo-reconnaissance role, here you can see the camera installation in the port outer gun bay, with two split obliques in the front and a long-focus high-speed oblique in the rear. The outboard cannon remains and is just visible on the left
(©Hawker Aircraft Ltd)

The prototype NF Mk I R7881 is seen here in its initial form with the three-blade propeller and the radar equipment housed in the 44Imp.Gal. drop tank under the port wing; the one under the starboard was just full of ballast

This is the revised layout of R7881, now with a four-blade propeller and the drop tanks painted black

In the fighter-reconnaissance role the inboard cannon were removed, but the stub for the starboard one remained as a camera looked out through a glass added into it. This is EK427 seen in late 1944

A closer look at the standard cannon barrel and the truncated one in the starboard wing of EK427, which was operated by No.268 Squadron in 1945

This is the port side of EK427 and you can see it only has the single cannon barrel in this wing

Appendix: I Tornado & Typhoon Kits

Below is a list of all static scale construction kits produced to date of the Hawker Typhoon and Tornado. This list is as comprehensive as possible, but if there are amendments or additions, please contact the author via the Valiant Wings Publishing address shown at the front of this title.

1/150th

- Sankyo, Japan [inj] 1/150th Hawker Typhoon Mk Ib #32 (late 50s-1968)
- Sankyo, Japan [inj] 1/150th Typhoon Mk Ib #N/K

1/144th

- Revell, Germany (ex-Crown) [inj] 1/144th Typhoon Mk Ib #H-1015 (1973) – Reissued in 1992 as #4026

1/93rd

- Eagle/Eagleware, UK (ex-Vulcan) [inj] 1/93rd Typhoon Mk Ib #9 (1950s to 1963) – Also released in the Eagleware 'Table Top Air Force' series in late 1962
- Sanwa/Tokyo Plamo, Japan [inj] 1/93rd Hawker Typhoon #1108 (1950s-60s)

1/72nd

- Academy, Korea [inj] 1/72nd Typhoon Mk Ib #1664 (1999)
- Academy, Korea [inj] 1/72nd Spitfire Mk XIVc & Typhoon Mk Ib '70th Anniversary, Normandy Invasion, 1944-2014' #12512 (2014)
- AER, Moldova (ex-Frog) [inj] 1/72nd Typhoon Mk Ib #7202 (1994->)
- Airfix, UK [inj] 1/72nd Typhoon Mk Ib Patt. No.107 (1959) – Renumbered #01027-8 in 1973; #61027-8 in 1982; renumbered #902072 in 1985; #02072 in 1986; issued in the 'All in One' series in 1997 as #92072; as #61027 in 1983; #961027 in 1985; #01027 in 1986; issued in the 'All in One' series in 1997 as #91027; included in 'The Historic Collection – WWII Fighter Classics' set in 1997 #9514; renumbered #A01027 in 2008 also issued as the new-style Gift Set in 2008 as #A50079; as the revised 'Starter Set' with paint, glue & brush in 2010 as #A50079
- Airfix, UK [inj] 1/72nd Focke-Wulf Fw 190A-8 & Hawker Typhoon Mk Ib 'Dogfight Double' #A50136 (2013)
- Airfix, UK [inj] 1/72nd Hawker Typhoon Mk Ib 'Starter Set' #A55208 (2013)
- Airfix, UK [inj] 1/72nd Hawker Typhoon Mk Ib #A02041 (2013)
- Airfix Corp. of America, USA (ex-Airfix) [inj] 1/72nd Typhoon Mk Ib #10-39
- Air Lines, Australia (ex-Frog) [inj] 1/72nd Typhoon Mk Ib #59900
- Alanger, Russia (ex-Frog) [inj] 1/72nd Typhoon Mk Ib 'Car door' #072026

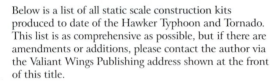

- Ark Models, Russia (ex-Frog) [inj] 1/72nd Typhoon Mk Ib #72015 – (2011)
- Aviation Usk, USA [ltd inj] 1/72nd Hawker Typhoon Mk Ib #AV-1005 (1989) – Reissued 1997
- Bienengraber, West Germany (ex-Frog) [inj] 1/72nd Typhoon Mk Ib #F209F (1969-74)
- Brengun, CZ [ltd inj/pe] 1/72nd Hawker Typhoon Mk Ib 'Mid-production with three-blade propeller' #BRP72003 (2013)
- Brengun, CZ [ltd inj/pe] 1/72nd Hawker Typhoon Mk Ib 'Mid-production with four-blade propeller' #BRP72004 (2013)
- Brengun, CZ [ltd inj/pe] 1/72nd Hawker Typhoon Mk Ib Car Doors 'Early Production' #BRP72006 (2014)
- Brengun, CZ [ltd inj/pe] 1/72nd Hawker Typhoon Mk Ib Car Door 'Early/Mid and Mid Production' #BRP72007 (2014)
- Brengun, CZ [ltd inj/pe] 1/72nd Hawker Typhoon Mk Ia 'Early & Late Production' #BRP72012 (2014)
- Chematic, Poland (ex-Frog) [inj] 1/72nd Typhoon #072104 (1996)
- CMR, Czech Republic [res] 1/72nd Typhoon Ib 'Early' #077 (1997 £13.95) – Reissued as Mk Ia/IIb 'Early version' with decals in 2003 #5077; as Mk Ib 'Early Version' once again in 2006 as #172
- CMR, Czech Republic [res] 1/72nd Typhoon Prototype/Mk IA #133 (2003) – Reissued in 2006
- CMR, Czech Republic [res] 1/72nd Typhoon NF Mk Ib #181 (2007)
- DFI, Russia (ex-Frog) [inj] 1/72nd Typhoon Mk Ib #U-3888 (1980s)
- Double Eagle Hobby, USA [vac] 1/72nd Typhoon Mk Ib – Announced in 1991 but never released, was to have been produced for them by JMK
- Eastern Express, Russia (ex-Frog) [inj] 1/72nd Typhoon #72279
- Frog, UK [inj] 1/72nd Typhoon Mk Ib 'Bubbletop' #389P (1959-1964) – Renumbered #F.389 (1964-1968) then #F.209F (1968-1974) before returning to #F389 (1974-1976)
- Frog, UK [inj] 1/72nd Typhoon Mk Ib #F.231 (Announced 1974, released Oct 1975 – 1977) – Initially listed as #F182 in the Spin-a-Prop range
- Frog 'Penguin', UK 1/72nd Hawker Typhoon FB.IB #101P (1946-1949)
- Heller, France (ex-Airfix) [inj] 1/72nd Typhoon Mk Ib #79727 (1995) – Classic Kit series
- Heller, France (ex-Airfix) [inj] 1/72nd Typhoon Mk Ib #59727 (2000) – Rapid Kit series
- Hema, The Netherlands (ex-Frog) [inj] 1/72nd Hawker Typhoon Mk Ib – Offered as part of the group kit set #15521104 (early 80s)
- Herna (ex-Frog) [inj] 1/72nd Typhoon Mk Ib #F209H
- High Planes Models, Australia [ltd inj/res/mtl/vac] 1/72nd Typhoon Mk Ib 'late war variant with rockets' #7234 (1997)

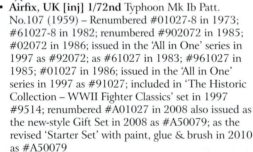
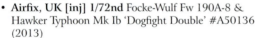

Tornado & Typhoon Kits   161

- **High Planes Models, Australia [ltd inj/res/mtl/vac]** 1/72nd Typhoon '2nd TAF Bombers, 1944' #7298 – *Due 2011*
- **JMK, Poland [vac]** 1/72nd Typhoon Mk Ib #N/K – *Announced 1991 but never released*
- **LF Models, Czech Republic [res]** 1/72nd Hawker Tornado [P5219] #7213 (2000)
- **Maintrack Models, UK [res]** 1/72nd Tornado Mk 1 conversion for the Airfix Typhoon kit #72:34 (1995)
- **Maintrack Models, UK [res]** 1/72nd Tornado 'Centauro' conversion for the Airfix Typhoon kit #72:38 (1997)
- **Maquette, Russia (ex-Frog) [inj]** 1/72nd Typhoon Mk Ib #7202
- **Master Models, The Netherlands (ex-CMR) [res]** 1/72nd Typhoon Mk Ib 'Early' #N/K (1990-1994)
- **Minicraft, USA (ex-Frog) [inj]** 1/72nd Typhoon Mk Ib #389 (1972)
- **Minix, Poland (ex-Frog) [inj]** Typhoon Mk Ib #F209M
- **Novo, Russia (ex-Frog) [inj]** 1/72nd Typhoon Mk Ib 'Bubbletop' #76004 (1977-1980)
- **Novo, Russia (ex-Frog) [inj]** 1/72nd Typhoon Mk Ib 'Car-door' #78078 (1980)
- **NovoExport, USSR (ex-Frog) [inj]** 1/72nd Typhoon Mk Ib 'Bubbletop' #76004 – (1977-1980)
- **NovoExport, USSR (ex-Frog) [inj]** 1/72nd Typhoon Mk Ib 'Car-door' #78121 (1977-1980)
- **Pavla Models, Czech Republic [ltd inj/res/vac]** 1/72nd Typhoon Mk Ib (Car Door) #72044 (2003)
- **Project-X, UK [vac]** 1/72nd Hawker Tornado Mk I #PX-034 – *Announced but never released*
- **R&D Replicas, USA [ltd inj]** 1/72nd Hawker Typhoon Mk I #A72.5 (1994-1999)
- **Roly Toys, Brazil (ex-Frog) [inj]** 1/72nd Hawker Typhoon Mk Ib #F.389 (mid-1970s)
- **RPM, Poland (ex-Frog) [inj]** 1/72nd Typhoon Mk Ib #72029 (1996)
- **Tashigrushka, Russia (ex-Frog) [inj]** 1/72nd Typhoon Mk Ib 'Car-door' #TG-65 (early 80s)
- **Xotic-72/Aviation Usk, USA [ltd inj]** 1/72nd Hawker Tornado #N/K – *Announced for 2004, never released*

1/48th

- **Bandai, Japan (ex-Monogram) [inj]** 1/48th Hawker Typhoon Mk Ib #8930 (1970s)
- **Hasegawa, Japan (ex-Monogram) [inj]** 1/48th Typhoon Mk Ib #HM13 (1990-1999)
- **Hasegawa, Japan [inj]** 1/48th Typhoon Mk Ib #JT59 (1998) – Reissued 2011
- **Hasegawa, Japan [inj]** 1/48th Typhoon Mk Ib 'Teardrop canopy' #JT60 (1999)
- **Hasegawa, Japan [inj]** 1/48th Typhoon Mk Ib with four-blade propeller #09311 (1999)
- **Hasegawa, Japan [inj]** 1/48th Typhoon Mk Ib 'Superdetail' #CH40 (1999) – *Limited edition, with KMC resin interior and flaps*
- **Hasegawa, Japan [inj]** 1/48th Typhoon Mk Ib 'Early' #JT183 (1999)
- **Hasegawa, Japan [inj]** 1/48th Typhoon Mk Ib Early Version 'No.56 Squadron' #09548 (2004) – *Limited edition*
- **Hasegawa, Japan [inj]** 1/48th Typhoon Mk Ib 'No.137 Squadron' #09379 (2001) – *Limited edition*
- **Hasegawa, Japan [inj]** 1/48th Typhoon Mk Ib 'No.193 Squadron' #09464 (2001) – *Limited edition*
- **Hasegawa, Japan [inj]** 1/48th Typhoon Mk Ib 'No.198 Squadron' #09862 (2009) – *Limited edition*
- **Italeri, Italy** 1/48th (ex-Hasegawa) Hawker Typhoon Mk Ib #2734 (2014)
- **Monogram, USA [inj]** 1/48th Typhoon Mk Ib #6136 (1969) – #6841 in 1973 catalogue and #5303 in the 1987 catalogue, 1991 as #5221, 11/1994 and 1997 as #5221
- **Monogram, USA [inj]** 1/48th Typhoon Mk Ib #85-6841 (1999) – *Limited edition reissue with original boxart in the 'Monogram Classics' series*

1/32nd

- **Model Design Construction, UK [res]** 1/32nd Typhoon Mk Ib #CV32037 (2005)
- **Revell, Germany [inj]** 1/32nd Typhoon Mk Ib #H-266 (1973) – Reissed in the History Makers series as #8616 in 1983, again in 1989 as #4782
- **Revell/USA [inj]** 1/32nd Typhoon Mk Ib #85-4663 (1996) – *This was the Revell-Monogram packaging for the US market*

1/24th

- **Airfix, UK [inj]** 1/24th Hawker Typhoon Mk Ib #A19002 (2014)
- **Airfix, UK [inj]** 1/24th Hawker Typhoon Mk Ib 'Car Door' #TBA – *Due in 2016*

```
Notes
inj         -   Injection Moulded Plastic
ltd inj     -   Limited-run Injection Moulded Plastic
mtl         -   White-metal (including Pewter)
res         -   Resin
vac         -   Vacuum-formed Plastic
(1999)      -   Denotes date the kit was released
(1994->)    -   Date denotes start of firm's activities, the exact
                date of release of this kit is however
                not known
ex-         -   Denotes the tooling originated with another
                firm, the original tool maker is noted after
                the '-'
CMR – This brand name is used to cover CzechMaster and Czech
Master Resin releases, as the former is the generic term used for
cottage industry production before the fall of the Iron Curtain,
while the later is the name used after this event by the particular
producer who previously offered the Typhoon under the generic
CzechMaster brand.
```

Appendix: II Tornado & Typhoon Accessories

QB72062 Typhoon Exhausts

Pavla S72036 Typhoon Pilot's Seat

Quickboost QB72460

BarracudaCast BR72136

QB72118 Typhoon Tailplanes

Aires 7315

Resin Art 7312

Below is a list of all accessories for static scale construction kits produced to date for the Hawker Tornado & Typhoon. This list is as comprehensive as possible, but if there are amendments or additions, please contact the author via the Valiant Wings Publishing address shown at the front of this title.

1/72nd

- Aeroclub 1/72nd [mtl] Hawker Typhoon Early Cannon Barrels #G040
- Aires 1/72nd [res] Hawker Typhoon Mk Ib Wheels and paint masks #7302
- Aires 1/72nd [res/vma] Hawker Typhoon Mk Ib Control Surfaces #7314 {Airfix}
- Airwaves 1/72nd [pe] Hawker Typhoon Detail Set #AEC72196 {Airfix}
- Airwaves 1/72nd [pe] Hawker Typhoon Flaps #AEC72197 {Airfix}
- Airwaves 1/72nd [res] Hawker Typhoon 1,000lb Bombs and Racks #AES72134
- Airwaves 1/72nd [res] Hawker Typhoon 45 Gallon Drop Tanks #AES72135
- Airwaves 1/72nd [res] RAF Mk 3 Rocket Rails x8 #AES72137
- BarracudaCast 1/72nd [res] Hawker Typhoon, Tempest Series I Main Wheels #BR72136
- Brengun 1/72nd [pe] Hawker Typhoon Mk Ib Air Intake Mesh #BRL72018 {Academy}
- Brengun 1/72nd [pe] Hawker Typhoon Mk Ib Detail Set #BRL72048 {Brengun}
- Brengun 1/72nd [pe] Hawker Typhoon Mk Ib Detail Set #BRL72057 {Airfix}
- Brengun 1/72nd [pe] Hawker Typhoon Mk Ib Air Intake Mesh #BRL72058 {Airfix}
- Brengun 1/72nd [pe/r] Hawker Typhoon Mk Ib 'Car Door' Detail Set #BRL72062 {Brengun}
- CMK 1/72nd [res/pe] Hawker Typhoon Mk Ib Interior #7022 {Academy}

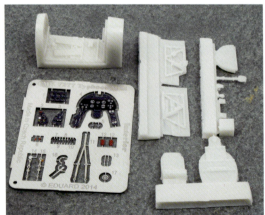

CMK 7277

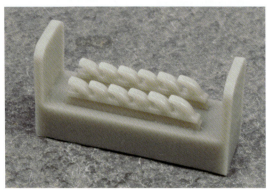

Quickboost QB72460

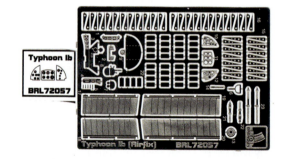

Brengun BRL72057

Scale Aircraft Conversions 72073

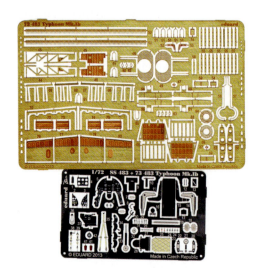

Eduard 72-483

Notes
br	-	Brass
ma	-	Die-cut Self-adhesive Paint Masks
mtl	-	White-metal (including Pewter)
pe	-	Photo-etched Brass
res	-	Resin
vac	-	Vacuum-formed Plastic
vma	-	Vinyl Self-adhesive Paint Masks
{Academy}	-	Denotes the kit for which the set is intended

Tornado & Typhoon Accessories 163

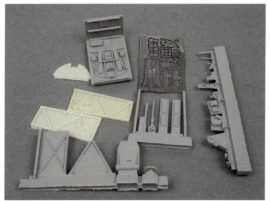
Aires 4366 Typhoon Car Door Cockpit Set

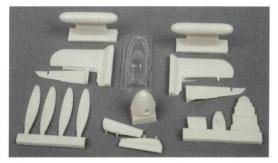
Pavla 7237 Typhoon Mk Ib Late Update Set

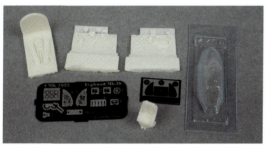
CMK 7022

QB72214 Typhoon Exhausts

Aires 4399 Typhoon Undercarriage Set

- CMK 1/72nd [res/pe] Hawker Typhoon Mk I 'Bubble Canopy' Interior #7277 {Airfix}
- CMK 1/72nd [res] Hawker Typhoon Mk I Armament Set #7278 {Airfix}
- CMK 1/72nd [res] Hawker Typhoon Mk I Undercarriage Set #7279 {Airfix}
- CMK 1/72nd [res] Hawker Typhoon Mk I Control Surfaces #7280 {Airfix}
- CMK 1/72nd [res] Hawker Typhoon Mk I Engine Set #7295 {Airfix}
- Eduard 1/72nd [pe] Hawker Typhoon Mk Ib Detail Set #72-304 {Academy}
- Eduard 1/72nd [pe] Hawker Typhoon Mk Ib Landing Flaps #72-567 {Airfix}
- Eduard 1/72nd [pe] Hawker Typhoon Mk Ib Detail Set, Pre-painted/Self-adhesive #73-483 {Airfix}
- Eduard 1/72nd [pe] Hawker Typhoon Mk Ib 'Zoom' Detail Set, Pre-painted/Self-adhesive #SS483 {Airfix}
- Eduard 1/72nd [ma] Hawker Typhoon Mk IB 'Car Door' Canopy & Wheel Masks #CX061 {Academy}
- Eduard 1/72nd (ma) Hawker Typhoon Mk Ib Canopy & Wheel Masks # CX363 {Airfix}
- Falcon 1/72nd [vac] RAF Fighters WWII Part 1 includes Hawker Typhoon Mk Ib Set #02
- Falcon 1/72nd [vac] RAF WWII Part 4 includes Hawker Typhoon 'Car Door' Set #22
- Freightdog 1/72nd [res] Hawker Typhoon Mk Ib Weapons Set #FDR72006 {Airfix}
- Freightdog 1/72nd [res] Hawker Typhoon Mk Ib 'Cuckoo Doors' #FDR72007 {Airfix}
- Kora 1/72nd [res] Hawker Typhoon Wheels, Early #D7285
- Master Models 1/72nd [br] Hawker Typhoon Mk Ib Early Type Cannon with uncovered barrels #AM-72-064
- Master Models 1/72nd [br] Hawker Typhoon Mk Ib Late Type Cannon with covered barrels #AM-72-065
- Montex 1/72nd [vma] Typhoon Mk Ib Canopy Masks #MM72038 {Academy}
- Montex 1/72nd [vma] Typhoon Mk Ib Canopy Masks #MM72202 {Airfix}
- Montex 1/72nd [vma] Typhoon Mk Ia Canopy Masks #MM72234 {Brengun}
- Montex 1/72nd [vma] Typhoon Mk Ib Canopy Masks #MM72235 {Brengun}
- Pavla Models 1/72nd [res] Hawker Typhoon Mk Ib (Late) Update Set #U7237 {Academy}
- Pavla Models 1/72nd [res] Hawker Typhoon/Tempest Pilot's Seat #S72036
- P-Mask 1/72nd [vma] Typhoon Mk Ib Canopy & Wheel Masks #Pk72006 {Airfix}
- Quickboost 1/72nd [res] Hawker Typhoon Exhausts #QB72062 {Academy}
- Quickboost 1/72nd [res] Hawker Typhoon Ib Exhausts #QB72460 {Airfix}
- Quickboost 1/72nd [res] Hawker Typhoon Mk Ib Late Stabilizers #QB72118 {Academy}
- Quickboost 1/72nd [res] Hawker Typhoon Exhausts #QB72214 {HobbyBoss}

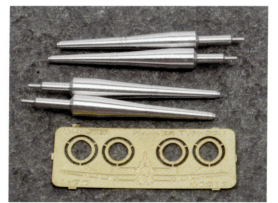
Master Model AM-72-065

Aires 7302

Resin Art 7315

Eduard 72-567

Master Model AM-72-064

Resin Art 7316

QB48264 Typhoon Cannon Barrels

CMK 4165

Cutting Edge CEC48150 Typhoon Exhausts

Ultracast 48074

Ultracast 48072

Ultracast 48057

CMK 4164 Typhoon Undercarriage Set

Ultracast 48178

Cutting Edge CEC48148 Typhoon Pilot Seats

Ultracast 48059

- Quickboost 1/72nd [res] Hawker Typhoon Exhausts #QB72460 {Airfix}
- Quick & Easy 1/72nd [res] Hawker Typhoon Mk I 'Bubble Canopy' Interior #Q72208 {Airfix}
- Resin Art 1/72nd [res] Hawker Typhoon Mk IB Radiator, Wheels & Pitot Tube #7312 {Academy}
- Resin Art 1/72nd [res] Hawker Typhoon de Havilland 3-blade Propeller #7315 {Academy}
- Resin Art 1/72nd [res] Hawker Typhoon Rotol 4-blade Propeller #7316 {Academy}
- Rob Taurus 1/72nd [vac] Hawker Typhoon 'Bubbletop' Canopy #72068 {Academy}
- Rob Taurus 1/72nd [vac/pe] Hawker Typhoon 'Bubbletop' Canopy & Detail Set #S72601 {Academy}
- Scale Aircraft Conversions 1/72nd [mtl] Hawker Typhoon Landing Gear #72073 {Airfix}
- Scale Resin (ex-Resin Art) 1/72nd [res] Hawker Typhoon Mk Ib Radiator, Wheels & Pitot Tube #RA7312 {Academy}
- Scale Resin (ex-Resin Art) 1/72nd [res] Hawker Typhoon de Havilland 3-blade Propeller #RA7315 {Academy}
- Scale Resin (ex-Resin Art) 1/72nd [res] Hawker Typhoon Rotol 4-blade Prop #RA7316 {Academy}
- Squadron 1/72nd [vac] Hawker Typhoon/Hawker Tempest Teardrop Canopy x2 #9110 {Airfix, Heller or Matchbox}
- Valiant Model Wings [res] Hawker Typhoon Detailing Set #MW0006
- Yahu Models 1/72nd [pe] Hawker Typhoon Mk Ib Instrument Panel #YMA7238 {Academy, Airfix & Brengun}

1/48th

- Airwaves 1/48th [pe] Hawker Typhoon Detail Set #AEC48079 {Monogram}
- Airwaves 1/48th [res] Hawker Typhoon 44 Gallon Drop Tanks and Pylons #SC48-35 {Hasegawa}
- Airwaves 1/48th [res] Hawker Typhoon Photo-Reconnaissance Conversion #SC48-53 {Hasegawa}
- Airwaves 1/48th Hawker Typhoon Fighter-Reconnaissance Conversion #SC48-54 {Hasegawa}
- Airwaves 1/48th [res] RAF Mk 3 Rocket Rails x8 #AES48105
- Aires 1/48th [res/pe] Hawker Typhoon Mk IB 'Car Door' Cockpit Set #4366 {Hasegawa}
- Aires 1/48th [res] Hawker Typhoon Wheel Bay #4399 {Hasegawa}
- Aires 1/48th [res/pe] Hawker Typhoon Mk Ib 'Car Door' Cockpit Set #4366 {Hasegawa}
- Aires 1/48th [res/pe] Hawker Typhoon Mk Ib 'Teardrop Canopy' Cockpit Set #4464 {Hasegawa}
- Aires 1/48th [res] Hawker Tyhoon Mk Ib Gun B Set #4506 {Hasegawa}
- Arba Products 1/48th [res] Hawker Tempest Tailplanes #N/K
- BarracudaCast 1/48th [res] Hawker Typhoon Mk Ib Cockpit Interior Set #BR48041 {Hasegawa}
- BarracudaCast 1/48th [res] Hawker Typhoon Mk Ib Intake and Exhausts #BR48042 {Hasegawa}
- BarracudaCast 1/48th [res] Hawker Typhoon, Tempest Series I Wheel Set #BR48138 {Hasegawa}
- Brengun 1/48th [pe] Air Intake Mesh for Hawker Typhoon Mk Ib #BRL48049 {Hasegawa}
- CMK 1/48th [res/pe] Hawker Typhoon Mk Ib Interior Set #4151 {Hasegawa}
- CMK 1/48th [res/pe] Hawker Typhoon Mk Ib Engine Set #4152 {Hasegawa}
- CMK 1/48th [res] Hawker Typhoon Undercarriage Set #4164 {Hasegawa}
- CMK 1/48th [res] Hawker Typhoon Separate Control Surfaces #4165 {Hasegawa}
- Cutting Edge 1/48th [res] Hawker Typhoon Fishtail Exhaust Stacks #CEC48150 {Hasegawa}

CMK 4151

Arba Tempest Tailplanes

QB48068 Typhoon Exhausts

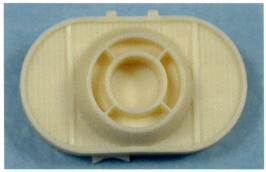
Ultracast 48058

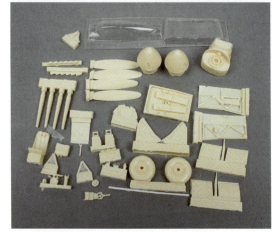
KMC 48-4018 Typhoon Car Door Update Set

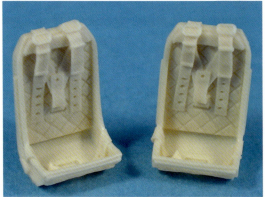
Ultracast 48018

Tornado & Typhoon Accessories 165

Engines & Things 48043 Sabre (Monogram)

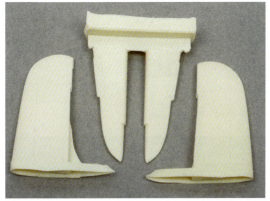

Ultracast 48080

Cutting Edge CEC48131 Typhoon Superdetail Set

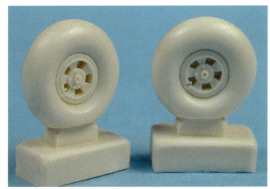

Ultracast 48073

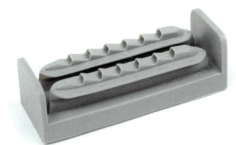

QB48276 Typhoon Exhausts

- Cutting Edge 1/48th [res] Hawker Typhoon Pilot's Seat x2 #CEC48184 {Hasegawa}
- Cutting Edge 1/48th [res] Hawker Typhoon Superdetailed Cockpit #CEC48131 {Hasegawa}
- Eduard 1/48th [pe] Hawker Typhoon Mk Ib Detail Set #48-275 {Hasegawa}
- Eduard 1/48th [pe] Hawker Typhoon 'Teardrop Canopy' Detail Set #48-297 {Hasegawa}
- Eduard 1/48th [vma] Hawker Typhoon Mk Ib Canopy & Wheel Masks #XF006 {Hasegawa}
- Eduard 1/48th [ma] Hawker Typhoon Mk Ib 'Car Door' Canopy & Wheel Masks #EX082 {Hasegawa}
- Eduard 1/48th [ma] Hawker Typhoon Mk Ib 'Teardrop Canopy' Canopy & Wheel Masks #EX090 {Hasegawa}
- Eduard 1/48th [pe/ma] Hawker Typhoon Mk Ib 'Big ED' detail sets & masks #BIG49117 {Has/Italeri}
- Eduard 1/48th [pe] Hawker Typhoon Mk Ib 'Bubbletop' Landing Flaps #48824 {Has/Italeri}
- Eduard 1/48th [pe] Hawker Typhoon Mk Ib 'Bubbletop' Detail Set, Pre-painted/Self-adhesive #49684 {Hasegawa/Italeri}
- Falcon 1/48th [vac] RAF Fighters WWII includes Hawker Typhoon Mk Ib 'Teardrop Canopy' Set #31 {Monogram}
- Engines & Things 1/48th [res] Hawker Typhoon Napier Sabre engine and firewall #48043 {Monogram}
- Jaguar 1/48th [res] Hawker Typhoon Detail Set #64811 {Hasegawa}
- Kendall Model Company 1/48th [res] Hawker Typhoon Car Door Update Set #48-4018 {Monogram}
- Kendall Model Company 1/48th [res] Hawker Typhoon 3-Blade Propeller & Spinner #48-5062 {Monogram or Hasegawa}
- Kendall Model Company 1/48th [res] Hawker Typhoon/Tempest 4-Blade Propeller & Spinner #48-5087 {Monogram, Eduard & Hasegawa}
- Master Models 1/48th [br/pe] Hawker Typhoon Mk Ib Early Type Cannon with uncovered barrels #AM-48-082 {Hasegawa}
- Master Models 1/48th [br/pe] Hawker Typhoon Mk Ib Late Type Cannon with covered barrels #AM-48-083 {Hasegawa}
- Montex 1/48th [vma] Typhoon Mk Ib 'Car Door' Canopy Masks #MM48019 {Hasegawa}
- Montex 1/48th [vma] Typhoon Mk Ib 'Bubbletop' Canopy Masks #MM48174 {Hasegawa}
- P-Mask 1/48th [vma] Typhoon Mk Ib Canopy & Wheel Masks #Pk48027 {Hasegawa/Italeri}
- Quickboost 1/48th [res] Hawker Typhoon Exhausts #QB48068 {Hasegawa}
- Quickboost 1/48th [res] Hawker Typhoon Mk Ib Cannon Barrels #QB48264 {Hasegawa}
- Quickboost 1/48th [res] Hawker Typhoon Exhausts - Shrouded #QB48276 {Hasegawa}
- Quickboost 1/48th [res] Hawker Typhoon Mk Ib Seat with safety belts #QB48268 {Hasegawa}
- Rob Taurus 1/48th [vac] Hawker Typhoon 'Car Door' early version Canopy #48053 {Hasegawa}
- Rob Taurus 1/48th [vac] Hawker Typhoon 'Car Door' early-mid version Canopy #48054 {Hasegawa}
- Rob Taurus 1/48th [vac] Hawker Typhoon 'Car Door' late version Canopy #48055 {Hasegawa}
- Rob Taurus 1/48th [vac] Hawker Typhoon 'Bubbletop' Canopy #48056 {Hasegawa}
- Scale Aircraft Conversions 1/48th [mtl] Hawker Typhoon Landing Gear #48161 {Hasegawa/Italeri}
- Squadron 1/48th [vac] Hawker Typhoon 'Teardrop' Canopy x2 #9510 {Monogram}
- Squadron 1/48th [vac] Hawker Typhoon 'Car Door' Canopy #9534 {Hasegawa}
- True Details 1/48th [res] Hawker Typhoon/Hawker Tempest Early Version Main Wheels with Smooth Tread #48036

Quickboost QB48468

Ultracast 48237

Airwaves SC48-35

KMC 48-5087 Typhoon 4 Blade Prop and Spinner

Ultracast 48056

Ultracast 48006

KMC 48-5062 Typhoon 3-blade Prop and Spinner

Tornado & Typhoon Accessories

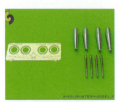
Master AM-48-082

MDC CV32019 Typhoon Wheels

MDC CV32018 Typhoon UC Legs

MDC CV32024 Typhoon Exhausts

Eduard CX363

Eduard LX001

Eduard 23-020

- True Details 1/48th [res] Hawker Typhoon Mk Ib Cockpit Detail Set #26014 {Monogram} ex-KMC
- Ultracast, 1/48th [res] Hawker Typhoon/Hurricane 44 Gal. Drop Tanks #48006
- Ultracast, 1/48th [res] Hawker Typhoon Seats with Sutton harness #48018
- Ultracast, 1/48th [res] Hawker Typhoon Control Surfaces #48056 {Hasegawa}
- Ultracast, 1/48th [res] Hawker Typhoon Exhausts #48057 {Hasegawa}
- Ultracast, 1/48th [res] Hawker Typhoon Radiator #48058 {Hasegawa}
- Ultracast, 1/48th [res] Hawker Typhoon Radiator with Dust Filter #48059 {Hasegawa}
- Ultracast, 1/48th [res] Hawker Typhoon/Tempest Seats with Mid-Late War 'Q' Type Harness # 48072
- Ultracast, 1/48th [res] Hawker Typhoon Wheels #48073
- Ultracast, 1/48th [res] Hawker Typhoon 4-Blade Propeller & Spinner #48074 {Hasegawa}
- Ultracast, 1/48th [res] Hawker Typhoon 'Tempest' Tailplanes #48080 {Hasegawa}
- Ultracast, 1/48th [res] Typhoon/Tempest Seats without harness #48178
- Ultracast, 1/48th [res] Typhoon Tail Wheel Well #48237 {Hasegawa}

1/32nd

- BarracudaCast 1/32nd [res] Hawker Typhoon Mk Ib/Tempest Series 1 Main wheels #BR32140 {MDC & Revell}
- BarracudaCast 1/32nd [res] Hawker Typhoon Mk Ib/Hawker Tempest Mk V Intake Ring #BR32141
- Model Design Construction 1/32nd [br] Hawker Typhoon Undercarriage Legs #CV32018
- Model Design Construction 1/32nd [res] Hawker Typhoon Wheels #CV32019
- Model Design Construction 1/32nd [res] Hawker Typhoon Three-blade Propeller & Spinner #CV32020
- Model Design Construction 1/32nd [res/mtl/pe] 3in 25lb AP Rocket Projectiles with rails [Mk 1] (Typhoon) x8 #CV32022
- Model Design Construction 1/32nd [res/mtl/pe] 3in 60lb HE Rocket Projectiles with rails [Mk 1] (Typhoon) x8 #CV32023
- Model Design Construction 1/32nd [res] Hawker Typhoon Exhausts #CV32024
- Model Design Construction 1/32nd [res/pe] Hawker Typhoon Cockpit Set #CV32030
- Model Design Construction 1/32nd [res/mtl/pe] 3in 60lb HE Rocket Projectiles with rails, Late War [Mk 3] (Typhoon) x8 #CV32035
- Model Design Construction 1/32nd [res/mtl/pe] 3in 25lb AP Rocket Projectiles with rails, Late War [Mk 3] (Typhoon) x8 #CV32036
- Model Design Construction 1/32nd [res] Hawker Typhoon Wings #CV32038
- Model Design Construction 1/32nd [res/mtl/pe] MC 500lb with Tail No.28 Mk 2 #CV32050
- Model Design Construction 1/32nd [res/mtl/pe] MC 500lb with Tail No.26 Mk 3 #CV32052
- Model Design Construction 1/32nd [res/mtl/pe] GP 1000lb with Tail No.29 Mk 1 #CV32053
- Montex 1/32nd [vma] Hawker Typhoon Mk Ib 'Car Door' Canopy Masks #MM32045 {Revell}'
- Squadron 1/32nd [vac] Hawker Typhoon 'Car Door' Canopy #9411 {Revell}

1/24th

- BarracudaCast 1/24th [res] Hawker Typhoon Mk Ib Seat with no seat belts #BR24200 {Airfix}
- BarracudaCast 1/24th [res] Hawker Typhoon Mk Ib Main Wheels #BR24201 {Airfix}
- BarracudaCast 1/24th [res] Hawker Typhoon Mk Ib

Jaguar 64811 Typhoon Detail Set

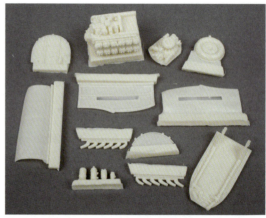
CMK 4152 Typhoon Engine Set

MDC CV32030 Typhoon Cockpit Set

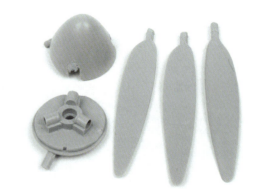
MDC CV32020 Typhoon Prop & Spinner

Tornado & Typhoon Accessories

MA-24001 – Etched

MA-24001 – Etched

Mk I Design MA-24001

MA-24001 – Brass

MA-24001 – Brass Rockets   MA-24001 – Metal

MA-24001 – Resin

Brassin 642001

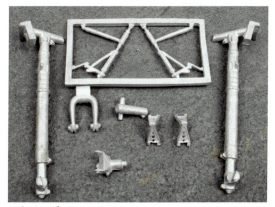
Scale Aircraft Conversions 24008

Brassin 642002

Eduard 23-016

- Carburettor Intake #BR24202 {Airfix}
- BarracudaCast 1/24th [res] Hawker Typhoon Mk Ib Gun Bay Upgrade #BR24203 {Airfix}
- BarracudaCast 1/24th [res] Hawker Typhoon Mk Ib Seat with belt #BR24204 {Airfix}
- BarracudaCast 1/24th [res] Hawker Typhoon Mk Ib Early Rockets #BR24206 {Airfix}
- BarracudaCast 1/24th [res] Hawker Typhoon Mk Ib Standing Pilot Figure, Mid-war #BR24208 {Airfix}
- Brassin 1/24th [res] Hawker Typhoon Mk Ib Wheels #624001 {Airfix}
- Brassin 1/24th [res] Hawker Typhoon Mk Ib Guns #624002 {Airfix}
- Eduard 1/24th [pe] Typhoon Mk Ib Seat Belts, pre-painted #23-016 {Airfix}
- Eduard 1/24th [pe] Typhoon Mk Ib Engine (Bay) Detail Set #23-017 {Airfix}
- Eduard 1/24th [pe] Typhoon Mk Ib Landing Flaps #23-018 {Airfix}
- Eduard 1/24th [pe] Typhoon Mk Ib Interior Detail Set, Pre-painted, Self-adhesive #23-019 {Airfix}
- Eduard 1/24th [pe/pa] Typhoon Mk Ib Seat Belts, Fabric #23-020 {Airfix}
- Eduard 1/24th [pe] Typhoon Mk Ib Wing Armament Detail Set #23-021 {Airfix}
- Eduard 1/24th [ma] Typhoon Mk Ib Canopy & Wheel Masks #LX001 {Airfix}
- Eduard 1/24th [pe/ma] Hawker Typhoon Mk Ib 'Big ED' detail sets & masks #BIG2401 {Airfix}
- HGW 1/24th [pe/pa] Seat Belts for Hawker Typhoon Mk Ib #124507 {Airfix}
- Mk 1 Design 1/24th [r/mtl/br/pe] Hawker Typhoon Mk Ib Detail Up Parts #MA-24001 {Airfix}
- Master Models 1/24th [br/pe] Hispano Mk II 20mm Cannon #AM-24-004
- Master Models 1/24th [br/pe] British 3in Rockets with 60lb SAP Heads x8 for Early Mk I Rails #AM-24-011
- Master Models 1/24th [br/pe] British 3in Rockets with 60lb SAP Heads x8 for Late Mk III Rails #AM-24-012
- Master Models 1/24th [br/pe] Additional Types of Warheads for British 3in Rockets [60lb Fragmentation, 25lp AP Mk I & II, 25lb SAP #AM-24-011
- Montex 1/24th [vma] Typhoon Mk Ib Canopy Masks #MM24016 {Airfix}
- P-Mask 1/24th [vma] Typhoon Mk Ib Canopy & Wheel Masks #Pk24001 {Airfix}
- RB Productions 1/24th [pe] Typhoon Radiators #RB-P24007 {Airfix}
- Scale Aircraft Conversions 1/24th [mtl] Hawker Typhoon Landing Gear #24008 {Airfix}

Eduard 23-019

BarracudaCast BR24202

BarracudaCast BR24204

Eduard 23-021

Eduard 23-018

Eduard 23-017

Master AM-24-004

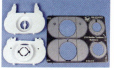
Master AM-24-011

RB-Productions RB-P24007

Appendix III: Hawker Typhoon Decals & Masks

Below is a list of all the decal sheets and self-adhesive paint masks produced to date of the Hawker Typhoon that we could find. This list is as comprehensive as possible, but there are bound to be omissions so if there are amendments or additions, please contact the author via the Valiant Wings Publishing address shown at the front of this title.

Decals

AeroMaster

1/48th #48-059 Storms in the Sky
- Hawker Typhoon Mk Ib, RB407, F3•T, 'Tess', No.438 Sqn, Holland, 1945
- Hawker Typhoon Mk Ib car-door, R8639, FM•B, flown by Fg Off Cedric Henman, No.257 Sqn
- Hawker Typhoon Mk Ib car-door, JP648, JE•D, flown by Fg Off K.A.J. Trott, No.195 Sqn, September 1945
- Hawker Typhoon Mk Ib, RB382, BR•M, flown by Fg Off A.E. Pavitt, No.184 Sqn, July 1945
- Hawker Typhoon Mk Ib, PD589, I8•R, No.440 Sqn, November 1944
- Hawker Typhoon Mk Ib, RB222, TP•F, No.198 Sqn during the Battle of Falaise Gap, mid-August 1944

1/48th #48-282 Storms in the Sky Part 2
- Hawker Typhoon Mk Ib, MN454, HF•S, flown by Sqn Ldr Scarlet, No.183 Sqn, early 1944
- Hawker Typhoon Mk Ib, MN518, R•D, flown by Wg Cdr R.T.P. Davidson, No.143 Wing, May 1944
- Hawker Typhoon Mk Ib, JR535, SF•B, No.137 Sqn, early 1944
- Hawker Typhoon Mk Ib, MN819, MR•?, flown by Sqn Ldr Jack Collins, No.245 Sqn, Holmsley South, 1944

1/48th #48-283 Storms in the Sky Part 3
- Hawker Typhoon Mk Ib, RB281, 5V•V, No.439 Sqn, 2nd TAF, early 1945
- Hawker Typhoon FR Mk Ib, EK427, •S, No.4 Sqn, 2nd TAF
- Hawker Typhoon Mk Ib, SW470, 'JB', flown by Gp Capt J. Baldwin
- Hawker Typhoon Mk Ib, RB455, FJ•H, 'Doreen', No.164 Sqn, 2nd TAF

1/48th #48-284 Storms in the Sky Part 4*
- Hawker Typhoon Mk Ib, RB248, ZH•B, No.266 Sqn, Hiddesheim, late 1945
- Hawker Typhoon Mk Ib, SW417, MR•X, No.245 Sqn, August 1945

- Hawker Typhoon Mk Ib, SW493, DP•S, 'Betty', No.193 Sqn, mid-1945
- Hawker Typhoon Mk Ib, SW411, PR•J, No.609 Sqn, September 1945
- *Main header marked as 'Part 3', but this was in fact Part 4 – Note that Parts 5, 6 & 7 dealt only with the Tempest, so are not included here

1/48th #48-372 Storms in the Sky Part VIII - car-door Typhoons
- Hawker Typhoon Mk I, R7648, US•A, 'Farquhar IV', No.56 Sqn, flown by Sqn Ldr Cocky Dundas, June 1942
- Hawker Typhoon Mk I, N/K, Z•Z, Duxford Wing, flown by Denys Gilliam
- Hawker Typhoon Mk I, R7752, PR•G, No.609 Sqn, flown by Sqn Ldr R.P. Beaumont
- Hawker Typhoon Mk I, R8893, XM•M, No.182 Sqn, November 1942
- Hawker Typhoon Mk I, DN406, PR•F, 'Mavis', No.609 Sqn

1/48th #48-373 Storms in the Sky Part IX - car-door Typhoons
- Hawker Typhoon Mk I, R8224, US•H, No.56 Sqn, Summer 1943
- Hawker Typhoon Mk I, EK270, EL•X, No.181 Sqn, flown by Sqn Ldr Crowley-Milling, June 1943
- Hawker Typhoon Mk I, R8871, EL•G, 'Cemetery Bait II', No.181 Sqn, mid-1943
- Hawker Typhoon Mk I, DN267, DP•B, 'Northern Star', No.193 Sqn
- Hawker Typhoon Mk I, EK273, JE•DT, No.195 Sqn, flown by Sqn Ldr Don 'Butch' Taylor

1/48th #48-436 Storms in the Sky Part X
- Hawker Typhoon Mk Ib, DN384, HF•D, No.183 Sqn, Exercise 'Spartan', March 1943
- Hawker Typhoon Mk Ib, JP504, DV•Z, No.197 Sqn, 1943
- Hawker Typhoon Mk Ib, RB742, EL•A, No.181 Sqn, Exercise 'Spartan', March 1943
- Hawker Typhoon Mk Ib, R7855, PR•D, A Flight, No.609 Sqm, RAF Manston, April 1943
- Hawker Typhoon Mk Ib, DN323, No.461 Sqn, Idku, Egypt, 1943
- Hawker Typhoon Mk Ib, DN421, EL•C, No.181 Sqn, April 1943
- Hawker Typhoon Mk Ib, R7881, RAE Farnborough, November 1942-March 1943
- Hawker Typhoon NF Mk Ib, EK273, JE•DT. No.195 Sqn, June 1943

1/48th #48-490 Storms in the Sky Part XI
- Hawker Typhoon Mk Ib, JP496, HH•W, No.175 Sqn, flown by Sqn Ldr R.T.P. Davidson, Lydd, September 1943
- Hawker Typhoon Mk Ib, MM987, TP•Z, No.198 Sqn, flown by Sqn Ldr J.R. Baldwin, RAF Manston, March 1944
- Hawker Typhoon Mk Ib, PD521, 'JBII', No.146 Wing, flown by Wg Cdr J.R. Baldwin, B.70 Antwerp, November 1944

1/48th #48-491 Storms in the Sky Part XII
- Hawker Typhoon Mk Ib, JP510, FM•A No.257 Sqn, flown by Sqn Ldr R.H. Fokes, RAF Warmwell, August 1943
- Hawker Typhoon Mk Ib, R8843, DJ•S, Tangmere Wing, flown by Wg Cdr D.J. Scott, September 1943

AeroMaster 48-282

AeroMaster 48-283

AeroMaster 48-373

AeroMaster 48-490

AeroMaster 48-436

AeroMaster 48-491

AeroMaster 48-284

Hawker Typhoon Decals & Masks 169

Aviaeology AOD24C08

Aviaeology AOD24S03

Aviaeology AOD24008 Part 1

Aviaeology AOD24008 Part 2

Airscale

1/24th AS24 TIFF Hawker Typhoon Mk Ib Instrument & Placard Upgrade Set {Airfix}

Aviaeology

1/72nd #OD72003 Sharksmouth Hawker Typhoon
- Hawker Typhoon Mk Ib, MP197, MR•U, No.245 Sqn, flown by H.T. 'Moose' Mossip and Tony Zweigbergk, 2nd TAF, 1944/45
- Hawker Typhoon Mk Ib, MP197, MR•U, No.245 Sqn, BAFO, 1945 in immediate post-war markings
- Hawker Typhoon Mk Ib, SW460, MR•Z, 'Zephyr Breezes', No.245 Sqn, flown by Geoff Murphy, 2nd TAF, 1944/45. *As there is no definitive information on this machine the alternative series SW560 is also included*

1/72nd #AOD72008 - 143 Wing (RCAF) Typhoons: 438, 439 & 440 Sqns - 1944 thru to Bodenplatte
- Same options as on sheets #AOD24008 Part 1 and 2

1/72nd #AOD72C08 Hawker Typhoon Mk Ib National Markings (Early to Jan 1945)

1/72nd #AOD72S03 Hawker Typhoon Mk Ib Airframe Stencil Data

1/48th #AOD48003 Sharksmouth Hawker Typhoon
- Hawker Typhoon Mk Ib, MP197, MR•U, No.245 Sqn, flown by H.T. 'Moose' Mossip and Tony Zweigbergk, 2nd TAF, 1944/45
- Hawker Typhoon Mk Ib, MP197, MR•U, No.245 Sqn, BAFO, 1945 in immediate post-war markings
- Hawker Typhoon Mk Ib, SW460, MR•Z, 'Zephyr Breezes', No.245 Sqn, flown by Geoff Murphy, 2nd TAF, 1944/45. *As there is no definitive information on this machine the alternative series SW560 is also included*

1/48th #OD48008 - 143 Wing (RCAF) Typhoons: 438, 439 & 440 Sqns - 1944 thru to Bodenplatte
- Same options as on sheets #AOD24008 Part 1 and 2

1/48th #OD48C08 Hawker Typhoon Mk Ib National Markings (Early to Jan 1945)

1/48th #OD48S03 Hawker Typhoon Mk Ib Airframe Stencil Data

1/32nd #OD32003 Sharksmouth Hawker Typhoon
- Hawker Typhoon Mk Ib, MP197, MR•U, No.245 Sqn, flown by H.T. 'Moose' Mossip and Tony Zweigbergk, 2nd TAF, 1944/45
- Hawker Typhoon Mk Ib, MP197, MR•U, No.245 Sqn, BAFO, 1945 in immediate post-war markings
- Hawker Typhoon Mk Ib, SW460, MR•Z, 'Zephyr Breezes', No.245 Sqn, flown by Geoff Murphy, 2nd TAF, 1944/45. *As there is no definitive information on this machine the alternative series SW560 is also included*

1/32nd #OD32008 Part 1 - 143 Wing (RCAF) Typhoons: 438, 439 & 440 Sqns - 1944 thru to Bodenplatte
- Same options as #AD24008 Part 1

1/32nd #OD320082 Part 2 - 143 Wing (RCAF) Typhoons: 438, 439 & 440 Sqns - 1944 thru to Bodenplatte
- Same options as #AD24008

1/32nd #OD32C08 Hawker Typhoon Mk Ib National Markings (May 1942 to Jan 1945)
- Same options as #AD24C08

1/32nd #OD32S03 Part 2 - Hawker Typhoon Mk Ib Airframe Stencil Data
- Same options as #AD24S03

1/24th #AOD24008 Part 1 - 143 Wing (RCAF) Typhoons: 438, 439 & 440 Sqns - 1944 thru to Bodenplatte
- JR500, 5V•X, No.439 Sqn, flown by F/O R.A. Johns, B.9 Lantheuil, mid July 1944.
- MN957, F3•N, No.438 Sqn, flown by Wg Cdr Davidson when he forced landing in enemy territory on 8th May 1944.
- MN716, 'Diane', F3•A, No.438 Sqn, flown by Flt Sgt R.G. Fox, B.78 Eindhoven, autumn/winter 1944.
- MP149, 'Pulverizer II', I8•P, No.440 Sqn, flown by F/O H.J. 'Harry' Hardy, B.78 Eindhoven, autumn/winter 1944.
- MN311 'Pulverizer', I8•P, No.440 Sqn, flown by Flt Lt H.J. Hardy mid-August to 6th September 1944.
- MN426, F3•H, No.438 Sqn, flown Sqn Ldr F.G. Grant through July 1944.

1/24th #AOD24008 Part 2 143 Wing (RCAF) Typhoons: 438, 439 & 440 Sqns - 1944 thru to Bodenplatte
- MP131, F3•J, No.438 Sqn, flown by F/O N.E. Dawber from the crossing of the Channel in late June through to 18th November 1944
- MN345, 'Peace River', 5V•G, No.439 Squadron, flown by F/O J.A. Brown, B.78 Eindhoven, October thorough to 6th November 1944
- MN413, I8•T, No.440 Sqn, flown by Flt Sgt N.L Gordon, B.9 Lantheuil, 1st August 1944.
- MN518, R•D, No.143 Wing, flown by Wg Cdr R.T.P. Davidson up to 8th May 1944 and Wg Cdr M.T. Judd afterwards.
- RB205, •FGG, No.143 Wing, flown by Wg Cdr F.G. Grant from 26th October to 24th December 1944.

1/24th #AOD24C08 Hawker Typhoon Mk I National Markings (May 1942 to Jan 1945)

1/24th #AOD24S03 Hawker Typhoon Mk I Airframe Stencil Data

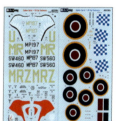
Aviaeology AOD48003

Aviaeology AOD32003

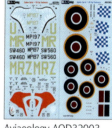
Aviaeology AOD48003 instructions

Airscale AS24

Dutch Decals DD2401

EagleCals EC159

EagleCals EC160

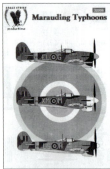
Eagle Strike 32006

Eagle Strike 72009

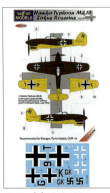
LF Models C72139

DP Casper

1/72nd #72003 Operation Bodenplatte Jan 1945
- Hawker Typhoon Mk Ib, QC•D, No.168 Sqn, Eindhoven
- Hawker Typhoon Mk Ib, NL•K, No.439 Sqn, Eindhoven

Dutch Decals

#DD2401 'Dutchies in the RAF'
- Inc. MP126, ZY•Y, No.247 Sqn, flown by Sqn Ldr Basil G. Stapleton

Eagle Cal

1/24th #159 Hawker Typhoon Part 1
- MN345, 'Peace River', 5V•G, No.439 Sqn, flown by F/O J.A Brown
- MP149, 'Pulverizer II', I8•P, No.440 Sqn, flown by F/O Harry Hardy DFC
- MN131, PR•M, No.609 Sqn, flown by Flt Lt L.E.J.M. Geerts

1/24th #160 Hawker Typhoon Part 2
- MP195, 'ZIPP X', Z•DP, No.193 Sqn, flown by Sqn Ldr J.C. Button
- MN951, 'The Uninvited', TP•A, No.198 Sqn, flown by Flt Lt Denis Sweeting
- MP126, ZY•Y, No.247 Sqn, flown by Sqn Ldr Basil G. Stapleton

Eagle Strike

1/72nd #72009 Typhoon Intruders
- Hawker Typhoon Mk Ib, SW417, MR•X, No.245 Sqn, August 1945
- Hawker Typhoon Mk Ib, SW470, 'JB', No.4 Sqn, 2nd TAF, Europe, 1945
- Hawker Typhoon Mk Ib, MN819, MR•?, No.245 Sqn, flown by Sqn Ldr J. Collins, Holmsley South, 1944
- Hawker Typhoon Mk Ib, SW493, DP•S, 'Betty', No.193 Sqn, mid-1945
- Hawker Typhoon Mk Ib, RB222, TP•F, No.198 Sqn, Battle of Falaise Gap, mid-August 1944
- Hawker Typhoon Mk Ib, RB248, ZH•B, No.266 Sqn, Hildesheim, late 1945

1/32nd #32006 Marauding Typhoon
- Hawker Typhoon Mk Ib, R8224, EL•G, No.181 Sqn, mid-1843
- Hawker Typhoon Mk Ib, R8893, XM•M, No.182 Sqn, November 1943
- Hawker Typhoon Mk Ib, R8871, US•H, 'Land Girl', No.56 Sqn, Summer 1943

Kora

1/72nd #Dec.72.265 Albion Lions in German Hands
- Hawker Typhoon Mk Ib Early in captured markings

1/48th #Dec.48.016 Albion Lions in German Hands
- Hawker Typhoon Mk Ib Early in captured markings

LF Models

1/72nd #C72139 Hawker Typhoon Mk Ib 'Zirkus Rosarius'
- Captured Mk Ib (Early) marked as T9+GK and operared by 2./Versuchsverband OKL, Köninsberg/Neumark airfield, flown by Fw. Herbert Gold, July 1944

1/48th #C74868 Hawker Typhoon Mk Ib 'Zirkus Rosarius'
- Captured Mk Ib (Early) marked as T9+GK and operared by 2./Versuchsverband OKL, Köninsberg/Neumark airfield, flown by Fw. Herbert Gold, July 1944

Model Alliance

1/48th #48204 WWII 2nd Tactical AF 1944-45
- Hawker Typhoon Mk Ib, JP671, XP•R, No.174 Sqn, Le Fresno-Camilly
- Hawker Typhoon Mk Ib, MN526, TP•V, No.198 Sqn, Plumetot
- Hawker Typhoon Mk Ib, MN639, QC•S, No.168 Sqn, Eindhoven

1/72nd #72204 WWII 2nd Tactical AF 1944-45
- Hawker Typhoon Mk Ib, JP671, XP•R, No.174 Sqn, Le Fresno-Camilly
- Hawker Typhoon Mk Ib, MN526, TP•V, No.198 Sqn, Plumetot
- Hawker Typhoon Mk Ib, MN639, QC•S, No.168 Sqn, Eindhoven

MPD/Mini Print Decals

1/72nd #72528
- Hawker Typhoon Mk IB, JP613, TP•N, No.198, flown by Sqn Ldr Jifi Manak

Superscale

1/72nd 72-719 RAF/RCAF Typhoon Ibs
- Hawker Typhoon Mk IB, JP148, I8•P, No.440 Sqn, 2nd TAF, Eindhoven, 1944
- Hawker Typhoon Mk IB, MN518, R•D, No.143 Wing, flown by Wg Cdr R.T.P. Davidson (RCAF), 1944
- Hawker Typhoon Mk IB, JR128, HF•L, No.183 Sqn, 1944
- Hawker Typhoon Mk IB, PD608, 5V•G, No.439 Sqn, 1945
- Hawker Typhoon Mk IB, SW564, HH•T, No.175 Sqn, 2nd TAF, 1945

1/48th 48-543 RAF/RCAF Typhoon Ibs
- Hawker Typhoon Mk IB, JP148, I8•P, No.440 Sqn, 2nd TAF, Eindhoven, 1944
- Hawker Typhoon Mk IB, MN518, R•D, No.143 Wing, flown by Wg Cdr R.T.P. Davidson (RCAF), 1944
- Hawker Typhoon Mk IB, JR128, HF•L, No.183 Sqn, 1944
- Hawker Typhoon Mk IB, PD608, 5V•G, No.439 Sqn, 1945
- Hawker Typhoon Mk IB, SW564, HH•T, No.175 Sqn, 2nd TAF, 1945

Techmod

1/72nd #72034 Hawker Typhoon Mk Ib
- Hawker Typhoon Mk IB, JP496, HH•W, No.175 Sqn, flown by Sqn Ldr T.P. Davidson, 1943
- Hawker Typhoon Mk IB, DN473, OV•E, No.179 Sqn
- Hawker Typhoon Mk IB, N406, PR•F, No.609 Sqn, RAF Manston, 1943

1/72nd #72042 Hawker Typhoon Mk Ib
- Hawker Typhoon Mk IB, JP510, FM•A, No.257 Sqn, flown by Sqn Ldr R. Fokes, RAF Warmwell, August 1943
- Hawker Typhoon Mk IB, R8925, •B, North Africa, early 1943
- Hawker Typhoon Mk IB, DN421, EL•C, No.187 Sqn, RAF Appledram, June 1943

- Hawker Typhoon Mk IB, R8781, SA•H, No.486 Sqn, flown by Sgt K.G. Taylor-Cannon, RAF Tangmere, December 1942

1/72nd #72061 Hawker Typhoon Mk Ib
- Hawker Typhoon Mk Ib, EK139, HN•N, No.175 Sqn, Spring 1943
- Hawker Typhoon Mk Ib, EK224, ZY•B, No.247 Sqn, RAF Bradwell Bay, June 1943
- Hawker Typhoon Mk Ib, EJ906, No.451 (RAAF) Sqn, El Daba, Egypt, 1943
- Hawker Typhoon Mk Ib, R7855, PR•D, No.609 Sqn, flown by A. Lallemant, Manston, February 1943

1/72nd #72062 Hawker Typhoon Mk Ib
- Hawker Typhoon Mk Ib, EK273, JE•DT, No.195 Sqn, flown by Sqn Ldr Don Taylor, Ludham, June 1943
- Hawker Typhoon Mk Ib, EK720, EL•X, No.181 Sqn, flown by Sqn Ldr D. Crowley-Milling, Appledram, June 1943
- Hawker Typhoon Mk Ib, R7752, PR•G, No.609 Sqn, flown by Sqd Ldr R.P. Beamont, Manson, February 1943

1/48th #48042 Hawker Typhoon Mk Ib
- Hawker Typhoon Mk IB, EK273, JE•DT, No.195 Sqn, flown by Sqn Ldr Don Taylor, Ludham, June 1943
- Hawker Typhoon Mk IB, EK270, EL•X, No.181 Sqn, flown by Sqn Ldr D. Crowley-Millington, Appledram, June 1943
- Hawker Typhoon Mk IB, R7752, PR•G, No.609 Sqn, flown by Sqn Ldr R.P. Beamont, RAF Manston, February 1943

1/48th #48043 Hawker Typhoon Mk Ib
- Hawker Typhoon Mk IB, JP496, HH•W, No.175 Sqn, flown by Sqn Ldr T.P. Davidson, Lydd, August 1943
- Hawker Typhoon Mk IB, DN473, OV•E, No.179 Sqn, May 1943
- Hawker Typhoon Mk IB, DN406, PR•F, No.609 Sqn, RAF Manston, March 1943

1/48th #48044 Hawker Typhoon Mk Ib
- Hawker Typhoon Mk IB, EK139, HH•N, No.175 Sqn, Spring 1943
- Hawker Typhoon Mk IB, EK224, ZY•B, No.247 Sqn, Bradwell Bay, June 1943
- Hawker Typhoon Mk IB, EJ906, No.451 Sqn, El Daba, Egypt, 1943
- Hawker Typhoon Mk IB, R7855, PR•D, No.609 Sqn, flown by A. Lallemant, RAF Manston, February 1943

1/48th #48045 Hawker Typhoon Mk Ib
- Hawker Typhoon Mk IB, JP510, FM•A, No.257 Sqn, flown by Sqn Ldr R.H. Folkes, RAF Warmwell, August 1943
- Hawker Typhoon Mk IB, R8925, •B, North Africa, early 1943
- Hawker Typhoon Mk IB, DN421, EL•C, No.187 Sqn, Appledram, June 1943
- Hawker Typhoon Mk IB, EJ981, SA•F, No.486 Sqn, flown by Sqn Ldr D.J. Scott, RAF Tangmere, June 1943
- Hawker Typhoon Mk IB, R8781, SA•H, No.486 Sqn, flown by Sgt K.G. Taylor-Cannon, RAF Tangmere, December 1942

1/32nd #32021 Hawker Typhoon Mk Ib
- Hawker Typhoon Mk IB, EK273, JE•DT, No.195, flown by Sqn Ldr Don Taylor, Ludham, 1943
- Hawker Typhoon Mk IB, R8781, SA•H, No.486 Sqn, flown by Sgt K.G. Taylor-Cannon
- Hawker Typhoon Mk IB, DN406, PR•F, No.609 Sqn, RAF Manston, 1943

- Hawker Typhoon Mk IB, JP496, HH•W, No.175 Sqn, flown by Sqn Ldr R.T.P. Davidson
- Hawker Typhoon Mk IB, EK139, HH•N, No.175 Sqn
- Hawker Typhoon Mk IB, EK270, EL•X, No.181 Sqn, flown by Sqn Ldr D.Crowley-Milling
- Hawker Typhoon Mk IB, R8925, •B, North Africa, 1943

Xtradecal

1/72nd #X72-149 No.1 Squadron 100 Years
- Inc. Hawker Typhoon Mk IB, R8752, JX•L, flown by F/Sgt W.H. Ramsey, RAF Lympe, 1943

1/72nd #X72-179 Hawker Typhoon Mk Ib
- MN317, ZY•B, No.247(China British) Sqn, No.124 Wing, RAF Hurn, 1944
- MN454 HF•S, No.183 Sqn, RAF Thorney Island, flown by Sqn Ldr the Honorable Felix Scarlett inspected by HM King George VI at RAF Northolt 3rd May 1944
- MN819, MR•?, No.245 Sqn, RAF Holmsley, 5th June 1944, flown by Sqn/Ldr J.Collins
- MP189, K•N, No.124 Wing, flown by Wg Cdr Kit North-Lewis, 1944
- MN855, WPB•, No.121 Wing, flown by Wg Cdr William Pitt-Brown, Volkel, 1944
- MN526, TP•V, No.198 Sqn, No.123 Wing, France, 1944
- MN639, OC•S, No.168 Sqn, 39 (Recce) Wing, Eindhoven, October 1944
- RB262, 5V•A, No.439 Sqn, No.143 Wing, Flensburg, 1945
- MN130, PR•M, No.609 Sqn, No.123 Wing, RAF Thorney Island, 6th June 1944
- JP602, XP•F, No.174 Sqn, No.121 Wing, Camilly, July 1944
- JP371, •A, No.268 Sqn, flown by F/O B. Rachinger, 1944

1/72nd #X72-194 D-Day 70th Anniversary Part 1
- Inc. Hawker Typhoon Mk Ib, NM293, TP•D, No.198 Sqn, flown by F/Sgt J.S. Fraser-Petherbridge, RAF Thorney Island
- Hawker Typhoon Mk Ib, MN625, MR•B, No.245 (Rhodesian) Sqn, flown by F/O W. Smith, RAF Holmesley South

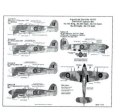

Superscale 48-543

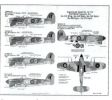

Superscale 72-719

Techmod 72061

Techmod 72063

Techmod 48042

Techmod 48044

Xtradecal X72149

Techmod 48045

Techmod 72042

Xtradecal X72194

Paint Masks

AMLM 33 009

AMLM 49 015

AMLM 73 011

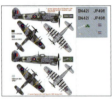
Montex K32291

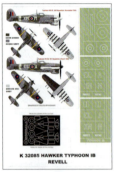
Montex K32085

Montex K48085

Montex MM48174

Note: For pure canopy and/or wheel masks, see the accessory section (Appendix II)

AML 1/72nd #AMLM 73 010
Hawker Typhoon Mk Ib 'Early Version' Camouflage Pattern Masks

AML 1/72nd #AMLM 73 011
Hawker Typhoon Mk Ib 'Late Version' Camouflage Pattern Masks

AML 1/48th #AMLM 49 014 [vma]
Hawker Typhoon Mk Ib 'Early Version' Camouflage Pattern Masks {Hasegawa}

AML 1/48th #AMLM 49 015
Hawker Typhoon Mk Ib 'Late Version' Camouflage Pattern Masks {Hasegawa}

AML 1/32nd #AMLM 33 008 [vma]
Hawker Typhoon Mk Ib 'Early Version' Camouflage Pattern Masks {Revell}

AML 1/32nd #AMLM 33 009 [vma]
Typhoon Mk Ib 'Late Version' Camouflage Pattern Masks {Revell}

Montex 1/48th #K48085
Typhoon Mk Ib 'Car Door' Canopy Masks plus 2x Marking Options
- RB893, XM•M, No.182 Sqn, November 1942
- RB742, EL•A. No.181 Sqn, March 1943

Montex 1/48th #K48086
Typhoon Mk Ib 'Car Door' Canopy Masks plus 2x Marking Options
- DN334, HF•D, No.183 Sqn, March 1943
- JP504, OV•Z, No.197 Sqn, flown by Sqn Ldr Holmes, RAF Tangmere, 1943

Montex 1/48th #K48087
Typhoon Mk Ib Canopy Masks plus 2x Marking Options
- DN334, HF•D, No.183 Sqn, March 1943
- JP504, OV•Z, No.197 Sqn, flown by Sqn Ldr Holmes, RAF Tangmere, 1943

Montex 1/48th #K48088
Typhoon Mk Ib Canopy Masks plus 2x Marking Options
- MN852, TP•Q, No.198 Sqn, July 1944
- JCB•, 'ZIPP-IX', flown by Wg Cdr J.C. Button, April 1945

Montex 1/48th #K48270
Typhoon Mk Ib 'Car Door' Canopy Masks plus 2x Marking Options
- DN421, HH•W, No.175 Sqn, flown by Sqn Ldr R.T.P. Davidson, RAF Lydd, August 1943
- JP496, EL•C, No.181 Sqn, Spring 1943

Montex 1/48th #K48272
Typhoon Mk Ib Canopy Masks plus 2x Marking Options
- MP149, 'Pulverizer II', I8•P, No.440 Sqn, flown by F/O Harry Hardy DFC
- MN518, R•D, No.143 Wing, flown by Wg Cdr R.T.P. Davidson, April 1944

Montex 1/48th #K48273
Typhoon Mk Ib Canopy Masks plus 2x Marking Options
- SW399, 'J-Babs VIII', HH•K, No.175 Sqn, Schleswig, Germany, July 1945
- MM987, TP•Z, No.198 Sqn, flown by Sqn Ldr J.R. Baldwin, RAF Manston, March 1944

Montex 1/48th #MM48019
Typhoon Mk Ib 'Bubbletop' Canopy & Kit Marking Options Masks {Hasgawa}

Montex 1/48th #MM48174
Typhoon Mk Ib 'Bubbletop' Canopy & Kit Marking Options Masks {Hasgawa}

Montex 1/32nd #K32085
Typhoon Mk Ib 'Car Door' Canopy Masks plus 2x Marking Options
- RB893, XM•M, No.182 Sqn, November 1942
- RB742, EL•A. No.181 Sqn, March 1943

Montex 1/32nd #K32086
Typhoon Mk Ib 'Car Door' Canopy Masks plus 2x Marking Options
- DN334, HF•D, No.183 Sqn, March 1943
- JP504, OV•Z, No.197 Sqn, flown by Sqn Ldr Holmes, RAF Tangmere, 1943

Montex 1/32nd #K32291
Typhoon Mk Ib 'Car Door' Canopy Masks plus 2x Marking Options
- DN421, HH•W, No.175 Sqn, flown by Sqn Ldr R.T.P. Davidson, RAF Lydd, August 1943
- JP496, EL•C, No.181 Sqn, Spring 1943

Montex 1/32nd #MM32045
Typhoon Mk Ib 'Car Door' Canopy & Kit Marking Options Masks {Revell}

Montex 1/24th #K24069
Typhoon Mk Ib Canopy Masks plus 2x Marking Options
- MP149, 'Pulverizer II', I8•P, No.440 Sqn, flown by F/O Harry Hardy DFC
- MN518, R•D, No.143 Wing, flown by Wg Cdr R.T.P. Davidson, April 1944

Montex 1/24th #K24070
Typhoon Mk Ib Canopy Masks plus 2x Marking Options
- SW399, 'J-Babs VIII', HH•K, No.175 Sqn, Schleswig, Germany, July 1945
- MM987, TP•Z, No.198 Sqn, flown by Sqn Ldr J.R. Baldwin, RAF Manston, March 1944

RB Productions 1/24th #RB-M24001
Typhoon Mk Ib Canopy Masks {Airfix}

Montex K24069

Appendix IV: Tornado & Typhoon Production

Tornado Prototype
Contract No. 815124/38
Hawker Aircraft Ltd, Langley
Quantity – 2
- P5219 & P5224

Tornado
Contract No. B12148/39
Hawker Aircraft Ltd, Langley
Quantity – 1,000
Cancelled and changed to 1,000 Typhoons, then amended to 200 Tornados & 800 Typhoons
- Serial Numbers – R7936-7975, R7992-8036, R8049-8091, R8105-8150 & R8172-8197

Sub-contracted to A.V. Roe & Co., with R7936 to R7938 as prototypes but in the end only R7936 was built

Tornado
Contract No. B97616/40
Cunliffe-Owen Ltd, Eastleigh
Quantity – 200
- Serial Numbers – X1056-1090, X1103-1117, X1166-1195, X1220-1264, X1297-1326 & X1343-1387

All subsequently cancelled

Tornado
Contract No. ACFT/944/C.23(a)
A.V. Roe & Co.
Quantity – 400
- Serial Numbers – DM594-642, DM664-709, DM727-776, DM794-842, DM857-900, DM921-856, DM975-999, DN112-134, DN148-197 & DN210-237

All subsequently cancelled

Tornado
Contract No. ACFT/944/C.23(a)
A.V. Roe & Co.
Quantity – 360
- Serial Numbers – EG708-747, EG763-810, EG819-845, EG860-897, EG915-959, EG974-994, EH107-156, EH171-211, EH228-261 & EH280-304

All subsequently cancelled

Tornado (Centaurus) Prototype
Contract No. SB21392/C.23(a)
Hawker Aircraft Ltd, Langley
Quantity – 1
- Serial Number – HG641

Typhoon Prototype
Contract No. 815124/38
Hawker Aircraft Ltd, Langley
Quantity – 2
- P5212 & P5216

Typhoon Mk Ia & Mk Ib
Contract No. B12148/39
Hawker Aircraft Ltd, Langley
Quantity – 800
Amendment to initial order for 1,000 Tornados, 800 of which were then changed to Typhoons.
- Only 515 built, remaining 285 (R8232-8621, R8275-8309, R8325-8364, R8377-8410, R8425-8468, R8484-8525, R8539-8572, R8590-8615) were cancelled
- 15 built by Hawker Aircraft Ltd (R8198-8200 & R8220-8231)
- 500 by Gloster Aircraft & Co. (R7576-7599, R7613-7655, R7672-7721, R7738-7775, R7792-7829, R7825-7890, R7913-7923, R7636-7975, R7992-R8036, R8049-8091, R8105-8150, R8172-8197, R8198-8200, R8220-8231, R8232-8261, R8275-8309, R8325-8364, R8377-8410, R8425-8468, R8484-8525, R8539-8572, R8590-8615, R8630-8663, R8680-8722, R8737-8781, R8799-8845, R8861-8900, R8923-8947, R8966-8981

A superbly atmospheric shot, showing a machine of No.183 Squadron running up prior to the mechanic handing over to the pilot for take-off. Note the groundcrew in the bottom left corner, fire extinguisher in hand!
(©Public Archive of Canada)

Factory-fresh Typhoon MN180 prior to a test flight at Hucclecote on the 10th January 1944 (©Gloster Aircraft Ltd/Crown Copyright)

'Fiji VI' (EK288) and 'Fiji V' (EK286) sit on the airfield at Hucclecote while a pilot prepares to get into the latter for a test flight in April 1943
(©Gloster Aircraft Ltd/Crown Copyright)

Car Door Mk Ib, EK286, 'Fiji V', Morris Hedstrom Ltd, Fiji' is seen at Hucclecote in April 1943. Note the factory-applied markings including roundels, fin flash, serial number, underwing ID stripes, fuselage band and Sky-painted spinner
(©Gloster Aircraft Ltd/Crown Copyright)

Typhoon
Contract No. B12148/39
Hawker Aircraft Ltd, Langley
Quantity – 570
- Serial Numbers – EJ175-222, EJ234-283, EJ296-334, EJ347-392, EJ405-454, EJ467-504, EJ518-560, EJ577-611, EJ626-672, EJ685-723, EJ739-788, EJ800-846 & EJ859-896

First 270 subsequently cancelled, all after EJ504 built as Tempest Mk Vs

Typhoon
Contract No. ACFT/943/C.23(a)
Gloster Aircraft Co., Hucclecote
Quantity – 425
- Serial Numbers – EJ899-934, EJ946-995, EK112-154, EK167-196, EK208-252, EK266-301, EK321-348, EK364-413, EK425-456, EK472-512, EK535-543, EK544-568

The last 25 (EK544-568) were subsequently cancelled

Typhoon Mk Ib
Contract No. ACFT/943/C.23(a)
Gloster Aircraft Co., Hucclecote
Quantity – 300
- Serial Numbers – DN241-279, DN293-341, DN356-389, DN404-453, DN467-512, DN529-562 & DN576-623

Typhoon Mk Ib
Contract No. ACFT/943/C.23(a)
Gloster Aircraft Co., Hucclecote
Quantity – 600
- Serial Numbers – JP361-408, JP425-447, JP480-516, JP532-552, JP576-614, JP648-689, JP723-756, JP784-802, JP836-861, JP897-941, JP961-976, JR125-152, JR183-223, JR237-266, JR289-338, JR360-392, JR426-449 & JR492-535

Typhoon Mk Ib
Contract No. ACFT/943/C.23(a)
Gloster Aircraft Co., Hucclecote
Quantity – 800
- Serial Numbers – MM951-995, MN113-156, MN169-213, MN229-269, MN282-325, MN339-381, MN396-436, MN449-496, MN513-556, MN569-608, MN623-667, MN680-720, MN735-779, MN791-823, MN851-896, MN912-956, MN968-999, MP113-158 & MP172-203

Typhoon Mk Ib
Contract No. ACFT/943/C.23(a)
Gloster Aircraft Co., Hucclecote
Quantity – 145
- Serial Numbers – PD446-480, PD492-536, PD548-577 & PD589-623

Typhoon Mk Ib
Contract No. ACFT/943/C.23(a)
Gloster Aircraft Co., Hucclecote
Quantity – 255
- Serial Numbers – RB192-235, RB248-289, RB303-347, RB361-408, RB423-459 & RB474-512

Typhoon Mk Ib
Contract No. ACFT/3864/C.23(a)
Gloster Aircraft Co., Hucclecote
Quantity – 300
- Serial Numbers – SW386-428, SW443-478, SW493-537, SW551-596, SW620-668, SW681-716 & SW728-772

Typhoon
Contract No. ACFT/3864/C.23(a)
Gloster Aircraft Co., Hucclecote
Quantity – 220
- Serial Numbers – TR864-905, TR918-956, TR969-999, TS113-158, TS172-205 & TS219-246

All subsequently cancelled

Typhoon Mk II Prototype
Contract No. ACFT/1640/C.23(a)
Hawker Aircraft Ltd, Langley
Quantity – 2
- Serial Numbers – HM595 & HM599

Both completed as Tempest Mk Is

Typhoon Mk II
Contract No. ACFT/1876/C.23(a)
Hawker Aircraft Ltd, Langley
Quantity – 100
- Serial Numbers – JN729-773, JN792-822 & JN854-877

All subsequently completed as Tempest Mk Vs

Typhoon (Centaurus) Prototype
Contract No. ACFT/1986/C.23(a)
Hawker Aircraft Ltd, Langley
Quantity – 6
- Serial Number – LA594 (cancelled), LA597 (cancelled), LA602 (Tempest Mk II), LA607 (Tempest Mk II), LA610 (intended as Tempest Mk III but became Fury X prototype) & LA614 (Tempest Mk III but cancelled)

Appendix V: Bibliography

The below list of Tornado & Typhoon related material is as comprehensive as possible, but there are bound to be omissions so if there are amendments or additions, please contact the author via the Valiant Wings Publishing address shown at the front of this title.

Official Publications

- **Typhoon Mk IA** – Air Publication 1804A
- **Typhoon Mk IB** – Air Publication 1804A
- **Pilot's Notes for Typhoon Marks IA and IB** – Air Publication 1804A – P.N.

Publications

- **Aircraft Archive – Fighters of World War Two, Volume 1** (Argus Books 1988 ISBN:0-85242-948-7)
- **Bodenplatte: The Luftwaffe's Last Hope** by J. Manrho & R. Pütz (Hikoki Publications 2004 ISBN: 1-902109-40-6)
- **Camouflage & Markings Royal Air Force 1939-1945** by M. Reynolds (Argus Books 1992 ISBN: 1-85486-065-8)
- **Fighter Command 1939-1945** by Ian Carter (Ian Allan 2002 ISBN: 0-7110-2842-7)
- **Fighter Squadrons of the RAF and Their Aircraft** by John D.R. Rawlings (Crécy Books 1993, ISBN: 0-947554-24-6)
- **Fighting Cockpits 1914-2000** by L.F.E. Coombs (Airlife Publishing Ltd 1999 ISBN: 1-85310-915-0)
- **Flugzeugtypen Vol 4 Military Aircraft of WWII** (Modelsport Verlag GmBh 1999 ISBN: 3-923142-12-9)
- **Ground Attack Aircraft of World War Two** by Christopher Shores (Macdonald and Jane's 1977, ISBN: 0-356-08338-1)
- **Hawker, An Aircraft Album No. 5** by Derek N. James (Ian Allan 1972)
- **Hawker FlyPast Reference Library** by Donald Hannah (Key Publishing Ltd 1982, ISBN: 0-946219-01-X)
- **Hawker Typhoon, Warpaint No.5** by Chris Thomas (Hall Park Books Ltd, 1996)
- **Hawker Typhoon** by F.K. Mason, Profile No.81 (Profile Publications 1966)
- **Hawker Typhoon** by S. Fleischer, Militaria No.126 (Wydawnictwo Militaria 2001 ISBN: 83-7219-103-X)
- **Hawker Typhoon, Tempest & Sea Fury** by K. Darling (The Crowood Press 2003 ISBN: 978-1-86126-620-0)

- **Hawker Typhoon Portfolio** by R.M. Clarke, A Brookland Aircraft Portfolio (Brookland Books/Business Press International Ltd 1986 ISBN: 1-86982-617-5)
- **Hawker Typhoon: The Combat History** by Richard Townsend Bickers (Airlife Publishing Ltd 1999 ISBN: 1-85310-908-8)
- **Hawker Typhoon/Tempest, Famous Airplanes of the World No.63** (Bunrin-do Co., Ltd 3/1997 ISBN: 4-89319-060-1)
- **Luftfahrt International No.18**, Nov-Dec 1976
- **RAF & RCAF Aircraft Nose Art in World War II** by C. Simonsen (Hikoki Publications 2001 ISBN: 1-902109-20-1)
- **RAF Fighter Command Northern Europe 1936-1945, Camouflage & Markings** by J. Goulding & R. Jones (Ducimus Books Ltd 1970-71)
- **RAF Fighters Part 2** by W. Green & G. Swanborough, WW2 Aircraft Fact Files (Jane's Publishing Co., Ltd 1979 ISBN: 0-354-01234-7)
- **Royal Air Force Losses of the Second World War. Volume 2. Operational Losses: Aircraft and Crews 1942-1943** by Norman L.R. Franks (Midland Publishing Limited 1998, ISBN: 1-85780-075-3)
- **Royal Air Force Losses of the Second World War. Volume 3. Operational Losses: Aircraft and Crews 1944-1945** by Norman L.R. Franks (Midland Publishing Limited 1998, ISBN: 1-85780-093-1)
- **Soldier in the Cockpit: From Rifles to Typhoons in WWII** by D.W. Pottinger (Stakcpole Books)
- **Hawker Typhoon** by Chris Thomas and Mister Kit, Spécial Mach 1 (Éditions Atlas 1980)
- **The Cold War Years: Flight Testing at Boscombe Down 1945-1975** by T. Mason (Hikoki Publications 2001 ISBN: 1-902109-11-2)
- **The Day of the Typhoon – Flying the RAF tankbusters in Normandy** by John Golley, An Airlife Classic (The Crowood Press 2000 ISBN: 978-1-84037-181-9)
- **The Hawker Typhoon and Tempest** by Francis K. Mason (Aston Publications 1988, ISBN: 0-946627-19-3)
- **The Secret Years: Flight Testing at Boscombe Down 1939-1945** by T. Mason (Hikoki Publications 1998 ISBN: 1-951899-9-5)
- **The Typhoon at War, A Pictorial Tribute** by Ken Rimell (Historic Military Press 2002, ISBN: 1-901313-14-X)
- **The Typhoon & Tempest Story** by C. Thomas & C. Shores (Arms & Armour Press 1988)
- **Typhoon Attack** by Norman Franks

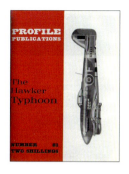
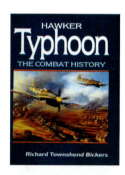

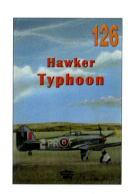
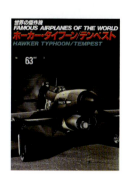

Bibliography

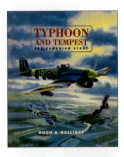

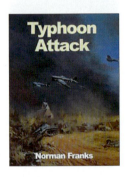
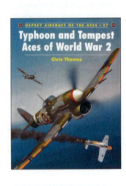

- **Typhoon/Tempest Aces of World War 2**
  by C. Thomas, Aircraft of the Aces No.27
  (Osprey Publishing 1999 ISBN: 1-85532-779-1)

- **Typhoon/Tempest In Action No.102** by J. Scutts
  (Squadron/Signal Publications 1990)

- **Typhoon and Tempest at War**
  by Arthur Reed and Roland Beamont
  (Ian Allan 1974, ISBN: 0-7110-0542-7)

- **Typhoon and Tempest – The Canadian Story**
  by Hugh A. Halliday (CANAV Books 1992/Howell Press 2000, ISBN: 0-92102-206-9)

- **Typhoon Wings of the 2nd TAF 1943-45**
  by C. Thomas (Osprey Publishing 2010
  ISBN: 978-1-84603-9737)

- **2nd Tactical Air Force Volume 1, Spartan to Normandy June 1943 to June 1944**
  by C. Shores & C. Thomas (Classic Publications)

- **21st Profile Vol.2 No.17**
  (21st Profile Ltd ISSN: 0961-8120)

- **Wings of Fame Volume 19**
  (Aerospace Publishing Ltd 2000
  ISBN: 1-86184-050-0/1-86184-049-7)

Periodicals

- Aero, No.156
- Aeroplane Monthly, June 1983, September 1983, October 1987, July 1991, May 1998 & September 1999
- After the Battle, No.51
- Aircraft Illustrated, November & December 1971
- Air Classics, Vol.10 No.3
- Airfix Magazine, April 1983
- Air Forces International, December 1989
- Air Pictorial, February 1969 & February 2000
- Airplane, Vol.12 No.143
- Aviation News, 31st December 1982 – 13th January 1983 & 8th-21st January 1988
- CAHS Journal, Vol.18 No.1, Spring 1980
- Fana de l'Aviation, No.182 January 1985, No.183 February 1985, No.184 March 1985, No.186 June 1985, No.187 July 1985, No.196 March, No.197 April, No.198 May, No.199 June, No.200 July & No.201 August 1986
- Flight International, 22nd June 1972
- Flypast, February 1990 & November 1996
- Imperial War Museum Review, No.2 (1987)
- Mushroom Monthly, Vol.7 No.4 April 1992
- PAM News, Vol.5 No.4
- Replic, No.34 (June 1984) & No.88 (December 1998)
- Rolls-Royce Magazine, No.54 (September 1991)
- Scale Aircraft Modelling, Vol.11 No.1 October 1988 & Vol.20 No.12 February 1999
- Scale Aviation Modeller International, Vol.6 Iss.12 December 2000 & Vol.11 No.5 May 2005
- Scale Models, Vol.5 No.2 February 1974, Vol.6 No.74 November 1975, Vol.7 No.76 January 1976 & Scale Models International, Vol.20 No.233 March 1989
- The Aeroplane, 11/02/1944
- Vintage News Annual, 1998-1999
- Wing Masters, No.10, May-June 1999
- Wingspan, No.80 (October 1991)
- 39/45 Magazine, 2nd Tactical AF

July 1944 advertisement featuring the Typhoon

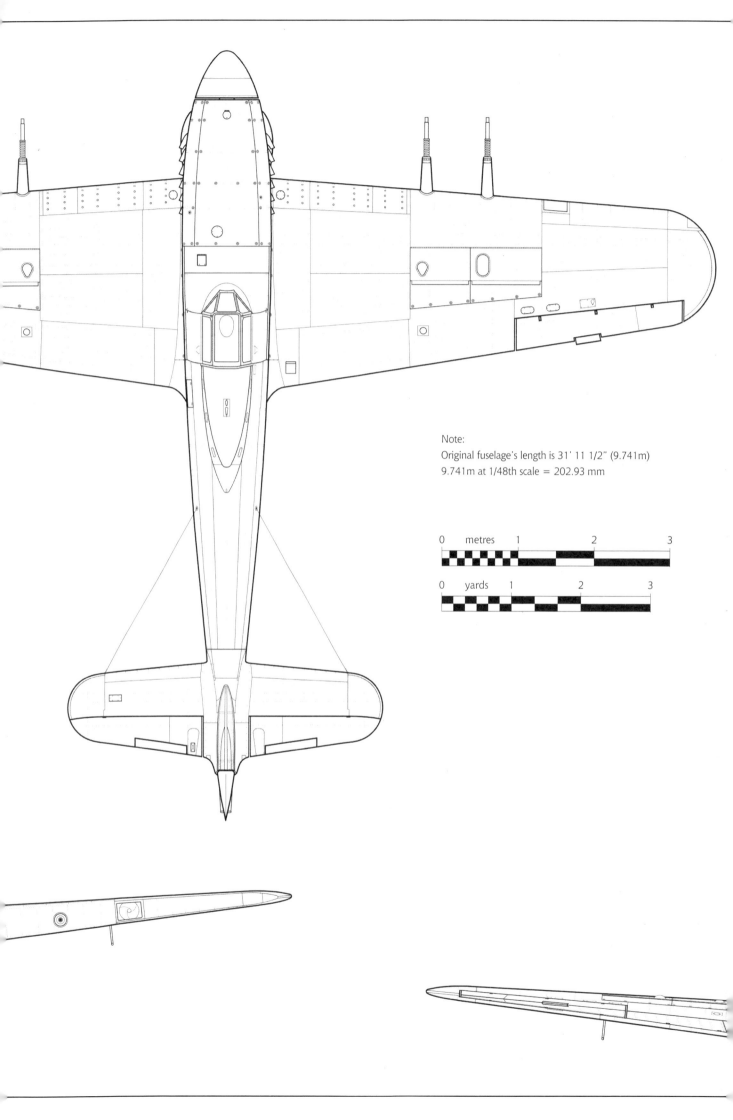

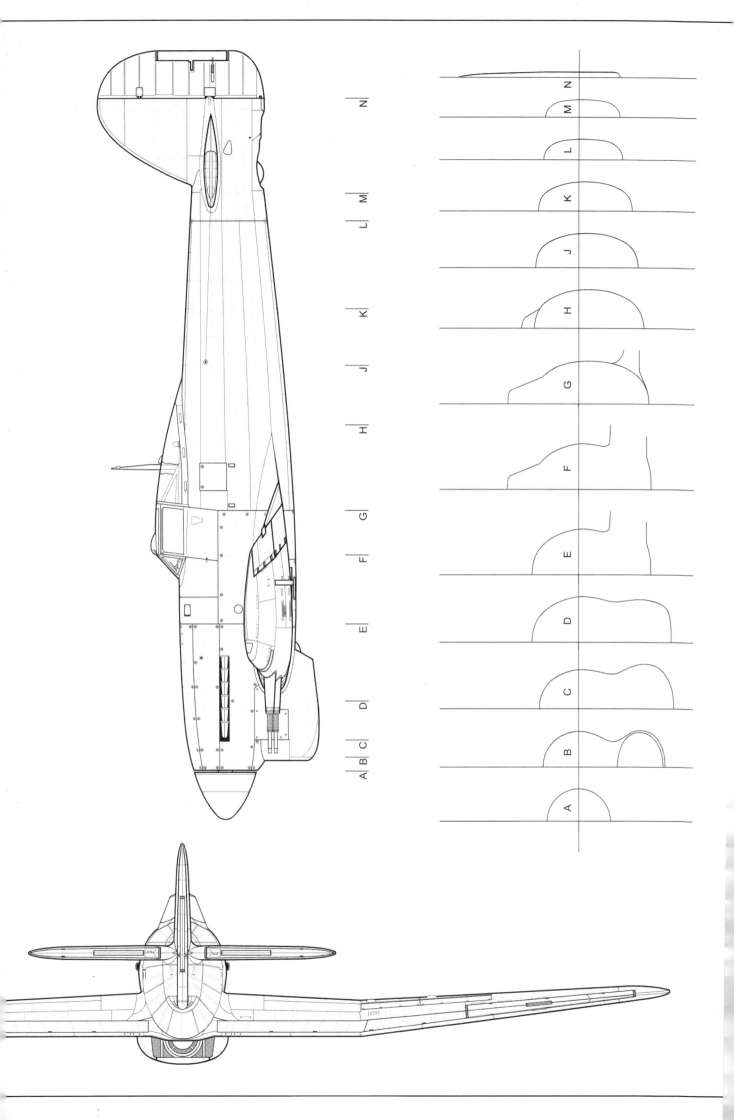

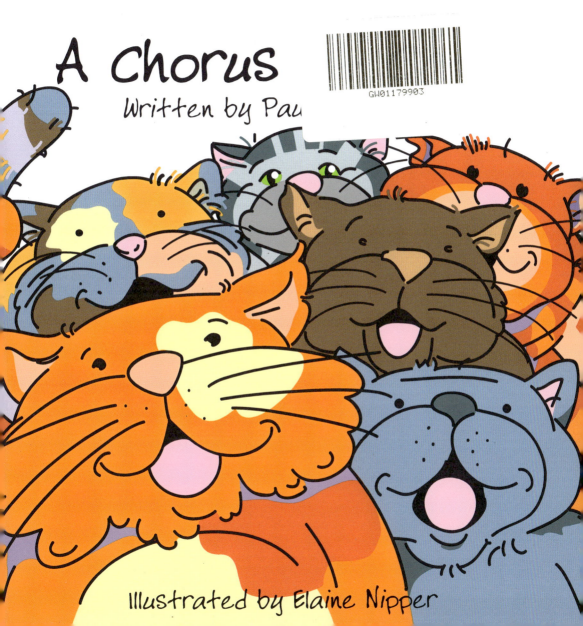

Copyright © text Pauline Travers 2012
Copyright © illustrations Elaine Nipper 2012

Pauline Travers and Elaine Nipper have asserted their rights
under the Copyright, Design and Patents Act, 1988
to be identified as the author and illustrator of this work

First published by Elaine Nipper in the United Kingdom 2012

ISBN 978-0-9569939-2-2

For further details about Pauline Travers as a visiting author
please contact her via e-mail at paulineat23@aol.com

www.elainenipper.co.uk

contents

Cats' Chorus	1
The Cat Who Lives Upstairs	2
Catastrophe	3
Gone Fishing!	4
Moon Cat	5
Purrsonality	6
The Pied Piper of Hamelin	7-10
Sleeping Cat	11
Fluffy	12
The Witch's Cat	13
Crazy Cat Claude	14
Cat Olympics	15
King of Cats	16
Lazybones	17
Claws	18
Sun Seeker	19
Super Cat	20

Look out for the killer cats

Cats' Chorus

Have you heard the cats's choir in the night?
It only sings when the moon shines bright.
The haunting tunes can keep you awake
Through the wee small hours, until day break.

The melodies screech and scratch your ears,
Worry your nerves and feed your fears.
Although you cannot hear the words
They're probably singing 'bout mice and birds.

The notes get higher and the pitch is shrill.
The chorus can make you feel quite ill!
So, open the window and do what you ought t'
And throw on the cats, a bucket of water!

The Cat Who Lives Upstairs

In through the window, he softly slides,
Over the sill he nimbly glides.
On to the bed, he jumps and lands,
Kneading with paws, while he stands.
Then checking it's safe, looks here and there,
He curls up to sleep without a prayer.
For he's the cat who lives upstairs.

He's scared of the dogs who live downstairs,
For they chase him and sniff him and nudge him off chairs.
He hates the cat flap, as it catches his tail,
And the children haunt him when they start to wail.
The grown-ups fuss him, knowing he's shy,
But he just wants a peaceful life, and that is why...
He's the cat who lives upstairs.

Catastrophe

Charles the cat is nimble and proud,
Tries all sorts of tricks that he's not allowed.
He pads along fences, climbs on to sheds.
Slips through windows, sleeps on neighbours' beds!

He fishes in ponds, catches mice by the dozen,
Miaows at chicken being cooked in the oven!
Climbs up chimneys, skates on the ice,
Rolls in the dirt and doesn't smell nice.

He's not scared of heights; he's always up high,
Sitting on roof tops, way up in the sky.
What if he slips, or by the wind's blown?
"What a catastrophe!" we will all groan.

Gone Fishing!

Lying lazily by the pool,
The soft grey cat looks sleek and cool.
Into the depths she dreamily stares.
No one notices, nobody cares.

But she is watching and making a note,
On the golden fish as they gently float.
She tests the water with her delicate paw,
Too warm? Too cold? Or should she ignore?

Seeing her shadow, fish fumble in fear,
As that menacing cat is lurking near.
Then swish, her paw dives in and grabs one small fish.
And grey cat has captured a nice tasty dish!

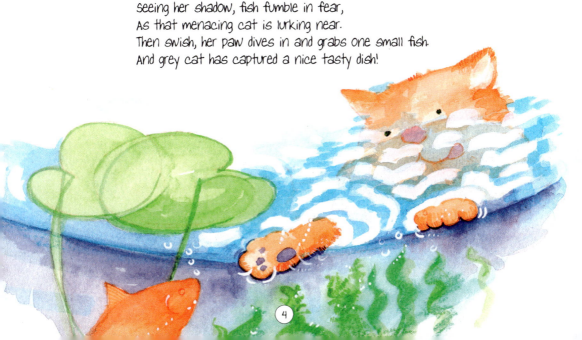

Moon Cat

Cat slips out when the moon is bright,
Never by day, always at night.
His delicate paws brush the moonlit fence
Into the garden where the shrubs are dense.

There he sits, statue still
Elegantly waiting for his kill.
His ears are pricked, his eyes shine bright
Dreaming of tasty mice tonight.

Then, SPRING! He pounces through the air,
His actions hardly turn a hair.
Neatly tucked beneath his feet
Is a poor little mouse just ready to eat!

Purrsonality

My cat is crazy, she's clever and bold.
And quite amazing for two months old!
She climbs the ladder against the wall,
sneaks in through the window and into the hall!
She jumps on my shoulder and licks my ear.
Slides down the banister, she has no fear!
She shimmies up curtains, swings on the rail,
Plays with my socks and with wool, leaves a trail.
She paddles in bath tubs and swims in the sink,
skates on iced ponds and thinks it's a rink!
But when she is sleepy, she curls on my lap
Purring and dreaming as she takes a nap.

The Pied Piper of Hamelin

The rats, the rats, they're everywhere,
The people of Hamelin cried.
They're in our homes! They're in the street!
They're getting underneath our feet!
We've put down poison, we've set many traps.
We've even trained hundreds of killer cats.
But it's no use, it's to no avail.
The rats of Hamelin still prevail.
Look out! Look out! For here they tumble.
The army of rats are on the rumble!

Yes! Here we are, the evil rats.
We don't like humans, we're not scared of cats.
Not tempted by poison, we'll dismantle traps.
So pay your respects and doff your caps!

The terrified people set off in a state,
To see the mayor, they were quite irate.
They rapped on the door of the great town hall,
And all together began to bawl.
"You must do something, to free us from rats,
We've now tried everything,
Even killer cats."
The mayor of Hamelin, looked out at the crowd.
Raised a hand and softly bowed.
"I promise to free you from these vermin.
Wherever they are, I'll send them squirming."

As if by magic, a piper appeared
To eliminate rats he volunteered.
To be paid in gold he set his price.
The mayor he nodded and took his advice.
Then shrill notes danced and filled the air,
And rats followed the piper without a care.
They darted from houses, erupted from drains,
Sprinkled down water pipes, frolicked down lanes.
Their bravado shattered, they began to quiver,
As the piper drowned them in the river.

"Hurray for the piper!" the people cried.
"He's saved our town he has not lied!"
"I'll collect my gold," the piper said.
"Now that all the rats are dead."
But the mean old mayor in his town hall sniggered.
"Pay you all that! I'll be jiggered."
So the piper turned and began to toot,
A different tune on his merry flute.

Out of the doors with a gallop and skip
Came children for this unplanned trip.
They followed the piper so merrily after,
Dancing and spinning with hearts full of laughter.
"Goodbye, mother, goodbye father.
Come on sister and little brother!"
The parents stood and were frozen with fear,
As they watched their children disappear.
All except one little boy, who was lame.
Who wept when he was left out of this game.
The piper was never seen again
But, his story lives on...
as does his fame.

Sleeping Cat

Black cat sat on the window ledge,
Cleaning his glossy fur.
The sun poured in through the window,
And he began to purr.
He licked his paws and wiped his face,
For cats should never be a disgrace!
Then stretched out long and closed his eyes,
A cat does not need lullabies.
Relaxed and gently breathing slow
His eyelids flickered to and fro.
And there he lay all afternoon
In his sun blessed window ledge cocoon.

Fluffy

Fluffy is a *fluffy* cat,
her fur is long and curly.
Her multicoloured markings
are brown and black and whirly.
She's cute and soft and cuddly.
She curls into a ball,
And looks just like a pom-pom,
when she's sleeping in the hall.
She likes to have her head scratched,
her tummy tickled too.

She loves it when you smooth her back,
she purrs and snuggles you.
But if she sees the cat brush,
she's off in just a flash,
and then you'll see that ball of fluff
in a hundred metre dash!

The Witch's Cat

A witch's cat is sleek and black,
With glossy fur and a high arched back.
With claws so sharp they can tear to shreds,
Carpets, chairs and covers on beds.

A witch's cat has a very long tail,
That can wiggle and wave and curl like a snail.
It has ears that can hear the slightest sound,
Even a leaf as it falls to the ground.

A witch's cat can even fly,
Up on a broomstick in the sky.
Cat guides the witch where she needs to go.
A fluffy sat. nav... didn't you know?

Crazy Cat Claude

Claude's got in a tangle,
he's wound up in wool.
He'll need my help,
with a jolly good pull.
He's climbed up the curtains!
He's crashed to the floor!
He's got his paw stuck
underneath the door!
He's licking the butter,
he's sipping mum's tea!
He's jumped on my lap,
claws dug in my knee.
He's pouncing on paper,
he's raced round the house.
He's killing my slipper,
he thinks it's a mouse!
This cat's a disaster
He's crazy and mad!
Now asleep in his basket.
Ah! ...He's not all bad!

Cat Olympics

There is a cat Olympics.
It's all around my house.
It happens quite often
when Puss chases a mouse.

He high jumps through the window,
he sprints across the floor.
The triathlon is just a breeze,
as he whizzes past the door.

Attempting now the javelin,
knives shoot into the air.
The table cloth is ruined.
He doesn't have a care!

He's out into the garden,
swims two lengths in the pond.
Marathons through flower beds,
of which I was quite fond.

He doesn't win a medal,
as he never gets a mouse.
And peace at last can be restored,
from the Olympics in my house!

King of Cats

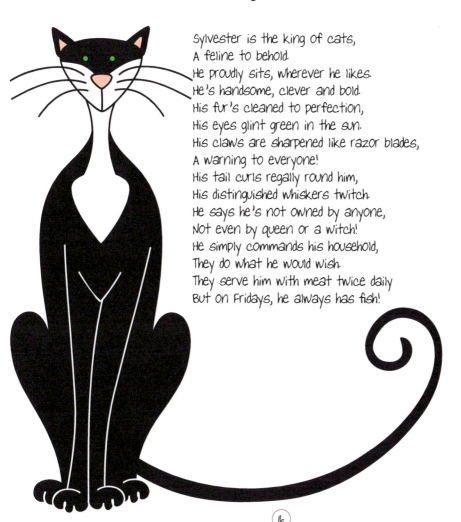

Sylvester is the king of cats,
A feline to behold.
He proudly sits, wherever he likes.
He's handsome, clever and bold.
His fur's cleaned to perfection,
His eyes glint green in the sun.
His claws are sharpened like razor blades,
A warning to everyone!
His tail curls regally round him,
His distinguished whiskers twitch.
He says he's not owned by anyone,
Not even by queen or a witch!
He simply commands his household,
They do what he would wish.
They serve him with meat twice daily
But on Fridays, he always has fish!

Lazybones

Stretched and yawning, cat lies
On the sun drenched window ledge.
Nose twitching, tightly closed eyes,
Fur shining in the mid-morning light.

He wakens gently from his drifting dreams
Extends his soft body and flexes his claws,
Rises and slinks to the cosy armchair
Where visions of mice and birds fill his head again.

Ears perk and he seems to smile as
His owner approaches to pet and stroke him.
He rolls on to his back and allows a hand
To smooth his chest as he contentedly purrs.

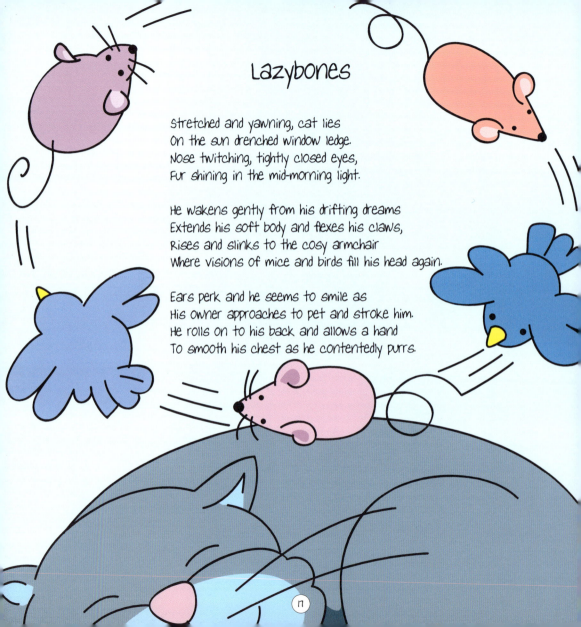

Claws

Claws is out on the town,
he's a gangster cat...
wears a dark fur coat
and a black fur hat.

He's light on his feet,
creeps up on his prey,
to surprise by night
and in light of day.

He terrifies kittens,
he even scares dogs.
The fish in the pond
are guarded by frogs!

Mice hide away,
birds don't sing or tweet.
When the gangster arrives
they beat a hasty retreat.

Claws is out on the town,
he's a gangster cat...
wears a dark fur coat
and a black fur hat.

You may just glimpse him
when he's out on the prowl.
Or hear the sound
of his gangster cat YOWL!

Sun Seeker

The sun shines down by the garden wall.
Who's warm as toast and curled in a ball?
It's Cosy Posy the tabby cat,
Not in her basket, well fancy that!

A streak of sun gleams on to the floor,
Who's basking and purring by the door?
It's Cosy Posy the tabby cat,
Not in her basket, well fancy that!

The sunlight warms the stump of the tree.
Who's soaking up sunbeams today, for free?
It's Cosy Posy the tabby cat,
Not in her basket, well fancy that!

She seeks the sun wherever it glows,
Warming her fur, her bones and her toes!
She's Cosy Posy, the tabby cat,
Not in her basket, well fancy that!

Super Cat

Super Cat
Agent number one,
(his mum just calls him 'Honeybun.')
He's strong, he's fierce
and incredibly clever,
so you must never, ever, ever,
tickle him underneath the chin,
set a task that he can't win,
or keep him in the house at night,
for Super Cat must defend and fight.
He likes to show that he is best,
in fact, it says so on his vest.

Super Cat,
Agent number one,
solves mystery cat crimes, just for fun!
He's like Sherlock Holmes,
with super powers.
He'll sniff out who's
trampled on the flowers.
He can catch the cat
who got the cream,
he'll spring into action
when kittens scream.
Some say they've even see him fly,
one paw outstretched, straight into the sky.
He's a judo expert,
never uses a gun.
He's Super Cat
Agent number one!

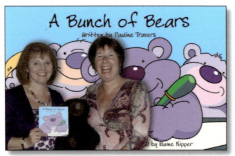

Pauline and Elaine at the very successful launch of 'A Bunch of Bears,' the first book in the series.

Pauline Travers is passionate about writing poems and the performance of poetry, especially for young children. She teaches verse speaking to help children understand their voices, to improve their diction and self confidence but most importantly, to instil a love of poetry. This is the second book in her poetry series and many of the poems have already won awards when performed by her young students.

Pauline is married to Jon and they have two grown up children. They live in Cheltenham, Gloucestershire.

For further details about Pauline Travers as a visiting author, please contact her via e-mail at paulineat23@aol.com

Elaine Nipper has enjoyed drawing since she was a child and has been illustrating professionally for several years. She is married to Chris and lives in Surrey.